Playfulness

Its Relationship to
Imagination and Creativity

EDUCATIONAL PSYCHOLOGY

Allen J. Edwards, Series Editor
Department of Psychology
Southwest Missouri State University
Springfield, Missouri

Phillip S. Strain, Thomas P. Cooke, and Tony Apolloni. Teaching
Exceptional Children: Assessing and Modifying Social Behavior

Donald E. P. Smith and others. A Technology of Reading and
Writing (in four volumes).
  Vol. 1. Learning to Read and Write: A Task Analysis (by Donald
  E. P. Smith)
  Vol. 2. Criterion-Referenced Tests for Reading and Writing (by
  Judith M. Smith, Donald E. P. Smith, and James R. Brink)

Joel R. Levin and Vernon L. Allen (eds.). Cognitive Learning in
Children: Theories and Strategies

Vernon L. Allen (ed.). Children as Teachers: Theory and Research
on Tutoring

Gilbert R. Austin. Early Childhood Education: An International
Perspective

António Simões (ed.). The Bilingual Child: Research and Analysis of Existing Educational Themes

Erness Bright Brody and Nathan Brody. Intelligence: Nature,
Determinants, and Consequences

Samuel Ball (ed.). Motivation in Education

J. Nina Lieberman. Playfulness: Its Relationship to Imagination
and Creativity

In preparation:

Donald E. P. Smith and others. A Technology of Reading and
Writing (in four volumes).
  Vol. 3. The Adaptive Classroom (by Donald E. P. Smith)
  Vol. 4. Preparing Instructional Tasks (by Judith M. Smith)

Harry Hom, Jr. (ed.). Psychological Processes in Early Education

Harvey Lesser. Television and the Preschool Child: A Psychological Theory of Instruction and Curriculum Development

Donald J. Treffinger, J. Kent Davis, and Richard E. Ripple (eds.).
Handbook on Teaching Educational Psychology

Playfulness

Its Relationship to
Imagination and Creativity

J. NINA LIEBERMAN

School of Education
Brooklyn College
Brooklyn, New York

ACADEMIC PRESS   New York   San Francisco   London   1977

A Subsidiary of Harcourt Brace Jovanovich, Publishers

ACADEMIC PRESS, INC.
111 Fifth Avenue, New York, New York 10003

United Kingdom Edition published by
ACADEMIC PRESS, INC. (LONDON) LTD.
24/28 Oval Road, London NW1

Library of Congress Cataloging in Publication Data

Lieberman, Josefa Nina,   Date
     Playfulness.

     (Educational psychology series)
     Bibliography: p.
     1.   Play.   2.   Imagination.   3.   Creative ability.
I.   Title.
BF717.L53   153.3   76-42975
ISBN 0−12−449450−1

To all who know how hard it is to play

Contents

Preface

Anyone interested in play has had to face the difficulty of capturing what it is. In this book, I deal with this question by asking *how* we play and by presenting data that identify a concept I labeled *playfulness*. By this I mean the lightheartedness that we find as a quality of play in the young child's activities and, later on, as the combinatorial play essential to imagination and creativity. I, therefore, see playfulness as behavior that goes beyond the childhood years; and, through its component parts of sense of humor, manifest joy, and spontaneity, it has major implications for childrearing practices, educational planning, career choices, and leisure pursuits. I present this point of view as my own formulation, while also building on existing research and theory and indicating how these data support my position.

My treatment of the subject starts with an historical perspective. Going beyond psychological source materials, it sets the stage for the thrust of my thesis, namely, that play and its quintessence, playfulness, arises in familiar physical settings or when the individual has the pertinent facts; that imagination enters by twisting those facts into different combinations, not unlike the operation of a kaleidoscope; and that the end product may, by the quality of its uniqueness, deserve the label "creative." The major portion of the book is devoted to a discussion of the play element in play, subdivided into sense of humor, manifest joy, and spontaneity. The approach is within a developmental framework and the setting is, to a large extent, the classroom. My own studies and the analysis of the research by others are based on the theoretical framework of Piaget and Berlyne; however, questions are raised about the ludic element as postulated by Piaget and the exploratory dimension as expounded by Berlyne. I emphasize a continuation of the ludic element in adolescent and adult thought, and I stress the differentiation between play and exploratory behavior based on familiar versus novel aspects in the factual givens—it is at that point that playfulness operates. My theoretical model indicates the role of playfulness in cognitive, affective, and social functioning, and specifically relates these links to imagination and creativity.

Because of the book's focus on playfulness as behavior at later stages of development, it shares with life-span psychology the stress on the influence of ecological variables on behavior. Sex differences, level of intelligence, and social class are some of the variables considered in relation to playfulness. In a wider framework, this specific view of play, with its emphasis on the interaction between developmental and historical time, relates to the fields of education and sociology. This relation is reflected in the discussion of everyday applications of playfulness in an individual's life cycle, which take us from the home to the school, to career choices, to on-the-job satisfaction, and, finally, to the use of leisure.

This book was written for professionals and advanced students in a number of disciplines. It will be of interest to developmental and educational psychologists as well as to educators in general and to graduate students. Colleagues in sociology and social work should find valuable information about the zeitgeist, the influence of cohorts, and the need for a positive approach in a group setting. Similarly, it will be helpful to psychotherapists since playfulness stresses joy, gentle humor, and spontaneity, all ingredients that contribute to the optimal functioning of the individual. In general, I hope the book will be not only a useful but also an enjoyable experience for its readers.

Acknowledgments

It is difficult to know where to begin with acknowledgments for a book such as this, which reflects my thinking over a decade and a half. Admittedly, one's growth is constantly affected by people around one and by one's successive experiences. To the extent that I am aware of these influences, these are acknowledged in this collective statement. There are, however, persons and experiences that call for special mention because of their decisive input at crucial turning points in my career.

Since I am a developmentalist by conviction and a history buff by avocation, I should like to record the influence of significant others in chronological order. When I first entertained the notion of doing my dissertation research on play and then formulated the concept of playfulness in play, Millie C. Almy not only encouraged me in my pursuit of what, at times, seemed a most elusive goal but predicted that playfulness would keep me busy at work for the rest of my life! When, at one of those crucial turning points, I was ready to give up on play, not only she but also Robert L. Thorndike led me back to my original commitment. There was one other person who, although not directly involved in my research efforts, gave me unwavering support in my professional endeavors. Gertrude P. Driscoll was not only a teacher and a colleague but also a friend whose wisdom, personal integrity, and warmth will continue to be an inspiration to me.

My own studies would not have been possible without the generous and fruitful cooperation of school officials and teachers, at both the kindergarten and secondary school levels. Among them, I want to single out Elsa Barnouw of the Gardens Nursery School and Kindergarten, Ruth Stronsky of the Israel Chipkin School, and Josephine A. Bliss of the Riverside Nursery School and Kindergarten, directors of their respective schools. At the secondary level, E. J. Cipolaro, Principal of the Mount Vernon High School, Mount Vernon, David Eliach, Principal of the Flatbush Yeshiva High School in Brooklyn, and Seymour Glassman of Ditmas Junior High School in Brooklyn were most helpful in allowing me to work with the teachers at their schools. Hyman Sardy of Brooklyn College, who acted as statistical consultant in the high school study, and Judith Garretsen, who assisted in the data analysis, were enthusiastic in their approach to the project and made many helpful suggestions. The studies were supported, in part, by three separate grants from the National Institute of Mental Health. The first was a Public Health Service fellowship MH-18, 219-01A1; the other two were Public Health Small Grants MH 13152-01 and MH 14426-01.

Throughout the years, I have been stimulated and encouraged by the writings of Daniel Berlyne, John Feldhusen, Nathan Kogan, Jerome L. Singer, and Brian Sutton-Smith, as well as by helpful personal exchanges of views I had with them. I was also fortunate in finding understanding and support from the editors at Academic Press.

Last but not least, I want to thank my husband, Meyer F. Lieberman, for his patience and forbearance during the trials and tribulations that were also part of writing this book. It was also he who, in tandem with our cat Ruby, pointed out the playful aspects in the act of writing so that in the end I allowed myself to enjoy working on the project.

Das Unbeschreibliche,
Hier ist's getan.

[*Faust*, Pt. 2]

1

Introduction

PLAY–IMAGINATION–CREATIVITY

A General Overview of Their Role in Psychological Research

It seems appropriate to start any discussion of play, imagination, and creativity with the question about the importance of the topics. Naturally, this cannot be done without referring to the concrete behavior that they denote. In a society like ours, based on the Protestant work ethic, can we allow ourselves the luxury of focusing on play? Similarly, in our pragmatically oriented culture, what role is there for imagination, which may seem only an idle passing of time, with no immediate tangible results? And lastly, in our democratically oriented society, what place is there for recognition of unique contributions or for the individual who does not fit the average mold?

We could, of course, refer to play as child's work and thereby gain respectability for our topic and, historically, there is precedent for such an interpretation (Dewey, 1913; Froebel, 1895b; Griffiths, 1935; Pestalozzi, 1898; Rousseau, 1964). We could defend our interest in imagination by pointing out the real-life value of role playing in the young child, of vocational decision-making by way of fantasizing in the adolescent, and of working through hostility by imaginary exploits and confrontations in the adult. And, again, there is concrete evidence for imagination aiding these aspects of behavior (Erikson, 1940; Jersild, Markey, & Jersild, 1933; Jones, 1968; Markey, 1935; Piaget, 1945; Singer, 1966; Symonds, 1942). Creativity, too, could be viewed from its lowest common denominator, and a case can be made that each and every one of us is creative to the extent that *we* discover things new to us, make things that *we* never made before, and bring our very own interpretation to the world around us. For this case, too, chapter and verse can be cited (Barron, 1969; Getzels & Jackson, 1962; Guilford, 1950, 1968; Jackson & Messick, 1965; Torrance, 1962; Wallach & Kogan, 1965).

Their Interrelationship: A Personal and Subjective View

Play

It is commonplace to talk about imaginative play in young children and about a creative person who is imaginative. This implies that, in naturalistic observation, we consider imagination to be part of play and creativity. Similarly, we often characterize an individual as playful, thereby implying that some ingredient of play is still part of the behavioral repertoire.

But play is a large and diffuse area of activity, and there is some truth in Berlyne's (1969) statement that "psychology would do well to give up the category of 'play' in favor of both wider and narrower categories of behavior" (p. 843). My investigations (Lieberman, 1965, 1966, 1967a,b) appear to meet Berlyne's critique. But this was not my primary rationale for the studies. The underlying assumption for studying playfulness, indeed for the formulation of the concept and the identification of the behavior labeled "playfulness," was based on the naturalistic observation that combinatorial play is an essential ingredient of creative thought. My first question, therefore, was how it was related to play at an earlier level of development. The second question was whether or not this type of approach survives play and becomes a personality trait of the player. The third question was what were the environmental variables that foster or stifle this tendency.

Imagination

To some extent, imagination shares with play the dubious distinction that psychologists were reluctant to study it, and the field was left largely to philosophers. In common parlance, when you say to someone you are imagining this, or this is a figment of your imagination, it means that there is no concrete objective reference in the environment or basis for the person's argument. It is understandable that scientists—and psychologists among them—have brushed aside imagination as something that is of no consequence to behavior or at least to the kinds of behavior in which they were interested.

Only recently, thanks to the ingenious work of Singer (1966) and Klinger (1971), have we a body of knowledge relating to the difficult-to-observe phenomena of daydreams and fantasy, especially in adults. We have, of course, earlier work by the British psychologist McKellar (1957), whose classification of thinking into the R-component (i.e., logical, reasoning) and the A-component (i.e., autistic) was helpful. But McKellar's influence on American psychology was only peripheral and was restricted to thought processes. With the rediscovery and acceptance of Piaget by American psychologists in the 1950s, his view of imagination greatly influenced child and educational psychologists. Since Piaget's own emphasis, however, was on the development of logical thought, imagination was considered mainly as part of early intellectual functioning and the ludic and symbolic elements were said later to disappear or to be transformed. It was the revived interest in creativity, also in the 1950s, that helped imagination to be considered again as part of the adult's thoughts.

Creativity

Creativity, like play and imagination, was another stepchild of psychological research. Interest in creative potential, divergent thinking abilities, and original or unique contributions was dramatically boosted by the advent of Sputnik in 1957. While Guilford and his associates (Guilford, Wilson, & Christensen, 1951) had been working on their model of the structure of intellect as early as 1950, particular attention was now being paid to the divergent production component in his model. Labeling, identifying, and then measuring the abilities stipulated to contribute to divergent production was a major step in the direction of operationally dealing with the elusive concept of creativity. As a result, ideational fluency and spontaneous and adaptive flexibility become dimensions for assessment of intellectual functioning.

Even this preliminary overview of the broad areas of play, imagination, and creativity suggests not only their relatedness but the need to introduce more narrowly defined concepts leading to dimensions of behavior that could be identified, measured, and experimentally manipulated. My own studies of playfulness, first investigated at the kindergarten level, were prompted by these very considerations.

PLAYFULNESS: ITS RATIONALE AND EXPLORATION

Well-meaning colleagues in psychology and related disciplines pointed out the hazards in pursuing a concept as elusive as playfulness. Yet, behaviorally, it could be seen in the play of young children and, at later developmental stages, as a personality trait of the individual.

The first impetus to look for this as yet unnamed behavior was a reference by Deutsch (1958) about the important ingredient of combinatorial play in the creative process. My starting point was determined by the rational conclusion that the element in play contributing to later creativity might be identified and measured at an age level that Griffith (1935) describes as the time when "play is the characteristic mode of behavior" (p. 319).

From 1959 to 1961, I spent considerable time observing preschoolers in nursery, kindergarten, and day-care centers. Most of these observations were made during play activities.

An example of a 5-minute observation will illustrate more graphically the course of the thinking that led to the conceptualization of playfulness.

Three five-year-olds are busy in the housekeeping corner. Susanna has sat down on a rocking chair and says to Diane and Edie: "Let's go to sleep." Her playmates are on a bed and chair now, and Susanna asks, "What do we dream?" This is echoed by the others in chorus, and Diane replies: "We sleep and we dream." But Susanna continues to ask, "About a witch or ghost?" and, looking somewhat annoyed at Diana, gets up and takes her by the hand. She is joined by Edie, and they all skip down to the other end of the room, still in dance rhythm. Then Susanna announces, "I saw a real witch," and bends forward and listens against the wall. There is low but animated conversation among the three, and once every so often at a higher pitch and louder, "then a witch . . . and a witch." A scurrying as they all imagine to see a witch through the window. More conversation and then the three, taking their cue from Diane, run back into the housekeeping corner, and Susanna is heard to say again: "Let's go to sleep again and let's dream." [Lieberman, 1964, p. 1]

A look at Susanna's behavior tells of her using realistic props for a flight of fancy, including her playmates; moving spatially out of the prop situation and taking the fantasy content of the dream with her; switching to an act of physical exuberance; elaborating the fantasy; and returning to the original place and original activity. All this suggests physical, social, and cognitive mobility in a spontaneous manner. The dancing could have been accompanied, at another time, by laughter and singing. There might also have been a little teasing and poking fun at the others. What emerges, then, is Susanna's way of acting in a play situation: the quality of her play or her style of play. I labeled this behavior "playfulness."

While the original stimulus to examine playfulness in play and its relationship to cognitive style came from outside the discipline of psychology and referred to adults, examination of studies with children and adolescents provided some support for hypothesizing such a relationship. Playfulness was one of the differentiating traits that Torrance (1961) found when he compared the most creative boy and girl in each of 23 elementary classrooms with children matched for intelligence, sex, age, teacher, and race. Getzels and Jackson (1962) used "playful attitude toward theme" when they categorized the fantasy production of 28 highly intelligent and 28 highly creative adolescents and found that the highly creative boys and girls scored significantly higher on this trait. Wallach and Kogan (1965) also found that their highly creative, highly intelligent fifth graders showed more playfulness in interpreting stick figures than their high-intelligent—low-creative sample. There was also playful behavior in the highly creative, low-intelligence sample, but reading the profiles of individual boys and girls in that category would suggest that they did not know how to channel their playfulness constructively. Indeed, it is one of the vexing questions about playfulness to know how and when it is appropriate and productive. A concrete illustrative example of such behavior is the introductory descriptive sentence of Ed as a "high-spirited boy whose clowning, foolishness, and fighting have earned him a reputation as a trouble-maker in school" (Wallach & Kogan, 1965, p. 258).

At a younger age level, the distinction between playful and impulsive behavior is a necessary, albeit difficult, distinction to make. Ward's (1968) study of reflective and impulsive kindergartners found the former scoring higher on divergent thinking. It seems, therefore, of paramount importance to anchor the concept of playfulness in concrete behavioral correlates that would obviate its confusion with impulsive and disruptive behavior.

Our own studies reported in Chapter III, which aimed at identifying and measuring playfulness and nonplayfulness in kindergartners and adolescents, are a beginning in this direction and led to operational definitions of this behavior in young children and adolescents. Central to it were physical, social, and cognitive spontaneity, sense of humor, and manifest joy.

PROPOSED THESIS FOR THE ROLE OF PLAYFULNESS AS A PLAY ELEMENT IN PLAY, IMAGINATION, AND CREATIVITY

If we assume that there exists a core of traits that constitute playfulness and if we assume that there is a developmental continuity of playfulness as behavior, then we may posit that playfulness survives play and becomes a personality trait of the individual. On a broader basis, in order to achieve the stated goal of this book, namely, to examine this play element in relation to imagination and creativity, it is necessary to look first into possible historical antecedents of what I label "playfulness." Chapter II will, therefore, probe for references and examples to this behavior from the point of view of adult versus child's play, the functional analysis of play, and, finally, the qualitative analysis of play, all in historical perspective. The review of the qualitative aspect of play will lead to the presentation, in Chapter III, of my own studies of playfulness in kindergarten-age children, in adolescents, and in adults. Guided by my findings about the importance of the component traits of playfulness, spontaneity, sense of humor, and manifest joy, Chapter IV will examine the current research literature for additions to, changes in, and modifications of my own conceptualization. This should lead to a clarification of the behavior subsumed under the label of playfulness (PF) and should be helpful in the subsequent evaluation of PF in a theoretical framework for a relationship among play, imagination, and creativity in Chapter V. Looking at the aspects from the point of view of the familiar versus the novel in these behavior dimensions and, at the same time, bringing in developmental and historical factors will highlight the role of PF in cognitive, affective, and social functioning. The viability of any theoretical model needs to be tested in applying it to current concerns. Chapter VI will explore the role of PF in selected areas of everyday activities. Again, my examination of its impact will be cast into a developmental framework. Before presenting conclusions and recommendations for future application in Chapter VII, the current scene will be reviewed in order to give sufficient backdrop to the questions that still need to be answered by further research and by theoretical formulations.

To recap the thrust of my aim in this book: I have been intrigued by a phenomenon in play that I consider to be a qualitative ingredient in play behavior, and which I labeled "playfulness." My own studies suggest that playfulness is made up of spontaneity, manifest joy, and sense of humor. My theoretical speculations and those of others, as well as evidence from my studies and those of other investigators, point to playfulness becoming a personality trait of the individual and a possible clue to cognitive style. The importance of playfulness as a psychological concept, its relationship to other psychological processes, and its impact on everyday living is underlined and documented. Its challenge for future research is self-evident.

II

Historical Clues to Playfulness
as the Play Element in Play

One of the great pitfalls of any endeavor is the temptation to think that no one has ever formulated similar concepts or advocated related approaches. Although I do not altogether subscribe to the rather pessimistic assertion in Ecclesiastes that there is nothing new under the sun, it must be admitted that many new things are different arrangements of old or known facts. In other words, most novel and creative work is based on appropriate rearrangement.

One of the hallmarks of play and one of the criteria that seems to distinguish it from exploratory behavior is that it operates in familiar settings. If we now further refine the behavior that we are looking for, namely, that which *makes* play distinctive or the play element in play, I think we are even more justified in stressing the influence and workings of the givens and the known. In fact, it is this type of behavior that I labeled playfulness and which I see as the connecting link between play, imagination, and creativity. My historical review will, therefore, be guided by looking for a manifestation of playfulness in adult as well as in children's play; it will seek to determine whether or not playfulness is part of the functional approach to play and, if so, to what extent; it will then view play from a qualitative point of view, underlining the question of how we play, and examine the role playfulness occupies in such a framework.

ADULT VERSUS CHILD PLAY: IS PLAYFULNESS
PART OF IT?

One of the intriguing questions that emerges as we look at play over time is the balance and sometimes change of emphasis between the play of the adult

[Handwritten annotation: Huizinga (1955) ↳ talks about Homo ludens = the playing man (not child) — Second time I've seen this tonight. also in "Rules of Play"]

and of the [...] my investigation, since the shifts from adul[t ...] [charact]erizing these play activities in a historical f[ramework ...] ontogenetic relationship between child and [...] idual. When we, for instance, look at the Oly[mpic ...] we are struck by the competitive overtones, [...] by the strict adherence to rules, some of th[em ...] held unalterable. Indeed, it is this agonistic element that Huizinga (1955) emphasizes as a civilizing element in man. It is understandable, therefore, that he talks about *Homo* ludens, the playing *man* and not the playing child. We need to contrast that with Albert Einstein's observation, cited by Deutsch (1958), as well as by others, that the creative process needs "combinatorial" or "associative play." That type of adult play emphasizes the aspect of spontaneity and nondirectedness, which we usually consider to be part of child's play.

The question then arises of whether these characterizations of adult play are historical or philosophical opposites. Little systematic attention or evaluation was accorded to the play of children before the Romantic age, and our knowledge of it is fragmentary. Limitations on the play of children may have been both biological and economic. Child mortality was high, and man's life span was much shorter; in addition, among the economically less favored classes, children and their labor were an economic asset throughout the Industrial Revolution.

Clues from Toys and Games

Despite these restrictive conditions, we have concrete evidence that children played, and it comes to us in the form of artifacts and paintings. One of the earliest recorded and most universally known aids in recreation was the ball; both children and adults have been depicted as playing with it. Also, in early times at least, both boys and girls played ball, and the Greeks valued it particularly for the elasticity it gave to the figure. Toy soldiers and toy weapons come to us from the Middle Ages lending support to the thesis that most physical action games and sports derived from competition and warfare. The latter explanation would also suggest a class distinction, since the underlying theory of imitation in play would point to the children of the nobility as being the ones practicing such pastimes. One notable record of play among the less privileged classes comes to us in pictorial format. In his painting, *The Games of Children*, the sixteenth-century artist Pieter Breughel the Elder, shows boys and girls playing leapfrog, hoops, tag, playing blind-man's buff, climbing on wooden horses, and piling up on top of one another. Most of the games are physical and outdoor activities. One or two, like games of chance (dice) and dress-up games, are placed either in the courtyards or at windows. From the way the children are dressed, one deduces that they are either peasant or working-class youngsters, and the rough-and-tumble aspect of their play is another clue to their status. But, historically, it leaves no doubt that children played in the sixteenth century and that some of the games played were the forerunners of, or were exactly the same as, those played by children today.

Another source of information about play is dolls. The types of dolls from ancient times suggest, however, that they may have been used more for religious than for recreational purposes. For instance, it is known that, in ancient Greece and Rome, girls consecrated their discarded dolls to Venus and Diana. The china dolls given to Hopi children were considered religious objects, and Hindu child brides would take their doll collections with them at marriage. All these uses seem to suggest an adult-oriented rationale. In Western Europe, the first infant dolls were introduced by Augusta and Richard Montanari in the late nineteenth century in England, although there were dollmakers as early as 1413 in Nuernberg, and fashion dolls were manufactured in Paris from about the same time on.

The Structured versus the Spontaneous Element in Play

It is interesting to note that there is little evidence of either doll play or ball playing in Western Europe during the Middle Ages. Were play and games, then, a domain restricted to adults in the privileged classes? And what about the spontaneous and imaginative aspects of play that these two types of play activities might suggest? Is the agonistic part of the play spirit reflected in the so-called "civilizing" influence of the privileged classes, while the aspect of joyous spontaneity is allowed in artists and fools? Perhaps a closer examination of the type of play predominant at that time may give us the insight and information needed to answer these questions.

A look at the Middle Ages will reveal to us essentially two kinds of playing. One would be the type represented by the tournaments engaged in by knights as approved pastimes and part of court life. The other type of playing engaged in by adults was in connection with church-related dramatic presentation and was thus part of religious life. When we examine them for their salient traits, we find in the courtly games, again, a striving for excellence within a highly competitive setting dominated by strict rules. The church drama also does not allow much leeway in interpretation of their subject matter, and one might speculate that anything spontaneous or playful would be a function of individual characterizations of parts rather than of deviations in subject matter. Still within the arena of drama, but with a more universalist cast, is the medieval morality play. In its cathartic effects, it can be likened to the Greek drama and, historically, is related to the psychoanalytic interpretation of play. We could make an adult–child juxtaposition here that probably can be extrapolated to present times. Both in the ancient world and during the Middle Ages, the adult was allowed uninhibited emotionality within the framework of play-acting. Today, the dramatic media—

theater, film, TV—still exercise cathartic influences on adults, but the same right and privilege is also extended to children. Moreover, as I shall explain in more detail, regarding the functional aspects of child's play in our present time, the catharses experienced through play today are used diagnostically and for therapeutic work.

For my own purposes of inquiry, there is yet another manifestation of play in the Middle Ages, one that is more filled with imagination and spontaneity and that is the "work" of the *troubadour* or the *minnesinger*. Here, in this play-acting of love, there is a much greater range for fantasy and subjective interpretation. It also introduces another aspect of play that we find in some current definitions, namely, the lack of seriousness that was accorded to the troubadour's productions. The threat was never real, or, at least, the pretense had to be kept that it was only play. Another character that represents the playful, not-to-be-taken-seriously aspect of an adult's behavior is the court jester. He also introduces another salient ingredient of playful behavior, namely, a sense of humor. Is the medieval fool, then, the type to whom we could apply the label "creative," by dint of the combinatorial play that he unquestioningly uses in his work? As Hamlet says of poor Yorick, the king's court jester, when he picks up Yorick's skull: "a fellow of infinite jest, of most excellent fancy." And we may go to Shakespeare again for an illustration of the fanciful speech of fools by quoting from King Lear, whose fool is master of the play on words in gruesome situations, lightening them with meaningful ditties such as these:

> *Her boat hath a leak*
> *And she must not speak*
> *Why she dares not come over to thee.*
> [Act III, Sc. 6]

The fool, in general, has permission to lighten dark, brooding moments and thus presents the comic counterpoint to the unfolding tragedy. He is the artist—philosopher and, at the same time, is given a child's license.

The Artist as Practitioner of Playfulness

Another approach to finding an answer to what was earlier posed as possible historical or philosophical opposites might be gained by looking at historical development through the life histories or biographies of artists. The evidence of their creativity is irrefutable. My endeavor here will be to find evidence of whether or not, and how, they played.

An appropriate starting point would be the Renaissance artist. The *Zeitgeist*, dominated by humanism and by the perfectibility of man, should have allowed for the element of spontaneity, one of the important characteristics of play.

Indeed, it is Huizinga (1955) who refers to the whole mental attitude of the Renaissance as one of play, considering it a combination of sophistication and spontaneity and an example par excellence of culture at play. When considering artists like Leonardo da Vinci or Michelangelo, a clear-cut distinction becomes evident between the frivolous and the playful, the latter helping to produce the kind of art forms that are novel yet allow their continuity to be traced from earlier forms, forms that are unfettered in their imagination yet disciplined in their execution. Another example would be Ariosto, of whom Huizinga writes that he is one of the best examples of the play spirit in poetry, with his gay and delightful people whom he endows with glorious mirth. An example of the blithe spirit that did pervade humanism can be found in the writings of Erasmus, which are sparked with irony and wit. And again, according to Huizinga, nothing could be more playful than Rabelais; indeed, he calls him the play spirit incarnate.

We do not necessarily have to accept uncritically Huizinga's general thesis that play is the matrix of culture and the play spirit is the civilizing factor in human development, but empirically, we know that play enters the creative process. This is not restricted to the plastic or literary arts. A very clear-cut example of the playful in the musician and in music is provided by Mozart in the following vignettes. In January 1787, Mozart wrote from Prague to his young friend, Gottfried von Jacquin, in Vienna:

> Well, dearest friend, dearest Hikkitihoki, that is your name as you must know. We all invented names for ourselves on the journey. They are: I am Punkititi. My wife is Schabla Pumfa. Hofer is Rozkapumpa. Adler is Notschopikitischibi. My servant Joseph is Sagadarata. My dog Goukerl is Schomanski. Madam Quallenberg is Runzifunzi. Mlle. Krox is Rumborimuri. Freistaetler is Gaulimauli. Be so kind as to tell him his name. [pp. 84–85]

Einstein, who quotes this passage in *Mozart, His Character and His Work* (1945), adds the following information: Gaulimauli even found its way into a canon by Mozart. It would be labor lost to penetrate into the deeper meanings of the names of this brother- and sisterhood (reference to the Freemasonry structure), but inventing them must have been a cause of endless delight to Mozart, a joy explainable only by their parodistic intent. Another anecdote known to me as part of Mozart folklore is the story that he had composed a piece of music where, at one point, both hands were at the right end of the piano keyboard and a note had to be struck at the far left. The challenge was that nobody could play this. Whereupon Mozart, who was blessed with a rather long and pointy nose, demonstrated that while his hands were at the other side of the keyboard, he could, with his nose, strike the note.

Certainly the last two examples would point to "child-like" behavior in some very special adults, but, paradoxically, qualities such as spontaneity, sense of humor, and joy would characterize the very play spirit that Huizinga regards as civilizing and, thus, part of adult behavior.

The Spontaneous in Play as Part of Education

Perhaps a bridge, and, at the same time, a breakthrough, can be established when we substitute "educational" for "civilizing" and explore Rousseau's visions in *Emile*, which suggest a new look at children's activities, including play. According to Rousseau (see Boyd, 1963), what a child learns is not acquired from the schoolmaster or from any other person, but comes to him without any consciousness of learning in the course of the spontaneous activities of play. Coupled with the emphasis on subjective experience as the basis for knowledge, this notion can, of course, lead to an overidealization of the self-made person, one who is untouched by so-called traditional civilization. Rousseau tempers his model by commenting that children should not be permitted to play separately according to their fancy but should be encouraged to play together in public, and that games especially, should be conducted in such a way that there is always some common end to which all aspire, thus "to accustom them to common action and to stir up emulation" (as quoted in Boyd, 1963, p. 22). One wonders whether this suggests an agonistic element, because the question that begs to be asked is whether it is common action for something or common action against someone or some other group. And when he speaks of emulation, is it of the adult? Does this, then, restrict the freedom and spontaneity originally prescribed? It seems at some points that the kind of freedom and spontaneity that Rousseau advocates is a departure from the set curriculum, an open classroom in an eighteenth-century romantic setting. Historically and philosophically, Rousseau laid the foundation for the educational theories of such nineteenth-century reformers as Pestalozzi and Froebel and, in the United States, John Dewey. Not only were spontaneity and freedom in play accepted as important characteristics of the child's activity, but they were also valued because of their influence on the emotional, social, and intellectual development of the growing individual. The need to integrate play as part of the curriculum is illustrated by Pestalozzi's (Kruesi, 1875) suggestion that, upon entry into school, children be allowed to continue at school the play activities which they have learned at home, "thus giving vent to their natural activity." Combined with his emphasis on joy in learning, Pestalozzi therefore transferred two characteristics of the play of children to the classroom atmosphere. As a footnote, one might add here that another one of Pestalozzi's concerns was the exclusion of the poor from education. From our earlier observations on the differential involvement of the social classes in play, we might go a step further and suggest that children of the poor were not only excluded from the benefits of education but also from the benefits of play. That this was not a total exclusion, however, might be deduced from Froebel's (1895a) collection of Mother Play Songs. These were mostly folk songs that were used in early mother–child interactions and which Froebel further developed for educational purposes. Examples would be the time song "Tick-Tock," the finger-counting game of "Little Thumb, I Say One," and, of course, the universally known baker's song "Pat-a-Cake," which involves motor play. This use of song games was an expression of Froebel's educational philosophy, which relates the child's activities in play to the growth of his mind and harnesses the spontaneity of play for this purpose (Froebel, 1895b).

As we move now through the nineteenth century, with the child at play becoming a more legitimate concern, we can already discern the preoccupation also with the functions of play, with which I will deal at greater length below. Here, I shall continue the focus on the emergence of the child as the principal player. While the early impetus of putting the child on center stage came from Europe, particularly from France and Germany, it was the writings and teachings of John Dewey in the United States that emerged as the most powerful influence in according respectability to a child's play. It becomes apparent that part of play is integrated into the classroom when Dewey asserts, in discussing *The Child and the Curriculum,* "Whatever is uppermost in his mind constitutes to him, for the time being, the universe. That universe is fluid and fluent; it tends to dissolve and re-form with amazing rapidity but after all it Is the child's own world" (cited in Dworkin, 1959, p. 93).

The Current Stance: A Change of Place
between Adult and Child?

The trend toward child-centeredness, begun in the eighteenth century and developed in the nineteenth, was further helped by the work of Freud and Piaget in the twentieth century. While their major interest was personality dynamics and the development of thought, respectively, their analyses of early childhood activities had, of necessity, to take in the area of play that, as we noted earlier, had by the 1930s become acknowledged as the characteristic mode of behavior in childhood.

Within the historical perspective, we can, therefore, say that the movement has been from adult games to child's play, and, correspondingly, the underlying philosophy has moved from a competitive, rule-dominated foundation to the spontaneity, freedom, and sense of fun associated with child behavior. If we add to this viewpoint the fact that play occurs in familiar settings, we can see the value of it as underlining the spontaneous, joyous aspect, a quality that might be lost in some of the agonistic applications of play. I am raising this question at this time because it is going to be part of the problem of PF in an educational setting. The answer is neither simple nor a direct "yes" or "no."

Parenthetically, we might note that there is now a possible reversal in the trend; namely, the elements of spontaneity, nonrestrictiveness, and fun are being culled from the child's activity and also are seen as essential ingredients in the growing leisure activities of adults in our own time.

THE FUNCTIONAL ANALYSIS OF PLAY, OR WHY WE PLAY: NO ROOM FOR PLAYFULNESS

As we looked at play from the perspective of adult versus child involvement, it became evident that the reasons we play or a justification for play were contained in some of the points of view and examples. At first mention, play is usually regarded as a useless or, at best, inconsequential activity, and it is therefore understandable that reasons or justifications for the behavior were sought and elaborated. From a moral point of view, activity without a worthwhile end was dangerous, if not evil; from a rational—deterministic point of view, it was irrational. It is not surprising, therefore, that the early attempts to explain play centered on its utilitarian aspects. Later, the so-called irrationality of play was found to have its hidden reasons, which the various schools of psychoanalysis were to use in diagnosis and therapy of behavior disorders. Another interesting aspect was that only when the focus was on child's play did the question of justification become more acute. The play of adults was in the service of God and King and thus did not need airtight alibis or raise questions. Support for such an interpretation comes again from Huizinga, who found that one of the most important characteristics of play was its spatial separation from ordinary life. His elaboration of that aspect led him to connect play with ritual, including magic and law. If we were to introduce Piagetan concepts at this point, we might be tempted to assert that play thus stimulated both the magical thinking associated with the child and the logical thought patterns of the adult. In this same vein, play was thus a proving ground for the demands of real life and, simultaneously, it served as a buffer against these harsh realities.

Even these very general and broad speculations about the functional basis of play highlight one of the difficulties and at, the same time, the fascinations of play as it relates to human development. It seems like the perfect paradox, or it is all things to all people. On that basis it would, of course, defy further analysis.

In order not to land in such a dead-end street, it is necessary and, hopefully, worthwhile to examine the paradoxes and the contradictions in the existing explanations of why we play and cull from them the best possible guidelines for further scientific investigation.

The Rationales of Some Established Theories of Play

A good starting point is to examine the theories of play, labeled the "surplus" and "deficit" energy models, respectively. At first glance, they sound contradictory in their approaches. An examination of the behavioral bases for their assertions will throw light on their subsumed functions.

Play as a Time to Discharge Energy

Two names are most prominently associated with the surplus energy model of play, that of the German poet Friedrich von Schiller and that of the English philosopher Herbert Spencer. Schiller's thinking about play was sparked by his concern about the aesthetic education of man, and it is in his letters on this subject (Wilkinson & Willoughby, 1967) that his theory of play is found. He relates degree of need satisfaction to serious or playful outlook, suggesting that bare satisfaction of physical needs leads to physical earnestness, while material superfluity (*Ueberfluss*) results in physical play, and, finally, aesthetic super-fluity culminates in aesthetic play. The absence of a goal that Schiller sees in play is perhaps better captured by the concepts of freedom and spontaneity (*Freiheit des Schoenen ueber die Fessel des Zweckes*) and sets down already qualitative aspects of play to which we shall refer later. His thinking, growing out of the Age of Enlightenment, is not unrelated to that of Pestalozzi and Froebel when they posited play as the child's natural activity. The fact that they claimed play also as the prerogative of the children of the poor can be related to Schiller's thinking that only after physical needs are satisfied is there enough surplus energy for play. This is a rather advanced social thesis which has empirical corroborations even today.

Spencer, building on Schiller's theory, elaborated about a century later the evolutionary rather than the social ramifications. He argued (as quoted in Millar, 1968, p. 15) that the lower the animal is on the evolutionary scale, the more its energies are engaged in finding food and escaping from its enemies. In his formulation, there is a direct correlation between amount of play and place on the evolutionary ladder. Man, considered the top of the hierarchy, would then have the most time for play and, logically, those whose bare necessities of life are taken care of would be more prone to play. We, therefore, touch again upon the social aspect of play and the difference in its availability and use as a result of social class structure. An interesting comment on this comes from Rousseau (1964), when he has Emile's tutor remark, "Je ne joue point du tout, étant solitaire et pauvre" (p. 434). Furthermore, he considers play the amusements of the idle, possibly with a negative overtone. The connotation that is conveyed, then, is that surplus energy may be available only to the higher-order animal and the leisure classes. If, as we assert, the play element is related to creativity, then this places an a priori restriction on the lower classes.

Play as a Time to Recharge Energy

What about the deficit model, the relaxation theory of play? The needs that play meet, according to this theory's chief exponents, Schaller (1861) and

Lazarus (1883), two nineteenth-century German thinkers, is to restore energy, to provide recuperation from work. Again, this particular formulation grew out of evolutionary theory. But, again, social aspects cannot be ignored. With respect to children, children did not work in the sense that adults earned their living; and the time set aside for adults to recuperate from work was certainly proportionate to their economic status.

When we compare the two "energy" models, their contradictions seem to be less apparent than their complementary nature, and one cannot help thinking of twentieth-century drive-reduction and arousal models, whose forerunners they are.

Play as Time to Practice Skills

Yet another functional analysis of play was influenced by Darwin's evolutionary theory. At the turn of the century, G. Stanley Hall (1906) proposed that play was used by the child to recapitulate phylogenetic behavior and thus acquire the skills of his ancestors for his own mastery of the environment. This interpretation, while in itself of short-lived significance, made two important contributions to the formulation of play theory. It linked child's play with the play of animals, and it also looked upon play in terms of stages. Today, ethologists study child behavior, including play, and apply the tools used in observing animals to the play of the human young. Dolhinow (1972) talks about the juvenile patas monkey jumping up and down in the tall grass; the monkey may seem to be enjoying a nice sport, but the full importance of these motor patterns is not obvious until you see an adult male patas jumping to divert the attention of a lion from the rest of the group. We can see that Dolhinow's type of thinking is congruent with what Karl Groos (1898, 1901), an early authority on the play of animals and on the play of man, talked about when he considered play the arena for the practice of later-needed skills. Groos, a professor of philosophy, was influenced, as were other thinkers of the nineteenth century, by the Darwinian point of view and based his explanation on the principles of natural selection; thus, he maintained that those animals survive who are best able to cope with prevailing conditions and that, if animals play, play is useful in the struggle for survival. Historically and philosophically, the approach to play as a domain for the practice of skills is, of course, very much in line with growth theories and with the explanations of later educational psychologists, who look upon learning through play as a preparation for later life: developing competence. In their functional analysis of play, both Lange (1901) and Claparede (1934) stress the ego-expanding and reality-meeting aspects of play. A contemporary elaboration of this view would be Erikson's (1950) formulation, seeing the child's play as "the infantile form of the human ability to deal with experience by creating model situations and to master reality by experiment and planning" (p. 194). Interestingly, he prefaced his own theory with the observation that "to be tolerant of the child's play the adult must invent theories which show either that childhood play is really work—or that it does not count" (p. 187). In an orthodox Freudian formulation (Waelder, 1933), play becomes associated with the repetition compulsion and, as such, its function is seen as constantly working over the same experience until it becomes assimilated into the child's functioning and thus leads to a sense of mastery over what might have initially been an overwhelming experience.

Play as a Time for Growth

It is usually hazardous to classify points of view by putting them into separate niches, even when categories are mutually exclusive. In our own case, here, Erikson and Waelder not only qualify as contemporary exponents of growth theories but also represent the stage theories that underlie the Freudian analysis of behavior. In this classification, their approach is related to that of Piaget, a foremost exponent of the stage theory in development. In the historical framework, we must concern ourselves with Piagetian theory in its relatedness to the past; in this respect, Piaget not only sees play in stages but sees it as a medium for developing the intellect: in particular, logical thought. We may, therefore, also connect him with the earlier skills approach to play as well as the growth theories.

What becomes apparent, then, in the historical overview of the functional approach to play is that the theories and speculations interlock, that they share certain assumptions, and that the later models are built on earlier approaches, with appropriate updating, thus bringing the earlier theories in line with the current Zeitgeist.

Similarly, there is no clear-cut division between the *why* and the *how* of play. As we, therefore, turn to the qualitative aspect of play, we must be aware of both the connectedness and the differences. In doing so, I should like to underline that, because of the implicit goal-orientedness of the functional analysis to play, the playful aspect is, of necessity, not accorded its rightful importance and influence on subsequent behavior. It is almost as if froth and frivolity were asked to legitimize their existence. It is easier either to deny that there is frivolity in play or to see that it does not interfere with the more sanctioned purposes of the behavior.

THE QUALITATIVE ANALYSIS OF PLAY, OR HOW WE PLAY: ENTER PLAYFULNESS

Speculations and investigations about the quality or style of play have been less central to the thinking about play and do not seem to go as far back into history as the rationale for playing.

The Balance between Fight and Fun

In his thesis of play as a major civilizing force, which would be the function of play, Huizinga refers to the "play spirit," which must be considered a qualitative aspect. "Joy," "fun," "pretend," and "nonseriousness" are key words in his conceptualization of play. While the fun element is seen as the part that resists all logical analysis, it is at the same time regarded as characterizing the essence of play. It is in the qualitative aspects that the paradox of play becomes even more apparent than in the functional analysis. At the same time that Huizinga refers to the fun and joy in early historical play activities, including its use in liturgy, he mentions the boastful, taunting ingredients demonstrated in the custom of potlatch. Such agonistic elements in play can, if allowed, be used for hostile purposes.

Conflict is also a central theme in the enculturation theory of games, formulated by Roberts and Sutton-Smith (1962). They were able to demonstrate a relationship between childrearing practices and the incidence or existence of games of physical skill, chance, and strategy. Emphasis on obedience training was related to games of strategy, responsibility training was connected to games of chance, and stress on achievement was related to games of physical skills. The inferences were that the conflicts engendered by the differing childrearing techniques were played out in different but predictable games.

As I look at these relationships and ask myself where playfulness would fit in, I could speculate that the youngsters who were held in by obedience found their enjoyment in outwitting the authority figure or an opponent in games of strategy; the children weighted down by responsibility found the spontaneity in chance, the exhilaration of not knowing where the pieces would fall, a source of fun and relaxation; the boys and girls exhorted to achieve, most likely in academic pursuits, found the feedback from physical prowess, or sheer kinetic feedback, a welcome arena for spontaneity and exhilaration.

Playing with the "Gang" or Playing by Oneself

Another qualitative aspect of play is whether it is solitary or group activity. While we can see fun, joy, and pretense as entering both solitary and group activity, it might be speculated that the elements of competition and strategy are more likely to be present when there are others on whom you can practice strategy or against whom you can compete. Paraphrasing Huizinga's "civilizing" effect of play, we might restate his thesis by examing the prosocial and antisocial aspects of play.

In my own investigations of playfulness at the adolescent level, I found it necessary to divide humor into "friendly teasing" and "hostile wit." Similarly, one might conjecture that, within the elements of strategy and competition, there is room for fun and enjoyment, the "glint-in-the-eye" behavior that characterizes the playful approach. Even playing a trick can have friendly overtones. A historical example is the story told by Cellini in his autobiography (undated) of how he disguised a young man as a girl and brought him to a party, introducing him as "Pomona," much to the glee of himself, of the young man, and, later on, of those duped. Similarly, the pretense and nonseriousness of troubadours and court jesters could be classified as prosocial and civilizing, even within the context of competition and strategy. But there is the other side of the coin—the boasting, the taunting, and the hurt in play. We might agree that these aspects can be civilizing, too, but might lead to discontent, a perspective that was well documented by Freud (1930). This, however, does not represent the play spirit mentioned by Huizinga and thus cannot be considered the quintessence of play. Perhaps to the extent that play behavior is more or less playful (i.e., has more or less spontaneity, joy, and humor in it), it is also more or less closely related to the quintessence of play.

While quality of play in groups and societies would be the central interest of social psychologists and anthropologists, the answer to the question of how an individual child plays in relation to his environment is the key to the clinicians's approach to diagnosis and therapy. This is a twentieth-century application of analyzing conflicts in play, and the qualities found are not usually the ones associated with the play spirit. On the contrary, it is deviation from the play spirit that is significant. Thus, we have Moustakas (1955) reporting on play therapy with normal children, whom he found to be happy, often singing and humming, and, in their actions, more decisive and spontaneous than the disturbed youngsters. Hartley, Frank, and Goldenson (1952) remarked about their nursery-school children that the well-adjusted children played as enthusiastically as the troubled youngsters, but their delight in the toys was greater.

A Dash of Joy

Contemporary developmental psychologists also refer to the qualitative aspects of play when they discuss the various phases of growth. Piaget (1945) distinguishes playful from merely imitative behavior and describes it as a process whereby the child incorporates external objects to his own thought schemata in a joyful manner. In a similar vein, Hunt (1961) finds function pleasure in play as a quality that frequently accompanies learning as a result of aimless activity.

While the conflictual quality of play has been more widely discussed because of its relationship to underlying functional needs, the aimless activity with a dash of joy comes closer to Huizinga's play spirit and thus to the essence of play. It would seem also to be the quality that Schiller refers to in his distinction between quantitative and qualitative superfluity. The key to the connection between play and the aesthetic impulse is not that the individual enjoys play more, but that he or she enjoys it differently. As an example, he cites the intrinsic value of ease of movement, an element that I have found to be an important component in my conceptualization of playfulness.

Whither with the Qualitative Approach?

Scientific thought has always been aimed at precision and explanation and, therefore, the most obvious way of analyzing play or of explaining any kind of behavior is to look for the underlying causes, an approach that I call the "functional" approach. It is a valid approach but, according to my own thinking, not the only fruitful one, especially with amorphous behavior such as play. The reasons we play have been given much consideration and also were the bases for numerous studies, especially in the more behavioristic framework, where we can use such variables as need reduction and need arousal, which are more amenable to measurement. The studies about how we play or the research based on questions of how we play can be found in the early descriptive literature of the 1920s, such as the Lehman and Witty (1927) study. It is only recently that this particular perspective has been adopted again by researchers, such as Rivka Eifermann (1971), who did an extremely detailed and comprehensive study of how children differ in their play—differ as a result of social class, type of school, and type of setting—and tried to relate it to the theses of enculturation. Other studies concentrated on what I called earlier the "nonplay spirit" within children's play. Again, this is understandable because of our interest in helping individuals to overcome both their hostility, aggression, and anxiety and/or to work them out in the play situation.

Recently, however, it has been more common and acceptable to concentrate on prosocial behavior, such as altruism, empathy, and affection (Aronfreed & Paskal, 1965; Dreman & Greenbaum 1973; M. L. Hoffman, 1975; Rosenhan, Underwood, & Moore, 1974; Staub, 1971; Yarrow, Scott, & Waxler, 1973), and to try to measure it. I say advisedly to try to measure it, because this is where the difficulty lies. It is much easier to observe, and then to tally, when a child pushes another child or calls another child nasty names, but how do we measure how much a child likes another child or enjoys his or her activity, or whether or not he or she has fun? Perhaps one of the reasons that so little research has been done in this area is because it is so fraught with difficulties in quantification. But this is only one reason. As I indicated earlier, the causal approach to relationships is the approach underlying scientific investigations. The question of "how" in behavior and trait clusters was considered a lower-order approach, especially if the question is not related to another trait or experience. Beach (1945), in his discussion on the then current concepts of play in animals, very cogently makes an argument against assessing that particular quality of play. He says, "Explaining a playful response by referring its occurrence to one assumed character common to all forms of play is equivalent to assuming that water boils because it is hot" (in Herron & Sutton-Smith, 1971, p. 202). I will take exception to this statement; I am suggesting that we go in a different direction by not trying first to explain a playful response. We accept the playful response as one of the characteristics of play, or as a response that occurs in play and that characterizes it as play, and then go beyond it and look for this type of response in other types of behavior, such as imagination and creativity. In these particular domains, we can then fruitfully relate the response to the types of imagination and the types of creativity that go hand in hand with what I consider more or less playful. In a way, this approach would be in line with the suggestions by Beach in his conclusions. What is needed in the analysis and research on play—and Beach connects it with any serviceable definition of play—is that "a number of predominating characteristics which combine to set it off from nonplayful behavior" (Beach, 1945, p. 209) should be isolated and tested. His own frame of reference is that these would be traits that, as an aggregate, lack immediate, biologically useful results. I would not necessarily agree, but then these statements were made in 1945, a time in psychology when creativity was hardly mentioned in the sense that we now use it both in psychological theory and in research as divergent thinking in the Guilford Model of Intellect (1956). In essence, I do not dispute the suggestion that play needs to be defined in the objective terms that comparative and experimental psychologists like Beach (1945) and Berlyne (1969) have been stressing repeatedly. My contention is that certain characteristics of play can be helpful in analyzing behavior other than play and/or can be related to cognitive dimensions at a later stage of development. Perhaps, in summation, one can say that we get different answers from the functional and the qualitative model of play, that both are necessary for the analysis of behavior called play, and that there are, naturally, areas where the two models not only intersect but also interact, so that the "why" and the "how" can lead to useful results in one and the same investigation. My concern is with the relative scarcity of investigations that try to capture the general exuberance and *joie de vivre*, as Frank Beach calls it, or the playfulness, as I label it, in play. Certainly, the difficulties of such attempts are acknowledged and will be illustrated in subsequent chapters, but this is no reason for not trying to identify and measure behavior which can give us important clues to type and style of thinking in later years.

III

Playfulness in Play and the Player: Developmental Studies of a Qualitative Aspect of Play

If we look at an accepted psychological definition of play, namely, "voluntary activity pursued without ulterior purpose and, on the whole, with enjoyment or expectation of enjoyment" (English & English, 1958, p. 394), its amorphousness and open-endedness is self-evident. It is, therefore, understandable and, indeed, necessary for researchers to define for themselves the aspects of play that they propose to study.

In my own approach to the study of play (Lieberman, 1964, 1965), I went beyond the play setting. I attempted—and to some extent succeeded—to cull from play what I perceived to be its quintessence and labeled this "playfulness." Furthermore, I hypothesized that playfulness as a quality of play would developmentally transform itself into a personality trait of the player in adolescence and adulthood (Lieberman, 1967a).

It was in preliminary, observational studies of *how* children played that the concept of "playfulness" emerged and was operationally defined as physical, social, and cognitive spontaneity, manifest joy, and sense of humor. Within the framework of play, it was seen as a quality of play. While in and of itself quality of play, or playfulness (PF), was important as part of the behavior repertory of the young child, its significance was seen to involve questions of a much broader nature:

1. whether PF as a personality trait is a unitary behavior dimension across physical, social, and cognitive functioning at various age levels;
2. whether the behavioral indices of PF are comparable at the various age levels;
3. what some of the childrearing antecedents are that influence PF;

4. what some of the variables in teacher personality and methodology are that influence PF;
5. whether PF gives a clue to the type of cognitive processes in an individual that have been labeled "divergent thinking."

In order to present the case for playfulness as it emerged from my studies, let me first describe the two major investigations. In addition, I will also report more briefly on some ancillary pilot investigations.

THE KINDERGARTEN STUDY: PLAYFULNESS AND ITS RELATIONSHIP TO DIVERGENT THINKING

My approach in 1960 was guided by the following observations:

1. The individual style of a child's play had not been given sufficient attention in the studies on young children's play activities.
2. The early identification of creative potential was becoming increasingly important. At that time, studies using Guilford's conceptual framework and tests based on his divergent thinking factors had not, to any extent, included the young child.
3. Empirical observations as well as theoretical formulation seemed to point to playfulness as a behavior trait that might manifest itself in the quality of a child's play and might relate to an aspect of thinking that is found in creative individuals.

The specific hypotheses tested were:

1. Playfulness in kindergartners is made up of different component traits, namely, physical spontaneity, manifest joy, sense of humor, social spontaneity, and cognitive spontaneity; and, through their intercorrelations, the component traits form a unitary behavior dimension of playfulness.
2. The more playful kindergartners do better on divergent thinking tasks.

The subjects were 93 kindergarten children (52 boys and 41 girls) from middle-class homes attending one of five private kindergarten classes in three New York City schools. The mean CA (chronological age) of the children was 5 years 6 months; the *SD* (standard deviation) was 4 months.

Measures of Evaluation

The three instruments used in this study were a rating scale for playfulness, a test interview for divergent thinking, and a standardized picture vocabulary test for an estimate of intelligence.

The Playfulness Scale produced ratings on each child on five behavior dimensions by two independent judges who had known the subject for some time. In this case, these were the child's teachers.

The Divergent Thinking Tasks gave separate scores for fluency, flexibility, and originality, on the basis of a structured, individually administered test.

The Peabody Picture Vocabulary Test yielded a mental age score and, thus, in Guilford's terms, provided a cognitive–semantic measure and, possibly, a control to the divergent-thinking semantic units and classes from the Divergent Thinking Tasks test.

The Playfulness Scale

The Playfulness Scale was developed by me for this study. It consists of five subscales corresponding to the five behavior traits of physical spontaneity, manifest joy, sense of humor, social spontaneity, and cognitive spontaneity. Each scale is divided into an A and a B part, referring to the quantity and the quality of the trait measured. These subdivisions were made in order not to contaminate frequency with degree or intensity of the trait measured. The further refinement was considered helpful to the raters. The division also indicated no prior assumption that quantity and quality were related. Ratings are made on a 5-point scale. Descriptive labels for the points on the scale are given as are sample behavior items for each trait to be rated. The samples of behavior for each trait were provided to ensure greater reliability for the ratings. As a check on validity, two questions not related to the behavior indices stipulated for playfulness were included. These scales asked for an evaluation of the child's intelligence and of his physical attractiveness.

Appendix A gives the Playfulness Scale, together with the rating instructions.

The Divergent Thinking Tasks

Three tests were administered, namely:

1. *Product Improvement:* a two-part test, each part with a time limit of 1 minute and 30 seconds, in which the child was asked to suggest ideas of how a toy dog and a doll could be changed to make them more fun to play with The test could be scored for ideational fluency, spontaneous flexibility, and originality.

2. *Plot Titles:* a two-part test, each part with a time limit of 2 minutes, in which two illustrated stories were read and shown to the child, and the child was asked to supply names for the stories. They were both about animals. The test could be scored for ideational fluency and originality.

3. *The Monroe Language Classification Test:* a three-part test, each part with a time limit of 30 seconds, in which the child was asked to list the names of animals, things to eat, and toys. The test could be scored for ideational fluency and spontaneous flexibility.

Two of these tasks, namely, Product Improvement and Plot Titles, were modeled after existing measures but were adapted to the age level. This involved making Torrance's Product Improvement a two-part test, with the addition of a doll. In the case of Plot Titles, I wrote original stories which were illustrated by a professional artist to make the test look like a book appropriate for 4- to 5-year-olds.

Here, a brief explanation note should be given of the order of presentation of the tests and the decision to time them. Arousing and holding the attention of 5-year-olds was the chief criterion for the sequence. Product Improvement was found good for establishing rapport. Plot Titles was then tackled more willingly, and the Monroe Test left most children with an apparent feeling of success. As to timing, the methodological necessity of securing comparable data required some standardization in the setting. As it was, in the adaptation of Product Improvement and Plot Titles, the time was shortened to make allowance for the limited attention span in kindergartners. No change was necessary in the timing of the Monroe Test.

The test interview concluded with some informal questions about work and play.

A special scoring guide was drawn up for the Divergent Thinking Tasks. As far as possible, the rationale was modeled after existing tests by Torrance (1960) and Guilford (1951, 1952), but the introduction of a new product, namely, the doll, and the original text of the stories called for specific guidelines for the answers obtained.

Interscorer reliability for the divergent thinking scores was established on a sample of 20 records and was uniformly in the high .90s.

Reliability of Playfulness Ratings

The reliability coefficients, obtained from the ratings of the two teachers for the five traits and considered quantitatively and qualitatively, under Parts A and B, ranged, with a Spearman–Brown correction, from .66 for frequency of sense of humor to .83 for frequency of physical spontaneity, with a mean of .70.

A correlation coefficient of .55 is considered typical for conventional rating scales. A Spearman–Brown correction for doubling would give a reliability coefficient of .71. Five of the playfulness subscales show corrected r's of .70 or better, while the other five are in the upper .60s.

Although the sizes of the correlation coefficients cannot be considered highly satisfactory, they can be accepted as an initial basis for the identification of the behavior. The differences among the correlations are not statistically significant, but the questions and comments from the teachers during the two briefing sessions allow some tentative interpretation of the stability of the observations. Closer agreement between the two raters on the quantitative dimension (Part A) on all traits except sense of humor can be attributed to the frequency of the activity being apparently more easily observable and less affected by subjectivity.

Unidimensionality versus Multidimensionality of Playfulness

According to the first of the two hypotheses listed earlier, playfulness in kindergartners is made up of different component traits, namely, physical spontaneity, manifest joy, sense of humor, social spontaneity, and cognitive spontaneity, and through their intercorrelations, the component traits form a unitary behavior dimension of playfulness.

The correlations among the combined ratings for Parts A and B show that the playfulness traits form a cluster of highly related behavior—the lowest r being .61, between sense of humor and physical spontaneity, and the highest being .86, between manifest joy and cognitive spontaneity. While the two additional ratings on intelligence and physical attractiveness are not so highly related to the playfulness traits as are the traits to one another, the obtained correlations still reach significance, as do those for CA and MA (mental age).

When centroid factors were extracted, as shown in Table 3.1, four of the five playfulness traits had almost uniform loadings in the middle .80s on the first centroid factor, the only exception being physical spontaneity, whose loading was in the high .70's. Ratings on intelligence and on physical attractiveness showed considerably lower loadings. Accepting the usual .30 as a level of practical significance, they were, however, still significant, as were, again, CA and MA.

TABLE 3.1
Centroid Factor Matrix for Playfulness Scales, MA and CA

Rating	Centroid factors			Communality h^2
	S_1	S_2	S_3	
Physical spontaneity	776	175	379	777
Social spontaneity	857	097	103	754
Cognitive spontaneity	887	182	139	839
Manifest joy	890	236	149	870
Sense of humor	847	−199	−040	759
Estimated intelligence	540	−355	−160	444
Physical attractiveness	369	311	134	251
CA	377	239	−283	277
MA	406	087	−190	209

Note: Decimal points have been omitted.

These findings support the first hypothesis of this study and provide a basis for computing a global score for playfulness. However, it cannot be overlooked that estimates of intelligence and physical attractiveness were also saturated with this factor, though to a considerably lesser degree. A similar pattern of saturation was shown by CA and MA. The fact that the two ratings came from the same source as the playfulness traits might account for some of the saturation, but this would not hold for the independent measures of CA and MA. The latter suggest the influence of development in playfulness. The slightly higher loadings on estimate of intelligence and MA might indicate that, as far as the behavioral dimensions of playfulness are concerned, intellectual abilities seem to carry greater weight than physical.

When due allowance is made for a certain amount of subjectivity in hand rotations and for the limited number of tests, the rotated factors give supplementary information. The results from the orthogonal hand rotations, which aimed at positive manifold and simple structure, suggest that three factors might explain playfulness. The pattern loadings indicate the spontaneities—physical, social, and cognitive—and manifest joy heavily saturated by Factor A. Sense of humor, estimate of intelligence, and physical attractiveness form a triad on Factor B, with significant loadings also being shown by social and cognitive spontaneity. Factor C accounts for the greatest amount of variance in CA and MA, with almost equally high loadings by social and cognitive spontaneity and manifest joy.

The behavior dimensions that contributed to the pattern loadings were used as guides in naming the factors. Factor A is called joyful spontaneity, Factor B is brightness and sparkle, and Factor C is maturation. In a way, Factor A is named in a somewhat circular fashion, which can be defended on the basis that it best describes the behavior characteristics rated. The pattern loadings of sense of humor, estimate of intelligence, and physical attractiveness, which contribute most heavily to Factor B, seem to suggest a child that, by a combination of clever sayings and good looks, catches the attention of the observer. This "being in the limelight" glow would also explain the carryover into social spontaneity and, to a lesser degree, cognitive spontaneity. Calling Factor C "maturation" is based on the inference that being older and brighter brings with it a certain feeling of competence that comes to permeate all areas of development except physical spontaneity.

In regard to the question of the dimensionality of playfulness, playfulness could still be applied to all three factors as an overall term for the behavior of joyful spontaneity (Factor A), brightness and sparkle (Factor B) and maturation (Factor C). This would then suggest a three-factor trait. Or, playfulness could be equated with joyful spontaneity alone and thus be considered a unitary trait. Brightness and sparkle, as well as maturation, would then be considered outside playfulness itself, but related to it.

As to the validity of the playfulness concept, the lower loadings of the estimates of intelligence and physical attractiveness scales on the first centroid factor and the nonsignificant loadings on Factor A, when rotated, suggest at least that playfulness traits have more in common with one another than with the other two measures.

The Relationship between Playfulness and Divergent Thinking

According to the second of the two hypotheses listed, the more playful kindergartners do better on divergent thinking tasks.

Table 3.2 shows the correlations among the five playfulness traits, namely, physical, social, and cognitive spontaneity, manifest joy, and sense of humor, and the three divergent thinking factors, that is, ideational fluency, spontaneous flexibility, and originality. Table 3.2 also gives the correlations with these factors when playfulness is treated as a global score. Correlations between playfulness—traits and global score—and the two separate orginality scores are also indicated. All are significant except the correlation between originality and physical spontaneity.

Additional information on the validity of the relationship between playfulness and divergent thinking came from computing correlations between ideational fluency, spontaneous flexibility, and originality, and the two questions aimed at testing halo on the rating scale. Correlations between physical attractiveness and ideational fluency, spontaneous flexibility, and originality were

TABLE 3.2
Correlation Coefficients between Playfulness Traits (Parts A and B Combined), Playfulness (All Five Traits Combined), and Divergent Thinking Factors (Combined Scores) and Originality (Weighted and Cleverness)

	Divergent thinking factors				
	Ideational fluency	Spontaneous flexibility	Originality	Originality (weighted)	Originality (cleverness)
Playfulness traits					
Physical spontaneity	$.29^c$	$.19^a$	.13NS	$.26^c$	−.02NS
Social spontaneity	$.35^c$	$.25^b$	$.25^b$	$.34^c$	.07NS
Cognitive spontaneity	$.35^c$	$.27^c$	$.21^a$	$.32^c$	.13NS
Manifest joy	$.33^c$	$.20^a$	$.22^a$	$.34^c$	.10NS
Sense of humor	$.30^c$	$.23^a$	$.22^a$	$.29^c$	.10NS
Playfulness (global score)	$.36^c$	$.26^b$	$.23^a$	$.35^c$	.09NS

[a]Significant at .05 level, one-tailed test, n = 90.
[b]Significant at .01 level, one-tailed test, n = 90.
[c]Significant at .005 level, one-tailed test, n = 90.

−.03, .00, and −.03, respectively. For the rating of estimated intelligence, the coefficients were .12, .16, and .20, respectively, none of which reach significance.

Before drawing any conclusions from the data, it is necessary to evaluate the reliability and validity of the measures for divergent thinking as used in this study.

As to the reliability of the tests themselves, the range of the reliability coefficients is from .56 for spontaneous flexibility on the Monroe Test to .87 for ideational fluency on Plot Titles, with a mean of .75, which can be considered satisfactory.

The question about the validity of the measures, however, calls for a closer examination of the interrelationships among the eight divergent thinking scores. What is immediately obvious are the high correlations among scores for different factors derived from the same test—to cite only one example, an *r* of .69 between spontaneous flexibility and ideational fluency on Product Improvement—as against the much lower coefficients between the same factor from different tests and the uneven pattern of correlations, though never too high, among different factors from different tests.

A comparison was made of the average intercorrelations or simple intercorrelations between the same factors from different tests and the average intercorrelations between different factors from different tests. The average correlation among the ideational fluency scores across tests of .24 is only slightly higher than ideational fluency's average *r* of .19 with spontaneous flexibility and .20 with originality. A similar breakdown for spontaneous flexibility shows an *r* of .24 between the spontaneous flexibility scores from the two different tests, namely, Product Improvement and the Monroe, against spontaneous flexibility's average *r* of .19 with ideational fluency, as already noted, and .17 with originality scores. Since both originality scores were derived from the same test—the *r* in their case being .69—they were omitted from this comparison. Average correlations for one originality score (cleverness) were also computed separately with ideational fluency and spontaneous flexibility. This lowers the average *r* between ideational fluency and originality from .20 to .17 and raises it between spontaneous flexibility and originality from .17 to .18 but, in essence, changes the picture little.

The most immediate impression is that while in all cases the same-factor relationship across tests is higher than that for different factors, the difference lies between .24 and a range from .17 to .20 and is thus slight. This raises the question of whether or not at this age level or with these measures the different divergent factors are really separable. Moreover, when the average intercorrelations between ideational fluency and spontaneous flexibility and the independent measure of intelligence, namely MA, were examined, the obtained *r*'s were .19 with ideational fluency and .18 with spontaneous flexibility. This indicates, again, only a slightly higher relationship among the divergent thinking factors themselves than their intercorrelations with the convergent abilities.

It is a moot question whether or not the overlap of divergent with convergent thinking abilities found in the present investigation nullifies or even modifies differences between them at this age level. Nor can a definite answer be given of whether or not divergent thinking factors are separable in kindergartners. What may be asserted from the findings is the presence of ideational fluency and spontaneous flexibility in kindergartners.

The relationship between playfulness and these two factors of divergent thinking, therefore, can be meaningfully considered. Both separately and as a global score, playfulness traits in kindergartners, as evaluated by teachers' ratings, and ideational fluency and spontaneous flexibility, as obtained from the Divergent Thinking Tasks, appear to have a common element, which makes for a significant relationship.

In trying to pinpoint this underlying common dimension, it might be claimed that joyful spontaneity in play gives a clue to a similar case of functioning when the child is faced with a more structured task that requires flow of ideas and shift of set. It must, however, be borne in mind that CA and MA were seen to influence both behavior dimensions, and thus the claim for a clear-cut relationship is weakened. One additional finding is of interest, especially in view of later follow-up studies examining possible sex differences: Inspection of the correlations of sex with the playfulness components (i.e., spontaneity, manifest joy, and sense of humor), as well as with global playfulness score and the divergent thinking factors, indicates that such sex differences as did occur could be attributed to chance.

THE HIGH SCHOOL STUDY: PLAYFULNESS AS A
PERSONALITY TRAIT IN ADOLESCENTS

Investigations of divergent thinking have periodically mentioned the term "playful" as a personality correlate. Getzels and Jackson (1962) found it to be a differentiating trait between creative and intelligent adolescents in their fantasy productions on the TAT (Thematic Apperception Test). The individual profiles presented by Wallach and Kogan (1965) underline the element of playfulness in their highly creative, highly intelligent youngsters. In our investigations (Lieberman, 1964, 1965), a relationship between playfulness as a quality of play in kindergartners and the divergent thinking factors of ideational fluency, spontaneous flexibility, and originality was found.

Empirical observations, experimental data, and theoretical formulations as shown by Lieberman (1967a), Piaget (1945), Rogers (1959), and Torrance (1962) lead to the assumption that playfulness as a quality of play survives the age of play and may become a personality trait of the player and possibly a clue to cognitive style, in particular, divergent thinking.

Theoretically and empirically, playfulness is part of the adolescent's behavior pattern. Cognitively, the adolescent is capable of "as if" thinking, which seems to be a prerequisite to toying with ideas and concepts as well as seeing remote connections. Emotionally and socially, there is an expanding of the horizon and a loosening of previous bonds. Physically, a new energy reservoir is opened up.

In planning the investigation of playfulness at the adolescent level, the underlying assumptions were as follows.

1. There is a resurgence of the joyful-spontaneity–sense-of-humor syndrome during adolescence.
2. This behavior syndrome is related to cognitive style and may be a clue to divergent thinking in adolescents.

Specifically, it was hypothesized that behavioral indices for spontaneity–physical, social, and cognitive—manifest joy, and sense of humor could be identified in adolescents in the high school classroom and that teachers would be able to rate adolescents along these traits. A corollary hypothesis was the dimensionality of playfulness. Furthermore, in order to round out the concept of playfulness, the dimension of nonplayfulness was introduced, without any prior assumption of complementarity.

Investigations into adolescent playfulness were carried out in two stages. The first stage was the formulation of the measuring instrument at the adolescent level, and the second was the testing of the instruments on large-scale populations.

Playfulness Observed in the High School Classroom

Phase 1: Formulation of the PF–NonPF Scale (A Format)

Once it had been decided to assess playfulness in the adolescent in relation to learning in the classroom, the question that needed to be tackled first was whether or not the behavioral correlates of the kindergarten level could be used in the high school classroom. An adaptation of the kindergarten scale was tried for adolescents. However, my visits to the high school classrooms during the spring of 1966 and follow-up discussions with teachers and fellow psychologists pointed to the need to establish behavioral criteria based on the way high school teachers in the classroom saw this behavior.

SUBJECTS AND PROCEDURE
Drawn from public and private schools in New York City and its suburbs and representing a range of subject matter areas, 115 junior high school and high

school teachers completed an open-ended questionnaire aimed at getting the following information:

1. their conceptualization of playfulness and nonplayfulness in general;
2. playfulness and nonplayfulness in a teenager;
3. behavioral traits or incidents by which playfulness and nonplayfulness could be observed in the classroom.

RESULTS

A content analysis of the collected data showed that the teachers' conceptualization covered intellectual, emotional, social, and motor manifestations as well as combinations of the above dimensions. A breakdown in direction (i.e., positive or negative connotation) on a sample of 36 questionnaires was the next step in ordering the data. They are markedly different from the results of the formulation of playfulness in the kindergarten scale, in which there were no negative elements in playfulness or positive mentions for nonplayfulness. Interestingly, though, two questions included for tapping a teacher's attitude toward playfulness and nonplayfulness, but not used for the formulation of the scale, indicated that, as a global concept, playfulness was seen more often as being stimulating to classroom learning (44 positive mentions versus 3 negative, and 8 suggesting a combination), and nonplayfulness was seen as inhibiting learning, especially creativity (46 negative mentions versus 6 positive).

The problem at hand now was to construct an instrument on what seemed, at first glance, a wide range of differing traits. A frequency count of the behavioral correlates mentioned by the teachers produced 294 mentions for playfulness and 260 for nonplayfulness. A preliminary sort of these correlates of playfulness–nonplayfulness as observed in the classroom produced 10 categories for playfulness and 21 for nonplayfulness. With the help of a graduate assistant, I aimed at establishing logically consistent profiles within the teachers' formulations and was able to reduce the 21 categories of nonplayfulness to 10. Inspection of these categories suggested a complementary trend on a continuum, and these 10 profiles for playfulness and nonplayfulness were matched and formed the basis of 10 playfulness–nonplayfulness scales. In addition to the profiles at each end of the scale, it was decided—for greater clarity and ease of evaluation by the teachers—to flag the extremes with descriptive traits, which referred to the most characteristic behavior sketched in the profile.

In order to help the rater make finer distinctions, the questions headlining each of the 10 subscales indicated either quantity or quality. Thus, five behavior dimensions—physical, social, cognitive, emotional, and a combination (sense of humor)—emerged, each of them subdivided into a quantity and intensity dimension. The final format was constructed after a pilot run involving 10 high school teachers (graduate students in an education course) to see whether or not descriptions and profiles were meaningful units.

Two questions not pertaining to playfulness—nonplayfulness behavior were added as ringers to test for the "halo" effect. These were directed to the achievement orientation and physical attractiveness of the student and make up Scales VI and VII of the playfulness—nonplayfulness instrument.

A copy of the final form of the rating scale and of the rating instructions are included in Appendix B. Both in dimension and in format, it was not much different from the kindergarten scale. The major difference lies in the behavioral correlates. These must be viewed in a developmental framework; they make sense in that light.

Phase 2: Trait Composition and Dimensionality of PF—NonPF in Adolescents

Since my first aim was to explore the "fun in learning" aspect of playfulness, I thought it legitimate to test the rating scale on a representative sample of high school students. The major thrust, therefore, was assessing PF—nonPF in the classroom.

Standardization of the PF—NonPF Measure

A cross-sectional representative sample of students in Grades 9 through 12 were rated by their teachers on the PF—nonPF measure. Since it is difficult at the high school level to find students who follow the same program and at the same time to get a representative sample, it was decided to increase the total sample, to get test—retest data on the total sample, and to use a subsample restricted to a private school and urban schools, where a combination of regular and student teachers was available for an interrater reliability check.

TEACHER SAMPLE

The raters were 22 teachers from 7 subject matter areas; 27 class groups were included. The subject matter areas were: English, social studies, science, mathematics, modern languages, secretarial studies, and shop.

Lists of teachers who had volunteered for the study were acquired, and the selection of those to be involved was based on the subject matter area of the teacher and the characteristics of the students. A group of students, as representative as possible in terms of age, sex, grade, and achievement level, was chosen. In one sample—the largest—a modified randomization was used in the selection.

Class rosters were obtained from each participating teacher, and all class members were originally included in the sample. Those students with whom the teacher felt too little acquainted or those who were chronically absent were subsequently dropped from the sample.

STUDENT SAMPLE

The final sample consisted of 610 junior high school and high school students from seven New York City schools and two suburban schools. Originally, data were collected for 643 subjects, but for 33 subjects of one class, data were incomplete and those subjects were only used for one special analysis of variance. Data for them were not included in the frequency distributions. The subjects were drawn from Grades 9 through 12 and were between 13.1 and 19.3 years of age. Since no IQ scores were available, classes at various homogeneous achievement levels, as well as several heterogeneous achievement groups, were selected to form a representative sample of high school students. The range of homogeneous class achievement levels was from "below average" to "above average." The distributions of subjects by age and sex, by grade, sex, and school location, and by level of achievement provided a sufficiently balanced population on which to base generalizations.

PROCEDURE

At least 6 weeks after school had started, briefing sessions of about 1 hour were held with the regular teachers at each of the cooperating schools and with the student teachers in my office. During these sessions, the rating instructions, a copy of the rating scale, as well as a sample of the trait rating sheet were distributed to the teachers. The scales were discussed one by one, and questions were invited. The teachers then were asked to observe the behavior of their students in the classes to be rated for the next 10 days to 2 weeks, after which they received the class rosters, listed separately on the trait rating sheets for each of the 10 subscales of PF—nonPF and the two ringer questions about achievement orientation and physical attractiveness. Special emphasis was placed on the instruction that, in the rating, they were to compare the students with one another as well as to keep in mind a general standard for these traits in adolescents in the high school setting. This emphasis, of course, was meant to reduce the halo effect.

A second briefing session of about 30 minutes was held before the retest, which was given after an interval of from 4 to 6 weeks. One additional feature in the second briefing session was the inclusion of a ranking sheet, on which the class was to be assessed according to the teacher's global perception of PF—nonPF before the second rating was carried out. The ranking was added as an internal validity check. This procedure was followed for all the teachers involved in the test—retest ratings.

A special subsample of nine teachers was involved in establishing interrater reliability on 158 subjects. Two school systems were involved, one public and one private; approximately half of the students came from each. Grades 9, 10, 11, and 12 were represented, and six sets of double ratings were obtained (that is, six sets of two teachers rated the same group of students so that their ratings could be compared). Of the nine teachers, three were student teachers and six were regular teachers. Three double ratings were obtained from the cooperating teacher and student teacher, who worked with the children at the same hour of the day and in the same subject matter area. Three other double ratings were obtained from regular teachers who worked with the same groups of students but at different hours of the day and in different subject matter areas. Altogether, teachers in four different subject matter areas were involved. An attempt was made to hold briefing sessions on a more intensified scale with these raters. In two or three cases, it was also possible to have a third session before the actual rating was done, in order to clarify any points that might have come up in sample ratings they had been asked to do. However, in the cases in which student teacher and regular teacher were paired, the briefing of the regular teacher was done "at second hand" (i.e., by written instructions and by word of mouth through the student teacher). Double ratings for all groups except one were obtained at the time of the test.

STATISTICAL PROCEDURES

Since the primary goal of the study was the construction and standardization of a measure to assess playfulness and nonplayfulness in adolescents as observed in the high school classroom, the statistical approach was aimed at defining playfulness and nonplayfulness by consensual agreement of the experts and then, on the basis of considering the emerging trait or traits continuous, using correlational analysis to determine the relationships among the separate PF—nonPF dimensions as well as among those of age, grade, and sex.

The dimensionality of PF—nonPF was explored by a principal components factor analysis and was reduced by varimax rotation to four factors. Since test—retest correlations were sufficiently high (in the .70s), it was decided to use only the test data for the PF—nonPF ratings and add to them the questions on achievement orientation and physical attractiveness as well as on age and sex of student, grade level of student, and sex of teacher, which constituted a 16 × 16 matrix.

Some mention should be made here of the nonplayfulness end of the scale. Since this behavior crystallized as a complementary dimension, there could be only indirect evidence on the clusterings from individual profiles and from the frequency distributions of percentage scores.

The newness of the concepts involved made it necessary to proceed with caution and to include validity and reliability checks at the various phases of the construction and standardization of the instrument.

The major correlation matrix for 610 subjects was a 35 × 35 table and consisted of the 10 PF—nonPF scores on test, the 2 ringer scores, sums of odd-numbered and even-numbered scales and total scale score, the retest scores on these 15 variables, age and sex of student, grade level, normalized ranking of PF—nonPF by teacher, and sex of teacher. Reliabilities could, therefore, be read directly from the matrix for each item with total score, and one aspect of item reliability could thus be established. Of course, a certain amount of spuriousness enters into these coefficients, and some caution must be exercised in their interpretation.

The reliability of the test itself was estimated by the Kuder–Richardson formula based on item statistics. Another check on reliability was obtained by correlating the quantity (A) scales with the quality (B) scales on the basis that frequency and degree of the same behavior should be equivalent. A stability coefficient was also available from the retest data, both for total test score and by item (component traits), which provided a more conservative estimate of item reliability.

A separate matrix was run for 158 subjects on which ratings from two teachers were available. These data provided a measure of interrater reliability.

Validity data on the instrument consisted of the logical validity based on the content analysis and the concurrent validity obtained through the correlations of test and retest, as well as separate items, with the rankings by the teachers of each subject on total PF–nonPF as conceived by the respective teacher.

Concurrent validity.   To determine concurrent validity of the test, a comparison was made between the normalized rankings the teachers assigned their students on overall playfulness and the students' scores on the playfulness measure. Although the teachers' rankings were obtained after the first test was administered, it can be considered an adequate criterion for the following reasons. First, the rankings were obtained at least 4 weeks after the first ratings, when the teachers' original scorings were not fresh in their memories. At the same time, having been asked to evaluate the playfulness of the students once on specific subscales, it can be expected that they were sensitized to behavior that might be termed "playful" and thus were able to evaluate their students more

TABLE 3.3

Correlations between Ss' Rank on Playfulness (Global) and Ss' Score on PF–NonPF Subscales for Test and Retest[a]

		Correlations with rank	
Subscales		Test	Retest
Total score		.69	.76
IA	Physically on the move–physically rigid	.58	.72
IB	Physically alert–physically apathetic	.44	.62
IIA	Enthusiastic–discouraged	.32	.35
IIB	Relaxed (spontaneous)–tense (constricted)	.59	.73
IIIA	Fun loving–humorless	.63	.71
IIIB	Accepting in wit–hostile in wit	.43	.51
IVA	Group oriented–self-oriented	.58	.68
IVB	Friendly–rejecting	.44	.54
VA	Intellectually alive–intellectually stagnant	.36	.35
VB	Erratic–conscientious	.33	.42

[a]$N = 610$.

discriminatingly. Further, it is assumed that the tasks of ranking all of the students on a global "playful" dimension on the one hand, and rating each individual student on each of 10 subscale continua on the other, are sufficiently different to minimize the biasing effect of one on the other. This interpretation is supported by the correlations between the rankings and the halo items, which were as follows:

Rank and achievement orientation (test):   .00
Rank and achievement orientation (retest):   −.07
Rank and physical attractiveness (test):   .21
Rank and physical attractiveness (retest):   .19

In contrast, validity coefficients as assessed by the correlations between teachers' rankings and total scale and subscale ratings on PF−nonPF components are uniformly high, as shown in Table 3.3.

Reliability. Total test scores, split-half scores, and item scores were analyzed for reliability. Data are, therefore, available for internal consistency, stability over time, and item consistency and stability. A special section deals with interrater reliability.

Reliability coefficients of internal consistency were obtained by using the Kuder−Richardson formula based on test variance. These were .87 on test and .90 on retest.

Since quantity and quality scales were considered equivalent, reliability coefficients by the split-half technique between A and B scales were .84 on test and .86 on retest. Corrected for length by the Spearman−Brown formula, the split-half reliabilities were .91 on test and .92 on retest.

TABLE 3.4
Item Reliability Coefficients between PF−NonPF Subscale Score on Test and PF−NonPF Subscale on Retest[a]

Scale		r
IA	Physical mobility	.68
IB	Physical alertness	.62
IIA	Enthusiasm	.64
IIB	Spontaneous joy	.68
IIIA	Humor	.67
IIIB	Wit	.55
IVA	Self−other orientation	.69
IVB	Friendliness	.59
VA	Intellectual curiosity	.68
VB	Erratic behavior	.60
Mean r		.64

[a]N = 610.

A coefficient of stability over time was obtained for the total test scores with total retest scores in the amount of .82. Test—retest coefficients were .80 for A scales, and .75 for B scales. Test—retest reliabilities for each scale (item stability) are shown in Table 3.4.

The correlations of each item score with total test score were also inspected for reliability data. Although these correlations are inflated because the subscale score is a component of the total score, the correlations further support the internal consistency of the measure. Item reliabilities on test ranged from .36 to .86, with a mean of .68. On retest, the range was from .34 to .89, with a mean of .74.

Mention should also be made of the reliability of the "halo" items, namely, Scales VI and VII. Test—retest stability for Scale VI, measuring achievement orientation, was .71, and for Scale VII, measuring physical attractiveness, it was .78.

Interrater reliability. For a subsample of 158 students, separate ratings by two teachers were obtained to investigate the interrater reliability of the instrument. Two school systems were involved, one public and one private; approximately half of the students came from each. Grades 9, 10, 11, and 12 were represented, and six sets of double ratings were obtained, three from private and three from public schools. Altogether, nine teachers were involved, of whom three were student teachers and six were regular teachers. Three double ratings were thus obtained from the cooperating teacher and student teacher who worked with the children at the same hour of the day and in the same subject matter area. Three other double ratings were obtained from regular teachers who worked with the same groups of students but at different hours of the day and in different subject matter areas. Altogether, teachers in four different subject matter areas were involved. This mixed sample was the only one from which double ratings could be obtained, and it was felt that interrater reliabilities from the sample might be minimal. The student population in the private school was much more homogeneous than was the entire sample of students, both in socioeconomic status of the home and in level of academic achievement; thus, homogeneity of half of the population was also expected to minimize interrater reliability.

The correlations between ratings by two teachers of the 158 students are shown in Table 3.5.

It is interesting to note that the highest interrater correlations occur for the dimensions "relaxed—tense," "fun loving—humorless," "group versus self-oriented," "intellectually alive—intellectually stagnant," and "ambitious—indifferent," the last a "ringer" item. Probably these qualities in students are the most easily observable for teachers, and, on the one hand, the student's intellectual liveliness and ambition are of special concern to teachers, who try to encourage these qualities in the students. On the other hand, the more disruptive

TABLE 3.5
Interrater Reliability Coefficients on PF–NonPF and Ringer Scales[a]

Scale		r
IA	Physically on the move–physically rigid	.30
IB	Physically alert–physically apathetic	.39
IIA	Enthusiastic–discouraged	.34
IIB	Relaxed (spontaneous)–tense (constricted)	.52
IIIA	Fun-loving–humorless	.47
IIIB	Accepting in wit–hostile in wit	.23
IVA	Group-oriented–self-oriented	.47
IVB	Friendly–rejecting	.28
VA	Intellectually alive–intellectually stagnant	.46
VB	Erratic–conscientious	.29
VI	Ambitious–indifferent	.54
VII	Beautiful (handsome)–plain (unattractive)	.31

[a]$N = 158$.

elements of the fun-loving and chatty, gregarious youngster seem to stand out equally clearly to the teachers.

Therefore, satisfactory interrater reliability cannot be claimed for the present data, either for specific ratings on PF–nonPF subscales or for an overall conception of PF–nonPF. In part, it may be assumed that the many differences within both student populations and raters contributed to the unreliability of the data. It may be, also, that students' behavior in various classes and in response to different teacher personalities led to consistent differences in PF–nonPF ratings of the high school student. While satisfactory reliability might be obtained eventually on some of the more "overt" scales, those scales that rely on more "covert" characteristics may remain unreliable when comparisons are made among teachers. There was an additional element that may have contributed to the low interrater correlations. A substantial number of the sample came from homogeneous, high-achieving classes in a private school.

Halo. Directly related to both validity and reliability is the question of bias in ratings, which from student to student may affect validity and in ratings of the same student may be a "generosity" error affecting reliability.

To assess any carryover that might occur from an overall general perception of the student on playfulness–nonplayfulness, to what were considered the "ringer" questions on "ambitious–indifferent" behavior and the trait of "beautiful (handsome)–plain," the correlations between these questions and total test coefficients on test and retest were inspected and are .17 and .12 for Scale VI, and .26 and .28 for Scale VII, allowing the deduction that there was only limited carryover.

Another indication of the halo effect or the lack of it can be found in the data on concurrent validity. Teacher ranking of playfulness–nonplayfulness as a global concept showed total test score coefficients of .69 and .76 on test and retest, respectively. The range of item validity coefficients was from .32 to .63 on test, and from .35 to .72 on retest, with respective means of .47 and .56. Coefficients on test and retest between achievement orientation and teacher rank was zero, and between physical attractiveness and teacher rank was .20.

The Nature of Playfulness and Nonplayfulness

Unidimensionality versus Multidimensionality of Playfulness–Nonplayfulness

The same question that was asked in the study with kindergarten children, namely, whether or not playfulness–nonplayfulness was a unitary trait, had to be explored at the adolescent level.

Because of intercorrelations in the 80s between A (quantity) scales and B (quality) scales at the kindergarten level, it was possible to combine the correlations and work with the five dimensions of physical, social, and cognitive spontaneity, manifest joy, and sense of humor as composite traits.

The pattern at the adolescent level was markedly different. Intercorrelations among individual A and B scales range from a high of .53 (between IVA and IVB) to a low of −.13 between VA and VB, the mean value among all five scales being .40. Translated into behavioral terms, this suggests that the quantitative assessment of the social playful dimension of "group-oriented versus self-oriented" showed a fairly high relationship to the qualitative ingredient of "friendly versus rejecting," but that if a student was rated in cognitive playfulness as "intellectually alive," there was a slight but hardly significant tendency for him to be rated "conscientious," a nonplayful quality. When the relationships between the quantity and the quality of each dimension are compared to correlations among A scales or all quantity scales, we find coefficients as high as .71 between Scales IA and IVA, while the lowest is between IA and IIA, a correlation of .16. Looking at the pattern of the B scales, we find that the highest r, .60, is between IIB and IVB, and the lowest, −.02, is registered for IB and VB. In view of these intercorrelations, no pooling of quantity and quality dimensions was carried out. Instead, the individual correlations were made the basis of the factor analysis. Since test–retest correlation was .82 for total test, and item test–retest correlations had a mean of .64, it was decided to use only test scores (i.e., the 10 ratings on PF–nonPF and the 2 ringer ratings on achievement orientation and physical attractiveness as well as age of student, grade, sex of student, and sex of teacher) for the factor analysis.

The results of the principal components factor analysis and the subsequent

varimax rotation to best fit may be examined for further clues to dimensionality. Four factors emerged, as shown in Table 3.6.

Since the standardization of the instrument called for a cross-sectional,
heterogeneous sample, certain cautions had to be applied in the interpretation of
loadings. The cutoff point for meaningful labeling therefore, was set at .60. On
this basis, distinct patterns can be seen to emerge in the first two factors. Factor
A consists of physical mobility–physical rigidity, spontaneous joy–tenseness,
humor–lack of humor, group orientation versus self-orientation, friendliness–
rejection, play–conscientiousness. Factor B is comprised by physical alertness
(energy)–physical apathy, enthusiasm–discouragement, intellectual curiosity–
intellectual stagnation, and the ringer question assessing ambition (achievement
orientation). The age and grade of student and the sex of student and of teacher
emerged as two separate factors, unrelated to each other and to the first two.

TABLE 3.6
Rotated Factor Matrix for PF–NonPF and Ringer Scales, CA, Sex of Student, Grade,
and Sex of Teacher[a]

Rating		Pattern loadings from varimax rotations to best fit				Communality h^2
		A	B	C	D	
IA	Physical mobility–physical rigidity	851	−050	−059	−023	732
IB	Physical alertness–physical apathy	412	687	−057	−087	653
IIA	Enthusiasm–discouragement	203	828	−025	005	727
IIB	Spontaneous joy–tenseness	735	451	006	−023	746
IIIA	Humor–lack of humor	803	278	021	−041	724
IIIB	Friendly wit–hostile wit	502	413	102	−077	439
IVA	Group orientation–self orientation	830	124	−071	077	714
IVB	Friendliness–rejection	601	448	119	061	581
VA	Intellectual curiosity–stagnation	213	810	−043	−068	707
VB	Play–conscientiousness	669	−484	−105	−059	697
VI	Achievement orientation–indifference	−260	825	−064	037	754
VII	Attractiveness–homeliness	198	349	142	155	206
	CA	−035	−041	951	−019	908
	Sex of student	−098	−012	080	803	661
	Grade level	−014	016	948	−069	903
	Sex of teacher	066	009	−161	737	574

[a]$N = 610$. Note that decimal points have been omitted.

The data from the factor analysis further support the decision not to pool A and B scales, since the first factor consists of Scales IA, IIB, IIIA, IVA, IVB, and VB, while the second factor is made up of Scales IB, IIA, and VA. The two clusters of items suggest that two different kinds of playfulness—nonplayfulness are observable at the adolescent level and that the dimensions comprising one type are not major components of the other. These two types of PF—nonPF have been characterized as "social—emotional" PF—nonPF, a broad, situation-spanning behavior characteristic, and "academic" PF—nonPF, which appears more readily in the school situation (and is therefore narrower or situation-specific). As observed by teachers in the classroom setting, one could conceivably see academic playfulness as the teacher-approved type of playfulness that is constructive to the learning climate. Social—emotional playfulness—nonplayfulness would, by the same criterion, be held as disruptive of the learning process.

That the age and grade of student and the sex of student and of teacher have no appreciable effect on playfulness—nonplayfulness ratings was already intimated by the correlational analyses. The manner in which they crystallized as separate factors further confirmed the findings of minimal relationships between these variables and playfulness—nonplayfulness ratings.

Some mention should be made of the scales that showed lower than .60 loadings, yet were above the .30 loadings that are considered a level of practical significance in the interpretation of factors. Most conspicuously among these are the loadings of Scale IIIB, which aims at assessing the part of wit and subtlety in the adolescent's sense of humor as shown in the classroom. There is an almost equal distribution of saturation between social—emotional and academic playfulness, and it might indicate that perhaps two different traits have been combined—one, the teasing and off-color remarks, and the other, the more intellectual one of punning and of finding analogies. In the original content analysis of the teacher questionnaire, the dimension "sense of humor (wit)" was seen as a combination of the other dimensions (social, cognitive, emotional, and physical playfulness). The equal loadings of Item IIIB on both PF factors suggests that such a combination was indeed being tapped. In a provisional formulation of PF as a self-rating instrument, the teasing and intellectual punning traits had been separated, and there was found a correlation of .50 between them. It might be worthwhile to consider such a dichotomy once more.

NONPLAYFULNESS

Because of the conceptual implications, the nonPF end of the scale was examined for further clues to the dimensionality of the trait. The question raised and to be answered is the nature of nonPF—complementary to PF or coexistent with PF.

The nonplayful ends of the scales were used by the teachers only slightly less frequently than were the playful ends. Over 20% of the students were rated "1" or "2," that is, primarily nonplayful, on each of the following scales: IA, IB, IIA, IIB, IVA, VA, and VB. For the remaining scales, the percentages rated 1 or 2 were as follows: IIIA, 18.3% rated primarily humorless; IIIB, 10.2% rated primarily hostile or lacking in use of wit in class; and IVB, 11.2% rated primarily rejecting of peers. On Scale VB, "erratic–conscientious," twice as many students were rated 1 or 2, conscientious, as were rated 4 or 5, erratic.

There were, nevertheless, no significant negative correlations among any of the PF–nonPF scales, indicating that nonplayfulness as assessed by these scales was not inversely related to the playfulness ends of the dimensions. In the rotated factor loadings, the only large negative loading was −.48 for Scale VB, erratic–conscientious, on Factor 2, the academic PF factor. This loading suggests that the adolescent who receives high PF ratings on the other items loaded on the factor is likely to receive a low PF, or "conscientious," rating on Item VB.

The conclusion to be drawn from the present data is that nonplayfulness does not exist as a separate entity identifiable through the pattern of intercorrelations.

In order to check on possible trends, the profiles of 40 nonplayful students, ranked by their teachers as the lowest 3 in 14 different class groups, were examined. When the ratings of these students were tabulated, 33 of them showed a clustering on the nonPF end of the scale. However, it is the 7 students whose profiles were uneven that may point to a less clean-cut division between PF–nonPF behavior. Translated into a percentage, it would mean that 18% showed an overlapping of traits, a finding that calls for further investigation.

Assessment of Playfulness–Nonplayfulness in High School Students by Trait Checklist

Some of the troublesome loose ends about the trait composition of PF in adolescents called for a follow-up, using a different but related approach which might refine and further crystallize the operational correlates of PF and possibly also throw more light on nonPF. For example, when being asked to rate a student on Scale IIIA, which was the dimension of "fun-loving" on the PF end and "humorless" on the nonPF end of the scale, the teacher had to take into account not only the overall thrust of the question "How consistently does the student show a sense of fun (humor) in class?" but also consider the profile of the student, described at the PF end as one "who is the entertainer, who constantly makes jokes, enjoys horseplay, clowns, engages in cross-sex teasing." While it had been hoped that the behaviors cited would be shown consistently in a cluster in any given individual, some of the raters raised the question of what to do when one or the other trait was absent. In addition, what we had conceptualized as the quantity and quality dimensions of the same behavior did not turn out to be so in the adolescent. For instance, the correlation between Scales IIB and IIIA is .73, one of the highest. Behaviorally, it makes sense for the boisterous, chuckling, and laughing student, showing his joy with ease, to be more likely the fun-loving entertainer and clown, whereas IIIB, subtlessness in wit, relates only to the extent of .51 with that specific quality of joy.

In order to resolve some of the difficulties encountered in the profiles and the leading questions, it was decided to develop a trait checklist, based on the same open-ended questionnaires completed by the 115 junior high school and high school teachers. A count of the most frequently mentioned attributes constituted a 40-item trait checklist for PF–nonPF in high school students. Operational trait definitions were given on a separate sheet. Ratings were made on a 5-point scale and the raters were told that we were trying to assess whether or not spontaneity can be found in the behavior of high school students in the classroom and also whether or not it was possible to measure how cheerful and how "full of the devil" these youngsters were. Seven teachers rated 201 subjects—about an equal number of males and females—attending Grades 9 through 12. A principal components factor analysis carried out on the 40 PF–nonPF traits, grade, and sex resulted in seven factors, as shown in Table 3.7. Again, because of the heterogeneity of the population, a conservative cutoff point was chosen—this time .50, since there were fewer subjects than in the rating scale study. The factorial data point to a highly differentiated structure and allow for meaningful and distinct labeling as follows: Factor A, intellectual alertness and commitment; Factor B, bubbling effervescence; Factor C, tense aloofness; Factor D, hostile and sadistic teasing. Sex and age teased themselves out as separate factors with no significant relation to the PF–nonPF trait clusters. Basically, the configuration of intellectual alertness and commitment is congruent with the academic PF on the rating scale, and bubbling effervescence is congruent with social–emotional PF, as shown in Table 3.8. This very fact provides congruent validity for the two major PF factors as well as more clear-cut information on the nonPF dimension. It would attest to a core of invariance of what classroom teachers consider playfulness on the one hand while, on the other hand, identifying intellectual alertness and commitment as behavior that may be related to PF, but needs to be separated from it in any further assessments. A brief comment is also in order about the two types of nonPF that seem to be part of Factor C, tense aloofness, and Factor D, hostile and sadistic teasing. It suggests a passive and an active component, an important differentiation in the classroom setting where, understandably, the teacher would be more concerned with the disruptive behavior subsumed under it.

Parenthetically, I want to mention an incident that happened when I was analyzing the data. A colleague who was quite unaware of the thrust of my studies but to whom the factor constellation of the trait checklist was shown for comment on the statistical configuration, came up with the following remark as he looked at Factor B: "I like this kid. Real playful." This is certainly not an orthodox validation, but after struggling to conceptualize, identify, and measure

TABLE 3.7
Rotated Factor Matrix for PF and NonPF Traits and for Sex and Grade of Student[a]

Traits	Pattern loadings from varimax rotations to seven factors							Communality h^2
	A	B	C	D	E	F	G	
1 Alert	886	123	-108	082	015	-092	-052	830
2 Aloof	-101	079	841	-137	-089	-058	-008	754
3 Apathetic	-622	-006	555	104	-007	-028	102	717
4 Attention-getting	246	729	-101	-365	087	021	-073	750
5 Always volunteering	793	246	-236	-074	055	-236	-069	814
6 Baiting and teasing	-021	529	011	-599	161	097	030	675
7 Bored	-653	216	329	-291	-075	-064	124	691
8 Bright	835	279	009	024	-097	061	167	817
9 Conscientious	892	-126	262	096	-003	004	-182	855
10 Disruptive by calling out	-061	637	-170	-512	-034	203	-093	751
11 Disruptive by calling to neighbors	-234	676	-063	-408	-290	-057	-082	776
12 Does not volunteer	-717	-044	337	136	-059	227	037	705
13 Entertainer	162	812	-113	-201	163	-042	-073	773
14 Enthusiastic	885	183	-144	016	029	-140	-107	870
15 Extroverted	370	636	-319	-081	-002	-264	-068	724
16 Friendly	560	445	-352	134	-086	-263	-175	760
17 Fidgety	-126	489	315	-262	-027	446	-261	690
18 Hostile	-149	350	357	-659	-007	053	055	712

19 Humorless	−277	−388	560	−074	037	261	−030	616
20 Imaginative	771	466	030	020	−079	124	120	849
21 Inquiring	872	197	−105	092	065	−086	022	830
22 Intent on having a good time	105	840	−080	−041	−13	−158	−107	778
23 Introvert	−127	−419	637	−018	−081	253	−102	679
24 Irritable in fun situations	−005	−138	651	−379	−234	035	−066	648
25 Joking	213	890	−085	−070	044	−030	−016	852
26 Knowledgeable	856	221	115	037	023	−142	083	823
27 Lacks spontaneity	−465	−362	575	037	127	044	−075	703
28 Lighthearted	073	825	−224	103	−130	−140	−055	786
29 Makes fun of himself	183	524	190	011	011	−075	−541	642
30 Mischievous	050	900	050	−149	044	116	−008	853
31 Needs reassurance	046	334	267	−113	−165	091	−741	782
32 Quiet	−184	−385	568	296	012	288	−137	695
33 Sluggish	−446	−026	561	−181	169	−073	−318	682
34 Sullen	−205	−078	577	−551	−135	050	−089	713
35 Takes work seriously	840	−158	132	136	004	084	−216	819
36 Tense	172	019	644	−009	060	425	−333	739
37 Unenthusiastic	−756	−072	364	−182	039	035	−124	760
38 Unimaginative	−765	−212	247	−095	067	−063	−334	819
39 Wants to hurt others	−175	206	137	−778	038	−064	−094	711
40 Witty	417	795	−035	002	035	−147	−011	831
Sex of student	138	−020	−417	287	540	243	231	680
Grade level	294	288	−206	030	015	−685	−041	683

[a]$N = 201$. Note that decimal points have been omitted.

TABLE 3.8

Factor Loadings[a] (by Trait) of Three Major Factors in Rotated PF–NonPF Trait Checklist Compared to Scale Factors of Rating Scale

Factor A	Scale factor	Scale	Factor B	Scale factor	Scale	Factor C	Scale dimension	Scale
Alert	B	IB	Attention-getting	A	IVA	Aloof	NonPF	IVA
Always volunteering	B	VA	Disruptive by calling out	A	IVA	Apathetic	NonPF	IB
Bright	B	VA	Disruptive by calling to neighbors	A	IVA	Humorless	NonPF	IIIA
Conscientious	B	VB (nonPF)	Entertainer	A	IIIA	Introvert	NonPF	IVA
Enthusiastic	B	IIA	Extroverted	A	IIB	Irritable in fun situations	NonPF	IIIA
Friendly	A	IVB	Joking	A	IIIA	Quiet	NonPF	IIB
Imaginative	B	VA	Lighthearted	A	IIB	Sluggish	NonPF	IB
Inquiring	B	VA	Making fun of himself	A&B	IIIB	Tense	NonPF	IIB
Knowledgeable	B	VI	Mischievous	A	IA & IIIA	Lacks spontaneity	NonPF	IA
			Witty	A&B	IIIB			
			Baiting and teasing	A	IIIA			

[a] Cutoff point = .50.

playfulness in adolescents, it was a shot in the arm for me. After all is said and done, are we not all interested in communicating our ideas?

Situation-Specific versus Situation-Spanning Aspects of PF–NonPF in Adolescents

Because of the recurring negative connotation of playfulness in the classroom, especially at later age levels, I undertook a smaller study investigating the labeling of academic PF as situation-specific to the classroom and social–emotional PF as situation-spanning. As part of their field experience in an adolescent development course, 27 undergraduate students observed 380 boys and girls, ranging in age from 10 to 18 years, who attended community centers on a voluntary basis. The data were collected in the form of anecdotal records on PF–nonPF in the adolescents observed. A content analysis of these write-ups produced 11 category sets for PF and 9 category sets for nonPF. Coder agreement in both analyses was in the mid-nineties. In order to compare these records with what teachers saw as PF–nonPF in high school students in the classroom, 27 questionnaires of the 115 completed by junior high school and high school teachers as part of the earlier study were randomly selected. Tables 3.9 and 3.10 compare the presence and absence of PF–nonPF traits in the community agency and in the classroom settings as seen by groupworkers and teachers, respectively. A rank-order correlation, based on frequency of mention by the observers, was calculated on the situation-spanning traits for PF and nonPF, both separately and combined. *Rhos* were found to be .60 for the PF dimension, .10 for nonPF, and .59 for the combined data for PF–nonPF. None

TABLE 3.9
Situation-Specific Traits That Constitute PF and NonPF as Seen by Group Workers and Teachers in the Community Agency and Classroom Setting

Community agency	Classroom
Playfulness	
Being involved in an activity or sport with others	Eager and energetic
Showing off	
Giggling, laughing	
Gossiping	
Rhythmic body activity	
Flirting	
Nonplayfulness	
Fun spoiler and disrupter	Conscientious and driving
Painful teasing	Noncreative approach to learning
Poor sportsmanship, poor loser	Sober, humorless; no appreciation for humorous attitude
Aggression	

TABLE 3.10

Situation-Spanning Traits That Constitute PF and NonPF as Seen by Group Workers and Teachers in the Community Agency and Classroom Setting

Community agency	Classroom
Playfulness	
Joke-telling and humorous exchanges	Humorous
Teasing; mimicry; role playing, pretending	Plays taunting pranks and teases
Encouraging, friendly, good sport	Gregarious and extroverted; at ease
Curious (experimenting)	Creative
Horseplay and making loud noises	Restless and fidgety
Nonplayfulness	
Good conduct	Well-behaved and cooperative
Bored, apathetic, sluggish	Sluggish and unconcerned
General truculence	Hostility
Introverted, being an isolate; unfriendly behavior	Quiet, sensitive (easily hurt)
Nonparticipation in a given activity	Nonparticipation in groups

of these results reached a significance level of .05, though a *rho* of .63 would have been significant for the combined data.

Looking at the results within the framework of continuity and change, it is evident that some behavioral correlates of PF–nonPF in adolescents differ as a function of the setting. However, the data allow the inference that there exists an invariant core to PF–nonPF as a personality trait. If we examine the behavior within the differential approach in personality structure (Emmerich, 1968), this would support a claim for structural consistency rather than change. Turning to the specifics, it is apparent that joke-telling and humorous exchanges, friendly teasing, curious–creative investigating, and horseplay and physical restlessness constitute major elements of playfulness both in the classroom and in the leisure-type setting. Interestingly, the nonplayfulness dimension divides itself also into an active and a passive syndrome, namely, truculent hostility and apathetic sluggishness. Moreover, the *rho* of .10 indicates a different emphasis by groupworkers and teachers, with teachers being more concerned with the quiet apathetic dimension.

The question now arises of whether or not there is a "pure" playfulness factor, corresponding to bubbling effervescence or social–emotional playfulness and being characterized by attention-getting, entertaining, joking, light-hearted, mischievous, witty, and friendly teasing behavior. Intellectual commitment would then be behavior situation-specific to the classroom. Perhaps some clues for such an interpretation could be sought from looking at the data within a developmental framework. This would allow comparing the factor obtained from the rating scale at the kindergarten level with those obtained from the rating scale and trait checklist at the adolescent level. In a schematic presentation, the cognitive element is seen to fall by the wayside, or is teased out, and instead of the overall saturation of all areas of development with playfulness seen at the kindergarten level, there is the much tighter syndrome of physical mobility, joy, humor, friendliness, and play (erratic behavior).

SOME PRELIMINARY FINDINGS ON POSTADOLESCENTS AND ADULTS

Within the framework of developmental continuity and change, some mention needs to be made of studies with postadolescents and adults, the former preceding the major study with adolescents.

Postadolescents

A self-rating scale was developed for use first with undergraduate students. It was modeled after the PF Scale at the kindergarten level and tapped the three aspects of spontaneity (physical, social, and cognitive) manifest joy, and sense of humor shown in a classroom setting. One major difference between the kindergarten (K) format and the PF (SELF) Scale format was the division of the sense of humor ratings into "punning," "seeing things as funny," and "being able to make a joke and also having fun poked at you." On the qualitative dimension of the sense of humor rating, I asked "What degree of sharpness (hostility) is mixed into your humor?"

I, as the instructor, rated the students as a validity check for the behavior of PF as formulated in the scale. The correlations, upon inspection, ran from .30 to .50, a result that could be considered satisfactory for a pilot study. The students were asked for comments on the trait and their own ratings. What emerged was that the majority felt that subject matter and the personality of the teacher influenced their manifestation of playfulness. While no immediate follow-up was undertaken with self-ratings of undergraduate students, the question of subject matter was built into the adolescent study that followed it. The findings on the sense of humor dimension may provide some pointers for further study. There were consistent discrepancies between "punning," "seeing things as funny," and "being able to make a joke and also having fun poked at you." One exclusively taps production of humor and the other consumption, while the third question addresses itself to a mixture and takes in the affective dimension of give and take. It might be helpful, though, to separate the questions so that a clear division emerges between production and consumption. Recently (Levy, 1975), a colleague used the PF (SELF) Scale for self-awareness training of undergraduate students preparing themselves for teaching in the secondary schools. An inspection of a random sample of the three-way split in the humor ratings found only a minimal relationship between punning and seeing things as funny. It also suggests a further subdivision between making a joke and being the butt of one.

Adults

Self-ratings were again employed with graduate students who were already teaching. The tentative data available on playfulness in adults are, therefore, restricted to teachers.

The aim of the study was to explore, in a preliminary format, whether or not playfulness could be identified in the behavior of a teacher and, if so, what effect, if any, it had on classroom climate and individual students.

Procedure

Sixteen teachers (seven teaching in lower primary grades, seven in the upper elementary grades, and two at the junior high school level) were given an open-ended questionnaire asking them to formulate 10 traits they would include under the label of "playfulness" in a teacher. Several briefing sessions were held in the process of formulating the behavioral correlates. These were used to clarify and refine the traits. In the second part of the exploratory study, the teachers were asked to observe their own behavior in terms of the indices developed and to comment on their effect in the classroom

Results

A content analysis of the completed questionnaires produced 27 different traits. Ranking them by frequency of mention produced the following behavioral syndrome of playfulness:

1.   sense of humor;
2.   kindness, sensitivity;
3.   cheerfulness, laughter;
4.   enthusiasm, active participation;
5.5 flexibility;
5.5 imagination;
7.   at ease, relaxation;
8.   entertainment.

Traits with mentions of three or below were not included. The descriptive write-ups, though not formally analyzed, supported, in their anecdotal records, the actual manifestation of the above traits. In the teachers' own evaluations, when these traits were shown, a reciprocity was induced in the children and, in several instances, examples of divergent thinking were described.

In a follow-up study, teachers were asked to keep a tally of their own behavior with respect to the traits listed above. As a corollary to this procedure, they were also asked to draw up a rating list for their own pupils to complete, evaluating their teachers along the dimension of PF. While it was possible to come up with a composite of themselves as more or less playful in terms of the traits supplied, only in one or two cases were the pupil questionnaires given to the pupils for rating the teachers. If this particular procedure is to be followed, a great deal more work needs to be done in refining the concepts from the pupil's point of view and having the questions made age- and grade-appropriate.

Another approach is now being pursued by me. A teacher self-rating questionnaire had been drawn up on the dimensions of PF mentioned by the original 16 subjects, counterchecked by my own criteria. A trial run of this instrument showed that it could be used in its present format, but, in addition to the six different behavior categories directly relevant to PF, it is felt that some ringer questions need to be added to test for social desirability. The items as they are now worded may be too attractive on the positive end of the scale, though some balance is provided. To illustrate the point, Scale I states "I find myself saying funny things, making puns, poking fun at myself, and, good-naturedly, at my pupils," and Scale II is worded, "I find myself going off my lesson plan, adding or leaving out material, as other things come to my mind or are brought up by my pupils." All scales are on a 5-point continuum going from "very often (5)" to "hardly ever (1)." Further work is now going on with this instrument.

SOME HIGHLIGHTS OF THE FINDINGS AND POINTERS FOR FURTHER RESEARCH

As is apparent from the sequence of the playfulness studies, my approach to the concept and to the behavior was developmental. In order to organize some of the significant data, it might be worthwhile, therefore, to do so with the help of the guidelines worked out originally for the direction of research and stated at the beginning of this chapter.

Is Playfulness as a Personality Trait a Unitary Behavior Dimension across Physical, Social, and Cognitive Functioning at Various Age Levels?

Perhaps a good way to start is to concretize the individual at the various age levels. We have the kindergartner who skips, hops, and jumps, who is likely to smile more readily, show glint-in-the-eye behavior, move easily among his or her peers, and be more imaginative in labeling his or her play products. The playful high school student seems to be two different types: One is physically alert, enthusiastic, and intellectually curious; the other is physically mobile, spontaneously joyful, humorous, group-oriented, and friendly. Additional information from the trait checklist might round out the picture of our first adolescent as being also bright, imaginative, conscientous, always volunteering, inquiring, knowledgeable, and taking work seriously. The other youngster emerges as attention-getting, disruptive by calling out and calling to neighbors, lighthearted, mischievous, extroverted, joking and witty, and intent on having a good time.

If we were faced with stating the results in a nutshell, we would be justified in saying that what has been labeled "bubbling effervescence" in the adolescent is the carryover from the kindergartner's all-pervasive playfulness. At the same time, an orderly age variation can be observed in line with the principle of differentiation of behavior, going from the simple to the complex, so that we may do either of two things: We may speak of two types of playfulness as suggested, with academic PF being more situation-specific to the high school classroom; or we may consider the emergence of a "pure PF factor" and look for relationships to some of the cognitive and physical manifestions which comprise academic PF. From the data of my study, we might infer that throughout adolescence, teachers do not see any difference in the playful behavior of their students. Another interpretation is that the teachers rated their classes by using only the particular age group in question as a reference group and thus rated each child relative only to that group. Only the rating on Scale VI, the ringer question of "ambitious—indifferent," showed a departure from chance expectation significant at the .01 level on a *chi*-square analysis. Younger students are more often rated "3" than are older students, and older students are more often rated toward one or the other end of the continuum than are younger students. It could be conjectured that, in the latter years of high school, this behavior becomes more salient.

In order to shed more light on this developmental puzzle, I underwent some introspection about my own playful behavior from age 11 to 17. The school system that I attended was the European gymnasium with no division into junior high and high school units. What remains uppermost in my recollections are more socially oriented pranks with peers in the early years, whereas the later years saw more punning on academic subject matter.

What seems to be indicated is a further developmental check on playfulness of early versus late adolescents. It might be fruitful to carry this out with the trait checklist. If it is done by rating scale, then factor scores for each individual student should be computed. This would also give added information about the combinations of social—emotional and academic playfulness in a specific population.

Some mention must also be made of nonPF in its developmental continuity and change and its relationship to imagination and creativity. In the young child, crying, irritability, and perseveration were seen as some of the operational indices of nonPF, though they were not incorporated into the rating scale. Thus, the kindergartner was seen as more or less playful, while the adolescent was assessed from highly playful to nonplayful, establishing a logical continuum in that manner. The factorial constellation of the rating scale suggests a social–emotional nonplayfulness and an academic nonplayfulness. This may be an artifact of the teachers' conceptualization, which suggested a complementary trait rather than coexisting behavior. The analysis from the trait checklist does produce a separate hostile dimension, and any follow-up could usefully employ factor scores to test experimentally whether or not the behavior is indeed complementary. More definite answers to this question would also help to evaluate the relationship of the nonPF dimensions to imagination and creativity. This would apply particularly to hostile versus friendly wit. To what extent is baiting and teasing corrosive of the individual's ability for constructive imagination and productive creativity? The fine-tuning suggested by the recent focus on prosocial behavior would perhaps lead to more specific answers to some of the perplexing questions posed by Freud (1955) and by others (Guilford, 1950; Lombroso, 1895; Terman, 1922) as they see genius in the social context. It also calls for an examination of the situational variables operating in the environment that could possibly "sour" imagination and "pervert" genius.

An indication of playfulness as being less acceptable in the adult is suggested in the tentative findings from the pilot studies with college students and teachers in the public schools. Physical and cognitive spontaneity seem to fall by the wayside; manifest joy and sense of humor may be tolerated at times.

Are the Behavioral Indices of Playfulness Comparable at the Various Age Levels?

There are a number of ways that elements of continuity and consistency can be analyzed. Such an attempt was made in a schematic presentation based upon a comparison of the teacher-observed and psychologist-referenced traits of playfulness in kindergarten children and junior high school and high school students. I find consistency most evident in manifest joy and sense of humor. In Form K of the PF rating scale, the operational description of the consistency of manifest joy is as follows:

> This may be judged by facial expression, such as smiling; by verbal expressions, such as saying "I like this," or "This is fun"; or by more indirect vocalizing, such as singing as an accompaniment of the activity, for example, "choo, choo, train, go along." Other behavioral indicators would be repetition of activity, or resumption of activity with clear evidence of enjoyment.

The qualitative aspect is assessed by the freedom of expression with which joy is shown, and the correlation between Scales IIA and IIB is .87.

The operational definition in Form A of the PF end of the scale is also a two-part one, but no longer is there a separate quantitative and qualitative aspect of joy. It is divided into enthusiasm and relaxed spontaneity, two qualitatively different dimensions, as shown both by the original correlation matrix and by the subsequent factor analysis by varimax rotation. The correlation between Scales IIA and IIB is only .50, and, factorially, IIA lines up with the academic PF factor (B), whereas relaxed spontaneity is part of the social—emotional PF factor (A).

If we hold with Griffiths (1935) that play is *the* characteristic (the emphasis is mine) mode of behavior in childhood, then quality of play is an individual's approach to the environment. It thus becomes a disposition or personality trait. Supporting evidence of this is the emergence of one centroid factor in the analysis of the five subscales on the playfulness rating instrument, Form K. While we are discussing one rating scale in particular, namely, joy, it is necessary to underline that the behavioral indices from the trait-list analysis indicate a core of "bubbling effervescence" made up of "lighthearted" "intent on having a good time," "extroverted"—indicative of joy—as well as of "witty," "joking," "mischievous"—indicative of sense of humor (Factor A). We know that, in general, there is a tendency for the expression of emotions to be changed, sometimes even to be disguised as the individual matures chronologically. Studies (Bridges, 1931; Goodenough, 1931; Jersild & Markey, 1935) have documented the progression of anger and hostility from physical to verbal expression. There is less hard evidence on what happens developmentally to joy and sense of humor, though there has been a growing interest in the modalities of humor expression (Berkowitz, 1970; Eysenck, 1942; Goodchilds, 1959; Graham, 1958; O'Connell, 1969).

A brief reference to the differentiation of sense of humor in the adolescent into good-natured (friendly) and hostile teasing is pertinent here. It is the prosocial element in friendly teasing that connects it with the joyful spontaneity in Subscale II of the playfulness dimension.

If we continue our examination for continuity in the playfulness syndrome, we find the social spontaneity dimension next in degree of similarity between kindergartner and adolescent. While group orientation was part of the behavior at both age levels, the behavioral expression of the underlying psychological process was different. The kindergartner would be judged on his or her joining different groups at any one play period and becoming part of them and their play activity and by being able to move in and out of these groups by his or her own choice or by suggestion from the group members without aggressive intent on their part. The socially playful adolescent emerged as the student who was busy passing notes, talking to neighbors, seeking attention, as well as pushing and shoving and calling out in class. When quality of social involvement was assessed—Part B of Subscale IV of the K and A formats—more positive or socially and situationally acceptable behavior was shown by the adolescent who was described as outgoing, friendly, and able to move from one group to another. Qualitatively, the kindergartner's social spontaneity was seen as a ready acceptance of the new situation, a lack of distress shown over the change, including even an ability to amuse himself or herself if left solitary after peer interaction. It is not surprising that situational determinants operate in the differential quality of social PF at the two age levels.

Looking at the two remaining dimensions, which, at the K level, were labeled "physical spontaneity" and "cognitive spontaneity," we find from the existing evidence that the emphasis shifts from continuity to change and differentiation. Whereas we have the kindergartner who hops, skips, jumps, and performs other rhythmic movements of the whole body or parts of the body, which could be judged as a fairly clear indication of exuberance, we have the adolescent in the high school classroom who is physically on the move—changing his or her seat, having trouble settling down, fidgeting with things, and mischievously throwing objects. The K form of Scale IB assesses the physical dimension as quality of motor coordination in the kindergartner, while the adolescent in the classroom is rated as physically alert, indicated by facial expression, waving of hands, and other gestures. Thus, very little remains the same over time from these overt indices of the physical component of playfulness. Is it an orderly age variation? If we use the gauge of "exuberance," possibly the element of mischievousness in IA might qualify. If we look for sameness of underlying process with only overt manifestations changing, we might possibly make a case for rhythmicity as the underpinning, but at best it is tenuous. The setting of the classroom would act as an inhibiting variable in the expression of physical exuberance. Rhythmic body activities do appear as a situation-specific trait of PF in adolescents in a leisure-type setting and would, on an empirical basis, be evidence of selective manifestation of this behavior. There was a suggestion that "fidgety" and "mischievous" might have some elements of horseplay in them, as observed in the community setting. From a theoretical point of view, we might have a better case to look for sublimation of physical activities into mental operations with concomitant signs of exuberance. If we accept this premise, the dimension of physical alertness represented in Scale IB could qualify as indicative of the same underlying process of physical exuberance with age- and situation-appropriate changes in expression.

An even more intriguing picture is presented by the dimension of cognitive spontaneity. Here, the evidence supports orderly age variation with psychological processes remaining the same but overt manifestations changing. The underlying process tapped in the assessment of cognitive spontaneity would be rearrangement of givens. Using a Piagetian framework, the kindergartner would still be at the preoperational stage, in which an accidental shape, a personal whim, or a suggestion from the peer group might cause a change in labeling play products in clay, sand, or paints. The adolescent whose overt manifestations of cognitive spontaneity are curiosity and inventiveness will be testing hypotheses in the propositional "if–then" manner, will go over his own thinking, and the reservoir of factual knowledge through the process of reversibility of operations, and may come out with unique solutions as a result of his "playing with ideas."

What is crucial in comparing the cognitive spontaneity of the kindergartner with that of the adolescent or the adult is the extent of the reservoir of knowledge or "density of cognitive structures," the term used by Kagan (1971) in his work with young children. Perhaps this may be one clue as to why the so-called "creative" kindergartner does not always develop into the "creative" adolescent or adult. How much knowledge the individual acquires and how comfortable the person is in moving around his storehouse of facts may very well be influenced by such variables as sex, intelligence, and possibly social class. While my own kindergarten study did not suggest sex as being a differentiating variable, some follow-up studies (Singer & Rummo, 1973) did, and there was in · my own study a trend favoring the boys in the adolescent study.

Some mention needs to be made of the factor of maturation as it relates to playfulness in the kindergartner and in the adolescent. Chronological age was related to PF in a sample of young children within a narrow age range and with comparable socioeconomic backgrounds. In the adolescent population, it emerged as a separate factor—and this in a population with an age range from 11+ to 19—spanning one of the crucial periods of physical, intellectual, and emotional growth. In addition, this was a heterogeneous population socio-economically. When we interpreted the finding at the kindergarten level, we related the influence of the maturational factor to a sense of competence. Piaget (1945) speaks about the young child first applying known facts to new situations, primarily for the purpose of mastering a skill. Only after competence has been achieved does the ludic or playful element enter. In everyday language, we might say that the young child needs to feel on top of things to be able to approach his or her environment with spontaneity, a chuckle, and a tease. That the maturational factor did not relate to playfulness in adolescents was contrary to expectations. I, along with other psychologists, had theorized that the older adolescent, feeling more comfortable with the newly gained sense of identity, would turn out to be more playful.

What Are Some of the Childrearing Antecedents That Influence Playfulness?

While, from a developmental point of view, this is a logical point at which to ask this question, the greater accessibility of the classroom made me first pursue the question of influences outside the home. This in no way diminishes the importance of the home and of the parents in the growth of the playfulness syndrome. My own hunches and studies of other researchers will throw some light on this question in my discussion of it in Chapters IV and VI.

What Are Some of the Variables in Teacher Personality and Methodology That Influence Playfulness?

At this point in my investigations, the findings from the two pilot studies with teachers provide some pointers, though not definitive answers. The underlying hypothesis was that situational variables influence the manifestation of PF in the student and that one way of encouraging that would be a corresponding behavior syndrome in the teacher.

Since the study was carried out with teachers who were attending a graduate course in the education of the gifted, it is particularly significant to note that sense of humor, understanding and flexibility, joy, enthusiasm, and imagination are seen as components of playfulness in a teacher. Once identified, it is also encouraging to note that, in their self-observations, the teachers displayed some of these traits. Also worth mentioning is the fact that, even on a descriptive basis, divergent thinking did occur in the pupils when the teachers were playful.

Interestingly, most of the participating teachers were in their twenties or early thirties and had, on the average, about 5 years of teaching experience. One student who extended her study to include the other teachers at her level of teaching (kindergarten) found considerable resistance among the older and more established colleagues. Some of them seemed quite distressed at the idea of "playfulness" in a teacher. This corroborates my earlier findings from data that were collected on the playfulness of high school students. There, too, the older and more established teacher had a more negative connotation of playfulness, even as it applied to high school students.

Teachers who may have seen the playfulness in adolescents as more a hindrance than an aid to learning thought that the junior high school student would emerge as the more playful. Parenthetically, when, at the beginning of the study, I approached one of the more prestigious high schools in Brooklyn for permission to work with students and teachers there, I was informed by the principal that I had better go to one of the junior high schools, since in his school, "the students were serious, college-oriented boys and girls." The following week, that school made headlines because of suspicious fires that had been started in the building by students. Was the fun that should have been in the learning transformed into mischief as an outlet of the "bubbling effervescence" in the high school student?

The emergence of two distinct factors in nonplayfulness provide further important insights into the vexing questions of positive and negative connotations of playfulness in the classroom. While there is less controversy about the aloof, tense, and apathetic traits, the dividing line between constructive and destructive teasing is particularly hard to evaluate in the classroom It is hoped that differentiating friendly from hostile wit will also aid the teacher in distinguishing the creative from the disruptive student.

Does Playfulness Give a Clue to the Type of Cognitive Processes in an Individual That Have Been Labeled "Divergent Thinking"?

To explore developmental continuity and change per se in playfulness is only the first step in our search for relationships to imagination and creativity. At the kindergarten level, significant relationships were found between the five separate subscales as well as among the global PF score and ideational fluency, spontaneous flexibility, and weighted originality. Singer and Rummo (1973), in their examination of behavioral style, which included dimensions taken from the Lieberman Playfulness Scale and Wallach and Kogan's (1965) teacher ratings, also found that playfulness relates to creativity, though only in male kindergartners. A replication, by Durrett and Huffman (1968), of the Lieberman study with Mexican–American children of kindergarten age confirmed the playfulness–divergent thinking relationship, with the exception of the originality score. In the Lieberman study, three originality scores were obtained—nonclever originality, weighted originality, and originality subtitled cleverness. The latter had more stringent criteria for relevant responses, and very few responses of this category were obtained, as illustrated by the fact that the weighted mean originality score was 6.45 and the cleverness score was only .48. None of the PF Scales showed significant correlations with the cleverness score. Some clues to developmental change can be obtained from the correlations between and among the divergent thinking abilities measured. The size of the correlations runs from a high of .94 between ideational fluency and originality in Plot Titles to a low of .03 between the two ideational fluency scores of Product Improvement and Plot Titles. It would suggest that, in 5-year-olds, there may not as yet be a clear differentiation between the various divergent thinking abilities as established by Guilford, Wilson, and Christensen (1952) in his adolescent and adult samples, and that the situational stimulus of the test produces greater perceptual cohesion. There is also the question of the contamination of the Divergent Thinking Tasks with the intellectual dimensions measured by the IQ. A reanalysis of my data by Singer and Rummo (1973), with MA held constant, found only the relationship between ideational fluency and the spontaneity, humor, and joy variables to be statistically significant. Piaget (1945) talks about the ludic element in a young child's play as the ability to carry on an activity without thinking of a definite goal, for the mere pleasure of it, with the mobility of schemata allowing the formation of real ludic combinations. In his own work,

Piaget relates this to the formation of intelligence, suggesting that, when the play activity becomes purposeful and dominated by the real properties of the stimulus, it loses its playful or ludic aspect. Based on these observations, Piaget holds that ludic behavior decreases with age and is replaced by experimentation. My contention is that the ludic or playful element is incorporated into experimentation. In the same way that Piaget distinguishes playful from merely imitative behavior and describes it as a process whereby the child incorporates external objects to his own thought schemata and thus is free to use "symbolic assimilation [as] a source of creative imagination" (p. 155), I postulated an analogue in adolescent thinking in which creative imagination and subsequent originality are a recombination of already existing factual knowledge. Staats, Brewer, and Gross (1970) come to a similar conclusion in their examination of cumulative—hierarchical learning within a longitudinal framework.

It is in this area that follow-up research needs to be carried out. Spontaneity, manifest joy, and sense of humor exist on a continuum in individuals, and it is to this extent, also, that degree of creativity can be established in a given individual.

IV

Playfulness in Studies of Play, Imagination, and Creativity

The developmental psychologist faces a double challenge when confronted with play. It is a matrix of behavior in general, while it suggests, at the same time, a quintessence that makes behavior either play or nonplay. Piaget (1945) notes that play enters every activity. By the same token, the essence of play, namely, spontaneity, manifest joy, and sense of humor, will guide my search for clues to playfulness in play, imagination, and creativity. I, therefore, shall look at investigations that use play as a setting in which physical, social, emotional, and cognitive aspects of behavior are tested; in addition, I shall examine those studies that are concerned with play itself as a legitimate area of analysis. I shall also look at research that deals with the salient aspects of play even in a nonplay setting.

This approach will allow me to focus on those aspects in the studies relating to spontaneity, manifest joy, and sense of humor, while not necessarily restricting me to the play setting. It will also serve as a basis to relate those specific characteristics of play to imagination and creativity.

SPECIFIC CHARACTERISTICS OF PLAY RELATING TO IMAGINATION AND CREATIVITY

A logical outgrowth of my interest in developmental continuity and change is a consideration of behavior that might already manifest itself at an early age in the play of the young child and become personality traits of the player in later life. I already indicated in my conceptualization of playfulness in play that these qualities or traits would be sense of humor, manifest joy, and spontaneity, and this was confirmed in my studies with young children, adolescents, and adults. It

63

is in no small measure due to the increase in studies in prosocial behavior that we now have a body of research dealing with both the cognitive and the emotional aspect of sense of humor. Studies of joy per se are more difficult to pinpoint. The majority have to be uncovered under "mirth, laughter, pleasure, and preference," and I shall need to extrapolate from them. The most difficult dimension in terms of precision of the behavior subsumed is spontaneity. Its close relationship to, and overlap with, flexibility of thought and actions will necessitate a discussion of their similarities and differences, in the light of the studies cited. As it is, it may be somewhat arbitrary to separate sense of humor, manifest joy, and spontaneity in my examination of pertinent studies. However, by doing so, I shall try to crystallize the salient points of each before combining them again in my discussions relating them to playfulness.

Sense of Humor

Humor as Identifiable Behavior

In the triad of major dimensions making up playfulness, namely, spontaneity, manifest joy, and sense of humor, the latter has been the one most directly investigated in studies and will, for this reason, be discussed first. Sense of humor, also, has more solid theoretical underpinnings than do spontaneity and joy (Berlyne, 1969, 1972; Goldstein & McGhee, 1972; Levine, 1969).

Does this mean that humor is easier to identify, or is it more interesting behavior? We can probably say "yes" on both counts. Even in a nontechnical approach to humor, we can easily see the expression of both cognition and affect. It is, therefore, not difficult to agree with Eysenck's (1942) formulation that humor may be divided into cognitive, affective, and conative aspects. Another vantage point from which humor can be viewed is that of considering an individual to be either a consumer of humor or a producer of it. Levine (1969) specifies that a playful, nonserious attitude is crucial to humor. Yet, we have hostile humor that may have serious consequences. It is my contention that the conceptualization benefits from being turned around, that is, that gentle humor and friendly wit must be teased out from the humor syndrome in general and that this type of humor becomes part of playfulness. As a component of playfulness, it may then contribute to the type of imaginative processes that result in creative products.

Humor Viewed in a Developmental Framework

There is very little disagreement that the appreciation, comprehension, and expression of humor shows a developmental progression in its manifestation. Theories have been built on this presumption (McGhee, 1972; Suls, 1972) and experimental data have been produced using these frameworks. One way of looking at developmental change is by analyzing existing productions of humor by children and adults. An example of such humorous products found at all age levels is the riddle. Shultz (1974) has approached the study of riddles on the basis of incongruity and resolution, that is, he looks at the riddle as a question followed by a surprising and incongruous answer. It is self-evident that, in riddles even of surface-structure ambiguity—such as the question "Tell me how long cows should be milked" and the answer "They should be milked the same as short ones, of course"—would be accompanied by signs of mirth such as laughter, guffawing, or chuckling. Riddles are a prime example of the combination of cognitive—affective functioning in humor. To cite another example from Shultz: "How far can a dog run into a forest?" The solution to this linguistic ambiguity is based on logic, that is, "Only halfway. After that, he will be running out." As we read this, we smile, and if we allow our imagination free range, we can hear the laughter of the one posing the question and the one who resolved it. In his interpretation of the findings, Shultz underlines that there is cognitive growth between the ages of 6 and 8, which allows for greater appreciation of the incongruity and thus for greater enjoyment of the humor in the question. However, as observed in the McGhee study (1971) a definite one-to-one relationship between Piagetian concepts of cognitive development and humor appreciation is as yet not possible.

In my interpretation, the knowledge available in existing cognitive structures forms a baseline of familiar material against which surprisingness, incongruity, and novelty need to be played. Therefore, it seems obvious that, in order to recognize something as surprising, incongruous, or novel, the individual would have to know what the expected or usual result or answer would be. That frame of reference is, of course, a function of developmental age and experiential exposure to facts and situations. From this point of view, the older and brighter individual should have more resources. The acceleration of the curve with age and experience would, however, be counterbalanced by set and rigidity of thought in adulthood.

The Cognitive Element in Humor

From my order of priorities, it seems natural to turn first to studies with a major focus on cognitive variables. As already indicated, many investigators look at incongruity, novelty, and surprise as key elements in the study of humor. These are, also, the variables that Berlyne (1960) includes in his list of collative properties of mediating processes, leading to arousal jag. McGhee (1971), Zigler, Levine, and Gould (1966, 1967), Shultz (1974), and Shultz and Horibe (1974) built incongruity, novelty, and, to some extent, surprise into their measures of humor. The resolution of incongruity was analyzed as being purely cognitive by McGhee and related to Piaget's concrete operational stage. Working with boys at three age levels—5, 7, and 9—he hypothesized that operational thinking would be necessary for the comprehension of incongruity elements in humor but not for the novelty features. While all three age groups understood novelty humor better than incongruity humor, there appeared to be no consistent relationship between age and humor appreciation for either novelty or incongruity humor. Do children laugh about something or can they find something funny without understanding it, or are there two types of laughter involved, one suggesting triumph, the other embarrassment? Zigler *et al.*'s findings suggest that a sense of mastery would need to precede enjoyment, a dimension that McGhee sees as less pure in cognitive content. From my point of view, it is interesting to note that Shultz' rationale in working with the humor variable is based on the apparent neglect of the playful side of cognition. While still working within the framework of the incongruity and resolution theory of humor, he looks for the appreciation of humor as the relevant developmental variable. Recording first the child's spontaneous mirth response and then obtaining a funniness rating assures the lighthearted side of humor some weight. Only as a second step is comprehension explored, for which four types of ambiguities are built into the riddles. Shultz uses Zigler's facial mirth score as a major indicator of appreciation, together with a preference ranking. In detailing these assessments, we are already alerted to the intertwining of humor and joy, though both theorists and experimenters agree that humor is not necessarily accompanied by laughter. It does underline the difficulty, however, of trying to separate the cognitive from the affective. Notwithstanding this, there are some aspects of cognition in humor that should be explored further. One of them is McGhee's (1972) differentiation between fantasy and reality assimilation in the cognitive approach to humor, and the other is Zigler *et al.*'s (1967) finding that a certain amount of cognitive challenge is necessary to appreciate humor. McGhee (1972, p. 65) describes the process of fantasy assimilation as one in which an individual incorporates or assimilates the source of inconsistency or expectancy disconfirmation into existing relevant cognitive structures without attempting to alter them or accommodate them, as would be the case in reality assimilation. In other words, holding reality in abeyance and allowing the fantasy elements to reign on a temporary basis seems to be a major ingredient in appreciating and perhaps also comprehending humor. On the basis of what we know about the playful element in the imagination of the creative individual, one might speculate that a matrix of knowns and givens (i.e., assimilated structures) is needed to set against what disturbs or unsettles through incongruity or novelty. Singer (1974) talks about the experience of joy or laughter that results from the reduction of an aroused condition triggered by listening to, or watching, comedians like Woody Allen and Charlie Chaplin, and underlines the importance of imagery as a cognitive function necessary to the appreciation of the humor. It would indeed be interesting to use Singer's (1966) measure of fantasy and establish experimentally whether or not high- and low-fantasy groups show differential appreciation and comprehension of incongruity humor irrespective of age. Since high-fantasy children were found to be able to wait longer in an ambiguous situation and also to show less aggression after viewing films that showed violence, it might be conjectured that they were able to be comfortable with what they know and to amuse themselves from stored knowledge. Therefore, they could tolerate incongruity more readily, be less defensive about themselves, and have greater appreciation of humor. Such studies would provide further data on possible links between sense of humor, fantasy, and creativity. Zigler et al.'s (1967) postulate of cognitive challenge as a factor in children's humor appreciation also points to a connection with creativity. If a sense of mastery and competence enters both the appreciation and the comprehension of humor, would it not be plausible to see the creative individual more comfortable with "getting the joke" in a cartoon? Conversely, the brighter and more inventive the individual, the more likely he would reject those not representing a cognitive challenge as just "baby stuff" or "silly." The humorless individual may, therefore, be seen as suffering from a cognitive deficit. The basis for not understanding humor is, however, different from that of rejecting examples of humor as age-inappropriate.

Zigler and his associates (1966) present a thesis of the operation of a "cognitive-congruency" principle and find support in their data of a significant positive relationship between cognitive level and cartoons sampled by their subjects in Grades 2, 3, 4, and 5. One of their measures was degree of mirth response, and they found that the humor stimuli that made few cognitive demands elicited less laughter. In a follow-up study (1967), they further elaborated on the element of cognitive challenge that makes for appreciation of humor. Presenting cartoons that were scaled from easy, moderately difficult, and difficult to impossible in comprehension, they found that moderately difficult cartoons were most appreciated for their humor. Pursuing their cognitive interpretation, they connect this phenomenon with the effectance motivation posited by White (1959). This would support my findings about the young child being more playful after mastery of the skill, or through experience. The PF scales, however, had separate dimensions for sense of humor and manifest joy, and, in view of the interpretation given, we might raise the question of whether the mirth shown was a function of appreciation of the humor or a function of joy over mastery. Zigler et al. also suggest an alternative interpretation, using an information-processing framework, in which case they hold that only the degree of congruence between the complexity of the humor stimulus and the complexity of the observer's cognitive structure is the decisive variable. In my efforts to look at the affective and cognitive variables in humor, this differentiation might lead to further clarification of the relative importance of the two dimensions. If preference can be seen as an affective determinant of behavior followed by enjoyment, then the work by Munsinger and Kessen (1964) would be important evidence of separating out the "joy" variable as well as of obtaining an age gradient dependent on cognitive structure. More recent data (Prentice &

Fathman, 1975) from a sample ranging from Grades 1 through 5 also suggest no significant relationship between enjoyment and comprehension of riddles. Yet, riddles of less complex cognitive structure were not enjoyed as much by brighter children.

The Role of Affect in Humor

Freud (1938c, p. 800) states that "the forms of humor are extraordinarily varied according to the nature of the emotional feeling which is economized in favor of humor." Since its formulation, this tenet has been the basis for analyzing humor for its underlying affect and for its use for displacement of otherwise unacceptable feelings—in particular, the aggressive and sexual drives. But even experimental psychologists, such as Berlyne (1969), introduce the concept of drive as part of the explanation for humorous behavior. Arousal jag as used by Berlyne is a state of excitement. Whether it has negative or positive valence depends on whether it generates feelings of distress or pleasure.

The problem in my treatment of affect in studies of humor is whether or not it can be separated from the motivational aspect or the direction at which the feelings are pointed. The subsequent question is whether or not this separation will pay dividends in terms of a better understanding of what constitutes humor. For this reason, I shall divide humor into its friendly and its hostile expression. D. L. Singer (1968) asserts that, in hostile humor, gratification comes not only from cognitive processes but from the expression of an impulse. His Negro subjects, aroused by "segregationists' " taped speeches, showed greater appreciation for antisegregationist humor than did those exposed to neutral humor. Rosenwald (1964) found that his labile or flexible high school students manifested a range of humor appreciation when presented with hostile cartoons. This is interpreted by the author as indication of the ego as a mediating variable, using external stimuli to determine degree of pleasure from the cartoon. At an earlier age level and in a cross-cultural setting, Smilansky (1968) found her disadvantaged preschoolers laughing *at* their peers rather than *with* them (italics in text). Situational variables and personality thus seem to determine the enjoyment of hostile humor. In less controlled settings, such as TV cartoons for children, the appeal to the child to identify with some of the slam-bang humor of physical assaults and the aggression of verbal insults is considered one of the underlying attractions of the programs. These examples that are cited as representative, though by no means exhaustive, of hostile humor underline the pervasiveness of its existence. Its usefulness will be explored when I take a closer look at the conative aspect.

What of friendly humor or gentle wit? In experimental settings (Rosenwald, 1964; Singer, 1968), the contrasting type to hostile humor was neutral humor. Thus, the opposite to negative affect is no affect? This, in itself, is revealing. Goodchilds (1972) calls her own first findings about the positive affect of humor in small group functioning "fortuitous," and only recently distinguishes between clowning and whimsical as against the sarcastic and biting elements of humor as part of her experimental design in studying the wit in groups. The PF scales at the kindergarten level directed the teachers to "glint in the eye" behavior and at the adolescent level asked them to assess friendly wit. Singer (1968) refers to the psychoanalytic premise that the full appreciation of humor needs a playful or somewhat disengaged psychological stance characterized by minimal defensiveness, and he uses this to explain why the Negro subjects whom he tested after the violent summer of 1963 found it more difficult to shift from anger to humorous enjoyment of the antisegregationist "jokes." Distance from the immediate demands of the task was also seen as differentiating the humor of male undergraduates rated as internal in locus of control, leading to an ability to accept themselves more readily as the object of a jest than do externally oriented subjects (Lefcourt, Sordoni, & Sordoni, 1974).

McGhee (1974b) adds another dimension to differential affect in the appreciation of humor. Using boys and girls at the heteronomous and autonomous level of moral development, respectively, he found that those showing more mature moral development judged the stories with less damaging outcomes as funnier. Here again we have conclusive evidence that not only can we differentiate between friendly and hostile humor but also that the type of humor shown serves as an index of maturity.

Going again to the natural setting (Cooper, 1974), namely, children's spontaneous use of riddles in a fourth-grade classroom, I find a positive affect in humor, possibly brought about by mastery as Zigler suggested. Examples of these spontaneous productions are: "What goes up when rain comes down? Umbrellas." "Which travels faster, heat or cold? Heat, because you can catch a cold." Shultz (1974) and Shultz and Horibe (1974) used riddles with surface-structure ambiguity and lexical ambiguity to tap developmental variables in the appreciation of jokes. This indicates more than a change in methodology; it reflects the zeitgeist of tackling humorous behavior from a prosocial point of view, since the measuring instrument itself has a positive valence. This is not to fault experiments looking for aggression and drive discharge, but it supports my argument that it is worthwhile to look at affect divorced from its motivational context.

The Conative Aspect in Humor

It could be argued that the cognitive–affective elements in humor combine as they give this behavior direction or purpose. But we must be careful here in the differentiation between a combination of any and all cognitive processes with any and all affective dimensions and the specific ones that might have a bearing on imagination and creativity.

In Berlyne's (1960, 1969) model of arousal increase and decrease, humor belongs to those behaviors that can trigger both arousal jag and arousal decrement. With the growing evidence that moderate rises in arousal are rewarding in themselves, we may classify humor as potentially intrinsically motivating. This quality is also inherent in imagination and creativity and may thus be considered a common element.

I already referred to Freud's suggestion about the varieties of expression that humor can take depending on the underlying affect. That the direction is crucial to the productive use of humor can be illustrated by looking at two defense mechanisms. One, "regression in the service of the ego," is used by Kris (1952) as a necessary ingredient to the creative process. The other sublimation is, by definition, the redirection of unacceptable drives into creative endeavors. From a directional point of view, it is intriguing to note that the creative individual needs to be able to go both forward and backward in his own developmental space to realize his potential. As we shall see in a closer look at the producing end of humor, both mechanisms can be seen operating there.

If we look again at the studies dealing with cognition and affect and now allow ourselves to ask to which end these functions are applied, we might reach a tentative overall conclusion. Cognition in humor serves the ends of comprehension and appreciation and thus can be said to achieve a sense of competence and mastery, as suggested by White (1959). Affect in humor serves the ends of tension reduction while at other times allows for moderate amounts of increase in excitement (Freud, 1938c; Berlyne, 1969). It may be argued that sense of competence and tension reduction both have as reinforcers a sense of satisfaction, of feeling good, and that here cognition and affect merge.

I said at the beginning that only specific cognitive dimensions and certain affective releases would lead us to the realms of imagination and creativity. One of the clues is provided in Goodchilds' (1972) statement about the differentiation of wit into a sarcastic and whimsical dimension; the other is D. L. Singer's (1968) reference about psychological distancing as a prerequisite to a playful attitude to humor appreciation. Remembering also that there is a "consumer" and "producer" approach to humor, we now have some essential building blocks for a connection between humor as conceptualized in playfulness and imagination and creativity. It becomes clearer that, in order to test for a relationship, we must focus on the producer of humor.

The Individual as a Producer of Humor

The majority of studies, especially those with an experimental framework, focus on the reaction of the consumer of humor. Equally important is the study of the producer of humor. As Eysenck (1972) points out, we must differentiate between the conformist meaning of sense of humor—that is, a person with a sense of humor laughs at the same things we do—and the productive meaning of the term—intimating the individual who is the life and soul of the party. It is the latter meaning that will lead us to the imaginative and creative individual. Even so, it is not a direct route. As I mentioned earlier, Goodchilds (1972) calls her own first data about the wit in small groups "fortuitous findings," a by-product of her research into group dynamics. Recently, she has made the production of humor more a focal point in her research and has attempted to isolate the "wittiness" in humor. Goodchilds' emphasis is on the audience as a facilitator in the production of humor and on the humorous individual, in turn, as a facilitator of the group processes that may lead to creative problem solving. The Observer Wit Tally (Smith & Goodchilds, 1959) is one way of assessing that type of humor. Another avenue is through some of the instruments used in the assessment of divergent thinking and associative creativity. Guilford's (1951) Plot Titles and Consequences and Unusual Uses, Wallach and Kogan's (1965) Line Drawings and Pattern Meanings, Torrance's (1960) Product Improvement and Circles and Squares are examples of tests that are scored for "funniness," as part of the weighting for creativity. Examples of such answers are found in Guilford's manual for scoring Plot Titles, such as a "Finnish Finish" for the following story.

> Rex was six feet seven inches tall, weighed two hundred and seventy pounds, and was a native of Finland. He was a midget auto racing driver and had entered the "Grand Prix Race," the most important midget auto race in the world. At the last lap of the race, Rex was several lengths ahead of the next car, but his motor "conked out" and his car rolled to a stop a few feet from the finish line. The next car seemed a sure winner, but Rex picked up his car and strode across the finish line, winning the Grand Prix.

Incongruity seems to be built into the study. No wonder that one of the answers in the manual given as an example of a clever response was a pun.

In other creativity tests, Wallach and Kogan's (1965) fifth-graders saw assorted dots or lines as "streams of ants," or "an alligator's open mouth." In my study with kindergartners, one of the stories was about Croaky the Frog, who was sunning himself and fell into the water after being tickled by a fly. One child suggested the title "Happiness is a Warm Frog." Although this is a *pars pro totem* answer, it can be regarded as both funny and original at age 5. It has also been my experience that, when demonstrating in class creativity measures, such as Torrance's Product Improvement (1960), Wallach and Kogan's Line Drawings (1965), or Guilford's (1951) Plot Titles, it triggered humorous responses. McGhee (1974a) realized the vacuum that existed in probing, developmentally, the ability of children to create the joking relationship. Among the results of his pioneering study was that the ability to produce successful wordplay humor increased through Grade 4, and then dropped slightly between Grades 4 and 6. This finding supports my theory of less playfulness in the early adolescent as a function of a greater state of flux in personality dynamics at that time.

The interrelatedness of wit and imagination in tests of adolescent fantasy production is also cited by Getzels and Jackson (1962). Humorous endings of fables included the one about the mischievous dog with the lines "This is your plight, you dogs that bite" or "For whom does the bell toll now?" In their own analysis of the humorous endings, Getzels and Jackson state that they most frequently contained incongruity or a sudden play on words, and add that unsuccessful attempts at humor commonly involved excessive hostility. The latter again underlines my contention for the need to differentiate "friendly" from "hostile" humor or wit. Support that such two types not only exist but can be identified comes from a study of class clowns among eighth-grade boys and girls in which Damico and Purkey (1976) found two distinct behavioral types emerging from the peer-nominated sociometric data. The first was the popular group-leader clown, seen by classmates as being "creative," "academically capable," and "well-liked." The isolate-type clown was the one that caused laughter at the expense of others, a fitting definition of what I called "hostile" humor or wit. For an even earlier age level, Groch (1974) was able to differentiate three types of humor in preschoolers which she labeled responsive, productive, and hostile. It is interesting to note that she found productive humor to be predominant in the free-play situation. A remark recently made by Sam Levenson as a Commencement speaker further underlines my point. He characterized his humor as "nonviolent," and his reputation as a humorist certainly goes to show that this type of humor has wide appeal.

An important consideration in any discussion of the production of humor is to what extent self-ratings and experimental conditions capture the ability of the individual in his or her spontaneous punning, joking, and witticism. Observation in the natural setting is necessary to supplement our laboratory studies. Children's playgrounds, classrooms, lunchrooms, and lockerrooms would lend themselves to ethological methodology in the natural setting. An example of the richness of this data pool is the list I received from one fourth-grade teacher (Cooper, 1974) when I asked her to bring in some currently used jokes in her classroom. Among these are the following:

Question: What goes up when rain comes down?
Answer: Umbrellas.
Question: Which travels faster, heat or cold?
Answer: Heat, because you can catch a cold.
Question: What is the beginning letter of yellow?
Answer: Y.
Retort: Because I want to know.

Admittedly, these are not original productions. But their use and application may be spontaneous and unique. Another way of tapping original authorship would be to look for variations on a theme or entirely new productions.

My own recent experience in a performance-based, field-experience-centered teacher education program, which takes me into a junior high school as a supervisor of college students in their observations and tutorials, has provided me with further evidence of this kind. The other day, I overheard one junior high school student saying to her friend: "Act your age, not your shoe size." The accompanying laughter made this friendly teasing rather than a nasty remark. On another occasion, one of my college students, reminiscing about her time at this very same junior high school, recounted a story about herself: She always was seen together with her girlfriend, who happened to have the same surname. When asked by teachers whether they were sisters, she answered, with a poker face, "No, brothers." That the classroom is not always the dull, uninspiring place that it is sometimes reputed to be is illustrated from the field notes of one of my students who reported that, in an English class, the pupils were encouraged to find phrases that could be translated into a two- or three-word rhyme. Her examples of the productions included: "child's bed—tot cot; favorite airplane—pet jet; million-dollar payoff—handsome ransom; wilted lettuce combination—pallid salad." Unmistakably, there are humorous overtones, and some of the productions are indeed creative. Picking up the *Knutty Knews* of the eighth-grade SPE class of that same junior high school, I found the following write-up, which I quote in its entirety:

RAPPING ABOUT ROCKS
by Liz Kaplan and Lisa Napoli

A rock for a pet?! Are you joking?! No we're not. People are actually buying them all over town. The cost is about $4. So don't think the lady pulling a pet rock on a "leash" just walked out of a bar. It's all for real.

Rocks are great pets. Mom doesn't have to worry about Fido scratching the furniture. No worry about pet stains. It doesn't even need food (an occasional few drops of water will freshen your pet up). You can even leave him when you go on a vacation and he won't be lonely. But they do cause problems. . . .

Yes! It seems that these "Pet Rocks" have even caused trouble. Trouble! you say. How could such wonderful, useful, well-trained pets cause Trouble?!

Well TROUBLE it seems these pets are getting people into. For some strange reason these pets seem to fall on people! Could it be that these pet rocks were made with a creative defect?! Or could it be the owner's fault for not training their pets with the Pet Rock Do It Yourself Training Kit?

So remember, whatever you do, you must always use the Pet Rock Do It Yourself Training Kit when teaching your pet rock how to behave itself.

An incident witnessed in a special summer school class for creative children in mathematics may further illustrate productive humor. The age range in this class was from 12 to 15. Even without the chronological age difference, the different stages of pubescence would make for a considerable variation in body build, height, and weight. One of the shortest students had just volunteered to put an example on the board. The board was full right to the top, and the boy had to erase most of it to gain space for himself. When it came to clearing the top, he had to jump and erase, much to the amusement of the rest of the class. This seemed to stimulate his sense of fun, as well, and he proceeded to clear the whole upper portion of the blackboard to the rhythm of "jump and thump" and the accompaniment of his own and the class's glee. Even faculty meetings are not immune from sense of humor. I recall an incident when the colleague in charge of grants and research was making a comment and a faculty member called out to him, "While you're up, get me a grant."

One advantage of viewing sense of humor within the playfulness conceptualization is that it allows us to examine the individual not only as a "consumer" of humor but also as its "producer." My "profiles" for the sense of humor scales put considerable emphasis on the production of humor and wit. It may have been one of the reasons teachers found it so difficult to identify that type of behavior in the high school student, since, traditionally, it would not be considered conducive to learning. Again drawing on my own experience of producing humor in the high school classroom, many a time the end result of the most infectious situations was an invitation by the teacher for me to leave the classroom and "stand outside the door." Remembering Goodchilds' observation for the need of the wit to operate in the social context, this was, of course, an immediate temporary depressant of the behavior, but, in the long run, did not extinguish it entirely. One of the reasons must have been, in Berlyne's term, the arousal jag that contributed to pleasure felt by the "producer" of the humor. It presents an educational problem even more so in the American school system, where the greater part of the day is spent in the school setting, and thus very little outlet is provided for the "bubbling effervescence" of the adolescent.

Manifest Joy

Joy as Identifiable Behavior

Play is commonly referred to as "voluntary activity accompanied by obvious enjoyment." Yet studies featuring joy as the major independent or dependent variable were practically nonexistent until very recently. We shall also find that, just as in the discussion of sense of humor, joy may not always be found in activities clearly identifiable as play. In some instances, the behavior of joy will be found under different labels, such as pleasure and happiness. But these, too, are abstractions, and it may be easier to work with operational correlates such as smiling, laughter, chuckling, singing, dancing, and facial expressions indicative of enjoyment. That these observable behaviors may be play-related is borne out by Aldis' (1975) assertion that the "first and most obvious function of laughter is to clearly distinguish play from nonplay situations" (p. 85). My own view would call also for an assessment of the nuance and the innuendo of the laughter to distinguish the benign chuckle from the gloating bellow. In other words, I agree with Piddington (1963) when he states that the laughter of play is to a large extent an expression of satisfaction or positive affect.

That we need to operationalize joy is also indicated by Berlyne (1973) when he talks about pleasure as an intervening variable but points to verbal, facial, or postural responses as ways of expressing this positive affect. This is certainly a more productive view than the one taken by Rest (1974), who asserts that the developmentalist "parts company with humanist psychologists who emphasize transitory affective feeling states" (p. 242) and lists openness, spontaneity, and joy as examples of the latter. Indeed, one hopes that aggression and hostility are also only transitory affective feeling states, yet psychological literature abounds with studies in that area. Why should more positively valenced feeling states be excluded from empirical and experimental investigations? The very fact that they exist makes a claim on us to study them.

In our search for precise measurement of enjoyment, the ethological method may provide a new approach as well as some hard data. McGrew (1972) speaks of a "play face" in nursery school children, characterized by laughter without the sound. He also calls it the only behavioral criterion distinguishing a playful interaction from an agonistic one. I agree that there is a need to tease out the *Schadenfreude* from the emotion of joy. The literal translation of the German would be the kind of joy derived from the damage or hurt to someone else. The closest to a translation of meaning would be to use the word "gloating." Such a separation is analogous to the attempts to differentiate hostile humor from friendly humor and might provide a fruitful avenue to test whether these positive affects can be used for prediction of constructive imagination and productive creativity.

At a time when technology should be harnessed more effectively for research, films and tapes would provide better opportunities to assess these differences. Aldis (1975) has made extensive and imaginative use of photographs and drawings in his discussion of play fighting. In general, ethologists and clinicians use auditory and visual data more frequently. It would seem to me that these are very fruitful techniques to capture the innuendos of affect in observing and analyzing the everyday behavior of normal children as well.

A more conventional approach is the questionnaire as a measuring instrument. Seagoe's (1970) question, "What do you like to play most?" in her Play Report Instrument taps the very stable dimension of preference which, if not a synonym, is certainly highly correlated with enjoyment in a normally developing individual. Other investigators (Pulaski, 1970; Singer, 1973) have found rating scales satisfactory indicators for measuring positive affect. In summary, as we look at the various methodologies listed, it is also important to realize that underlying the conventional and the more technologically innovative approaches is the crucial skill of observation. As we seem to be moving into more naturalistic settings for our data gathering, the basic skills of observation and analysis are highlighted and need to be developed and expanded further.

Joy Viewed in a Developmental Framework

One of the earliest indicators of joy and, at the same time, one of the most constant, is the smiling response. It is also behavior that, like imagination and creativity, is species-specific to *Homo sapiens*. It is interesting to note that the first stimulus that elicits smiling in the human infant is the human face (Wilson, 1963; Wolf, 1963). The primary interpretation of this stimulus—response connection has been as a facilitator of socialization in the infant and young child (Rheingold, 1956; Rheingold and Bayley, 1959). Since play is frequently the setting for the socialization process, it is worth mentioning here the two elements found to characterize the laughter of play (Piddington, 1963). For one, laughter is the product of a habit, formed in infancy, of expressing pleasurable satisfaction, and, second, laughter subserves the need of communicating to, and inducing in, the playmate the state of mind described as the "play mood."

Another variable that seems to affect smiling in infants is birth order. First-born and widely spaced infants were found to smile less (Collard, 1968). This is not surprising, since we know that the human face is a stimulus to smiling behavior. It can be inferred that siblings, especially chronologically close ones, peering into crib and carriage provide added stimulation by cooing and indulging in other play-like activities. A provocative question that suggests itself is whether or not we can also infer from frequency of smiling that these are happier children and that this disposition would continue into later life. Numerous studies starting from the pioneer studies of Terman and Oden (1959) have underlined that bright and creative individuals tend to be better adjusted than their average peers. At the same time, we know that there are a disproportionate number of first-born and only children among any specified groups of gifted youngsters or adults. At this point, I just want to note it as a puzzling phenomenon, but we might allow ourselves the speculation that smiling as a sign of feeling good in the company of others or of the joy that comes from social attachment (Gewirtz, 1965; Harlow, 1958) may need to be differentiated from the joy and exhilaration that comes from cognitive absorption and achievement.

A recent follow-up (Sears & Barbee, 1975) assessing "joy in living" among 430 women of the original Terman sample of 671 selected in the 1920s suggests that these women found a great deal of satisfaction in their work and, in a larger frame, with life in general. Parenthetically, we might want to make a note of this group of highly intelligent individuals who seem to be able to use their intelligence for the expression of joy. It is something that will feed into my discussion of intelligence as a variable in playfulness applied to work and leisure.

Joy in Cognitive Mastery: Playing with Ideas

The existence of a relation between cognitive mastery and "function plea-sure" has already been observed in the infant by such pioneers as Buehler (1918) and Piaget (1945). The usefulness of play to further cognitive development is also seen in an orthodox Freudian formulation (Waelder, 1933). Play is seen as associated both with the pleasure principle and with the repetition compulsion, and its most important function is one of working over experiences as a preparation for activities that must be mastered for the reality of living. The naive hedonism by which young children are guided in learning right from wrong followed by the "good boy" and "good girl" syndrome, as spelled out by Kohlberg and Kramer (1969), in the stages of moral development is another example of the relationship of joy to learning.

That there is gratification arising from a cognitive challenge and finding its resolution is also shown in the previously cited studies in which children were asked to solve cartoons and riddles (Shultz, 1972; Shultz & Horibe, 1974; Zigler, Levine, & Gould, 1966). In these investigations, joy is a by-product of sense of humor. There is a thin dividing line between the relatively unpleasant state of cognitive tension in trying to solve a riddle and the arousal jag that should be engendered by increased excitement prior to solution. Berlyne (1960) suggested that an intermediate level of arousal is more likely to result in pleasingness, and this is borne out by the enjoyment shown in solving cartoons and riddles of moderate difficulty by the subjects ranging in age from 8 to 12 years. If the riddle is not beyond the individual's cognitive level, then being at ease in the situation and the familiarity with the intellectual climate should lead to a playing with ideas, allowing for a recombination of the given data. We could then expect the kind of pleasure that accompanies both increase and decrease of arousal. Studies in the natural setting when youngsters tell one another jokes or pose riddles might provide valuable added data on the pleasure component in this cognitive process. Recent studies have addressed themselves more directly to pleasure as a specific outcome of cognitive challenge and mastery (Harter, 1974, 1975; Harter, Shultz, & Blum, 1971; McCall, 1972). The major indicator measuring enjoyment in these studies was the smiling response. Unexpected "fall-out" of laughter, jollity, and apparent happiness were found in the training of 4-year-olds by an adult model in imagery and fantasy games related to television viewing (Singer & Singer, 1974). These researchers present an original twist in looking at the influence of television for generating differential affect.

A clue to a predictive relationship between joy and intellectual ability may lie in Bayley's (1968) discovery that 2- and 3-year-old boys scoring high on the happiness dimension of a rating scale are likely to earn high verbal scores later. It is of significance here that "happiness" was actually identifiable as a personality characteristic in young children and was correlated with an intelligence factor at a later age.

A rather different problem related to pleasure derived from learning is presented by behavior modification studies and behavior modification techniques in the classroom. Certainly, youngsters like to get rewards, but the question has been raised of whether the extrinsic motivators, rather than the activity itself, namely, the learning accomplished, are the source of pleasure. Some investigators (Lepper, Green, & Nisbett, 1973) even found that young children who originally derived intrinsic reward—or enjoyment, in my terminology—from drawing had their interest undermined by extrinsic rewards. Similarly, fifth-graders' enjoyment of team games was found to be lowered by receiving a prize. The explanation offered was that the reward distracted from intrinsic attributions of causality (Kruglanski, Alon, & Lewis, 1972). Researchers (Chadwick & Day, 1971; Medland & Stachnik, 1972; O'Leary, Poulos, & Devine, 1972) committed to the behavior modification approach claim that there is a generalization effect working from the extrinsic reward to generating intrinsic enjoyment of the learning activity itself. It seems to make sense, both from a research and a common sense strategy, to use token reinforcers only for establishing new behavior and to rely on intrinsic drives within the organism to maintain this behavior. Levine and Fasnacht (1974), in their challenge of this approach, performed a service to the research community by allowing both sides to state their positions. The crucial element would seem to be the type of behavior established. If it goes beyond the molecular unit of learning both in the classroom and in therapy, then we may expect a general sense of mastery and coping to develop that would, in my view, be likely to generate feelings of goodness or joy. Borrowing a term from the Gestaltist vocabulary, the "aha-effect" and its accompanying elation should generalize from the specific incident to a restructuring of one's approach to problems in general. One of the results of such relearning would be the emergence of a more playful style in dealing with the environment. It should be underlined here that the relearning encompasses both the cognitive and affective dimensions.

That positively valenced fantasy may assist in the conquering of environmental problems is indicated in Sheehan's (1972) summary of the Singer and Antrobus studies of daydreaming. Those college students who emerged as "happy daydreamers" were also more thoughtful, speculative, and curious about people. Their inner life was characterized as richly varied but enjoyable. We certainly have not heard the last of this controversy, and this is encouraging (Ford & Foster, 1976; Levine & Fasnacht, 1976). As long as pleasure, enjoyment, and intrinsic rewards are investigated, we may get to know more about these elusive ingredients in our behavior.

Joy in Social Role Playing

That joy is linked to social variables was already indicated in my discussion of the development of the smile. As I noted, it is the human face that triggers it.

Even in everyday situations well beyond infancy, it is easy to demonstrate that joy needs a social setting, that it is affect that needs to be shared with others. Occasions such as the birth of a child, the graduation of a young man or a young woman, and a marriage ceremony are concrete illustrations of joy in social role playing.

Children's games form a special category as we look at them for evidence of joy in a group setting. The elements of cooperation and competition are crucial. What Roberts and Sutton-Smith (Roberts & Sutton-Smith, 1962; Sutton-Smith & Roberts, 1967) called "strategy games" might have less of the pure joy element in them than games of chance, while the physical skill games might generate the most exuberance. Age as a variable of "when to enjoy what" cannot be brushed aside, and some of the goodness that one feels about bodily competence at a younger age might translate itself into the pleasure that goes into the planning of a strategy game. I purposely avoided saying "winning" at a strategy game, because here again we may have a positive and negative type of joy involved. In a review of numerous studies of cooperative behavior in children (Cook & Stingle, 1974), coalition formation during play was found to be accompanied by more positive affect, such as smiling, and this trend was evident across cultures as well. In an extensive study of the games of Israeli children (Fifermann, 1968, 1971), 75% of the unstructured games were accompanied by "good spirits."

When we move to the experimental setting, we again find that joy is rarely the major focus of the outcome but more often is only an incidental by-product. There are, however, encouraging signs of change; one is Sherman's (1975) examination of what contributes to a school group's well-being as overtly expressed through signs of happiness or joy. Working with preschoolers, he measured "group glee," which tended to occur most often in groups of seven to nine children of both sexes. Elementary school children also manifested pleasure as part of behavior whose main thrust was cooperation and helpful concern for others in the classroom (Crockenberg, Bryant, & Wilce, 1976). Reinforcement from parents has also been found to be a variable in degree of enjoyment both of play and of more structured learning. Bishop and Chace (1971) were interested to know how the parents' view of their child's playfulness affects his or her creativity. Tolerating the child's singing and dancing as well as allowing the child to play with an opposite-sex toy were found to relate to the creativity scores of 3- and 4-year-olds. Early socialization practices that include a rejection, or at least a modification, of sexual stereotypes may perhaps already lay the foundation to less rigidly defined, or crossover of traditional, male and female characteristics found in creative individuals in the adult stage. Further evidence to that effect comes from a study by Bary (1974), who reported that when parents approved, enjoyment of playing with a sex-inappropriate toy was evident. Interestingly enough, she also found that the boys—all of them 4- to 5-year-olds—reported a higher degree of enjoyment than the girls. Are these already portents of boys being more at ease with "deviant" behavior, which would help to explain the higher proportion of males in all domains of creative endeavor? Social stereotypes may, however, also influence the manifestation of enjoyment toward a more traditional expression. The elementary school boys with whom Crockenberg, Bryant, and Wilce (1976) worked showed more enjoyment in a competitive than in the cooperatively structured learning setting. On the other hand, studies by DeVries and Edwards (1974a,b), using same ability but mixed sex groups in their Teams—Games—Tournament approach to classroom learning, seem to indicate that elementary and high school students preferred cooperatively structured learning environments. Looking at the photographs accompanying the manual, it is also very apparent how much joy is captured in the facial expressions of laughing and smiling and in the body expressions of waving arms. It is therefore of paramount importance, when we compare joy derived from competition as against cooperation, that we ask ourselves if we can differentiate between enjoyment that includes the "besting" or hostile ingredient from the one that is more intrinsically motivated. As already suggested, photographs, films, and tapes might help to distinguish the prosocial and antisocial elements in the same behavior. Even at the college level, students in an English composition class (Troyka & Nudelman, 1975) not only were found to benefit in improving their writing and organizational skills through a game setting, but were seen to have fun while doing their work.

That setting has an effect on the expression of affect is shown in a recent study by Davie, Forrest, Hutt, Mason, Vincent, and Ward (1975), in which they compared the amount of laughing and weeping in 3- and 4-year-olds during play at home and in nursery school. The mean incidence of both laughter and crying was consistently higher in the home, with laughter being shown three times as often. It may very well be that, to the young child, the home environment is more conducive to expressing both positive and negative affect more freely. The fact that more time is spent at home in fantasy play than at the nursery school would support my view of the element of playfulness arising in the more familiar surrounding and stimulating the child's fantasy. Admittedly, when the fantasy production was divided into representational play and complex fantasy, the difference disappeared in the category of complex fantasy. However, the researchers themselves explained this by the influence of setting and age, and this would certainly seem a plausible interpretation. A different facet to an examination of joy is brought into the picture when it is viewed from a psychoanalytic frame of reference. Josselyn (1955, p. 94), writing about the "happy child," looks at this youngster at the middle-childhood level and finds that his sources of gratification are "in interpersonal relationships with his own age group as well as [in the] pleasure that [comes] from combining fantasy with reality" in his play activities. Another perspective on social control at a later developmental level comes from a study of the expression of humor in undergraduates (Lefcourt, Sordoni, & Sordoni, 1974), in which it was found that young men characterized by internal locus of control were able to smile and laugh more than externally oriented subjects, especially when at times the joke was on them. When we get older, part of maturing may be the placement of our amusement gyroscope, and it would seem that internal locus of control connects with imagination and creativity.

Joy in Physical Play or Activity

Both from a developmental point of view and from the standpoint of observable behavior, manifest joy is, of course, more easily identifiable when it accompanies physical aspects of behavior. The spontaneous laughter accompanying the hop, skip, and jump of the kindergartner can readily be interpreted as manifest joy. Watching a group of teenagers dance also provides indices of enjoyment in the smiles that come from the rhythmic activity itself, possibly enhanced by social stimulation. The latter does not necessarily come from heterosexual involvement. I have seen young girls dance by themselves and show positive affect from the feedback of bodily competence. I would say even that at the preadolescent stage, 11- and 12-year-olds may feel more comfortable among their same-sexed peers and thus be more relaxed and open in their expression of enjoyment. Another arena for the expression of joy is the baseball diamond or football field. Here, even men are allowed to jump up and down and hug and kiss each other in an overflow of affect. This is a powerful aspect of playfulness shown in natural settings and it again impresses upon me the advisability of using the ethological method in any future studies of the playfulness syndrome.

What of the traditional methods of the past? Observation ratings such as the ones used by Singer and his collaborators (Singer, 1973; Pulaski, 1970; Freyberg, 1973) cover the dimensions of positive affect in a general sense and elation in a separate evaluation in ongoing physical play. Nursery school children between the ages of 2 and 5, who were rated as high-imaginative, showed a significantly higher amount of elation in their free play. That this surmounted class differences is shown in the data of Freyberg, who found improved affect in her sample of disadvantaged kindergartners accompanying their increase in fantasy and make-believe. Pulaski, who worked with boys and girls from kindergarten age through second grade, found positive affect ratings to be influenced not only by high-fantasy versus low-fantasy producers but also by minimally structured toys in a free play setting. What these data indicate is that joy derived from physical activity may also be rooted in a sense of mastery; that it indicates an ability of restructuring materials into a fantasy context; and that the observable product can be rated along the dimension of originality in the use of toys and play materials.

There is another aspect of physical activity, investigated by Zern and Taylor

(1973). They studied rhythmicity in nursery school children and found that it produced positive affect. An extrapolation of the results led to the suggestion that the enjoyment of dancing might indeed have its roots in such early manifestation of the goodness of this behavior, based on the postulate that rhythmic activities are the earliest response in the neonate, and based on the findings that it is a soother and analgesic. On a more speculative basis, one might raise the question of whether or not females have a less positive body image as a result of the psychoanalytic view that they are incomplete males. Could this deficit view of the body be another factor that undercuts the sense of mastery, coping, and achievement that is necessary to the creative process?

There are many instances of descriptive physical joy in infrahumans. Loizos (1967) discussed the occurrence of play faces among chimps, which he considered a playful *signal* leading to playful *action* patterns. These observations recall two experiences of my own when I saw physical joy in the natural setting in humans. In an introductory session of a course in the education of the gifted, a discussion of convergent and divergent thinking processes was in full swing, with the inclusion of theoretical constructs and definitions. Then, as an illustration, these adults, most of whom were teachers, were asked to give me "unusual uses" for a paper clip. Their faces literally broke into smiles, there was some overt laughter, accompanied by arm waving and body movements denoting joy. The other instance was when I watched a TV coverage of "unusual activities." A young engineer had perfected a plastic, bubble-type contraption for "walking on water." As he emerged from the demonstration, he was smiling and swinging his arms, thus conveying his joy through mastery in a physical sense.

Spontaneity

Spontaneity as Identifiable Behavior

As in the case of manifest joy, spontaneity is difficult to define in behavioral terms and even more difficult to measure. In order to clarify my own conceptualization, I found it necessary to draw a line—albeit somewhat thin—between spontaneity and flexibility, and helped myself by connecting the two behavior dimensions with play and exploration, respectively. I would hold that spontaneity, like play, occurs in familiar surroundings. Flexibility, like exploration, operates in applying oneself to a new situation. Spontaneity, however, is seen as intrinsically motivated. Flexibility is more likely to be extrinsically motivated. Behaviorally, spontaneity and flexibility may very often seem to be the same— that is, a change in direction of ongoing involvement, whether it be physical, social, or cognitive. Naturally, some overlapping will occur, and there are instances in which the two labels may be used interchangeably. As a matter of fact, in reexamining my own wording for the PF scale at the kindergarten level, I found just such an instance when we asked, under the assessment of social spontaneity, 'How often does the child show flexibility in his interaction with the surrounding group structure?'' However, the behavioral description of Scale IV leaves no doubt that we are tapping spontaneity, that is, changing from one familiar setting to another. Examples cited by Piaget (1966) in his Stage 3, the Secondary Circular Reaction, especially reproductive and recognitory assimilation, which aim at making interesting things last, are good illustrations of the workings of spontaneity. If something is interesting, it needs to have been assessed as such in a previous experience. Extrapolating from the sensorimotor stage to concrete and formal levels of operations, I suggest that the ludic element transcends the sensorimotor stage and contributes to creative production at later developmental stages. Since familiarity implies having a previous knowledge of facts and ideas, the cognitive input that must precede spontaneous behavior becomes evident. Staats, Brewer, and Gross (1970) give an excellent working definition of spontaneity when they talk about the process of recombining facts already known. Spontaneity, if we want to draw a comparison, operates like the whirl of the kaleidoscope. The bits and pieces of glass are the givens or familiar facts. The twist of the hand produces ever-different pictures with the same components. If we add to this the recombining of the components into unique and original patterns, we have spelled out the relationship between spontaneity and the creative product.

Spontaneity in a Developmental Framework

More often than not, spontaneity and spontaneous behavior are considered more appropriate at earlier age levels. There is both a common sense and a research basis for such a correlation. Usually we see the young child as more unfettered, more prone to do things on the spur of the moment, and more given to engage in activity that may seem aimless to the spectator. Theory and research (Bowlby, 1951; Freud, 1938b; McGraw, 1946; Montessori, 1936), too, show the developing organism as more malleable and less set in its ways, as expressed in such terms as sensitive and critical periods. Yet, by our definition of spontaneity, it presupposes informational input and, by this token, the older the individual, the larger should be the reservoir of knowns at his disposal. This leads me to suggest that, while the potential for spontaneous behavior increases with age, this attitude toward it as age-appropriate in later years may be the damper that makes it decline. Since spontaneity is an important and necessary ingredient in creative production, a survey of some of its manifestations at various levels of development may help us rescue it from becoming trampled underfoot.

It is one of the more difficult, but certainly necessary, tasks for the developmental psychologist and educator to differentiate between spontaneous and impulsive behavior. At the same time that the playfulness concept was being identified and measured, Sutton-Smith and Rosenberg (1959) were formulating a scale to identify impulsive behavior in children and ended up with 25 items of both positive and negative valence, such as "I make friends quickly" (No. 2), and "I play hooky sometimes" (No. 14). It also includes cognitive aspects of impulsive behavior, such as "I usually say the first thing that comes into my head" and "I often act on the spur of the moment without stopping to think" (Items 24 and 25, respectively). Thus, "impulsivity," as shown in these questions, portrays a youngster who does not take the time to check what is in memory storage. But I can see a child who may be a fast but not hasty processor. At the same time, this does not obviate the boy or girl who takes time over an answer. Type of problem and environmental setting would be additional variables that should be taken into account before we call spontaneous behavior impulsive.

Another, and perhaps even more important, factor is mental age. In my conceptualization of the element of spontaneity in playfulness, I hypothesized a greater amount in the young child and a recharging of this behavior in the adolescent. I considered the middle-childhood child to be more reflective and more matter-of-fact in terms of the Piagetian framework of cognitive growth as well as in terms of Erikson's model of ego development. Support for such an approach comes from a recent study (Achenbach & Weisz, 1975) correlating both MA and CA with the impulsivity–reflectivity dimension in children in nursery and day-care settings. They found a developmental influence; therefore, they caution against interpretation of "impulsive" versus "reflective" as a trait without taking into account the mental and chronological age of the child. Other studies (Denny, 1973; Maw & Maw, 1970; Ward, 1968a,b) underline the need to scrutinize impulsiveness in its relationship to conceptual style and creativity and to differentiate cognitive flexibility and spontaneity from impulsive thinking styles.

I have said repeatedly that cognitive spontaneity is also evident in the combinatorial play of the creative person. It is from this vantage point that studies using tests of divergent thinking may be analyzed for cognitive spontaneity. The Circle and Squares Test and Product Improvement—either verbal or graphic—in Torrance's (1960, 1966) Creative Thinking Tests are just two examples of the play-like activities that are involved in these tests. Wallach and Kogan's creativity tasks may be viewed as games, and the setting in the original Wallach and Kogan (1965) study was structured to be game-like without any time limit and in a one-to-one relaxed atmosphere. Even Guilford's Divergent Thinking Task of "naming all the things that are red more often than not," which taps ideational fluency, is an example of playing with ideas and concepts, even though it is timed. The play element may be seen to be operative because the individual goes to his or her stored information and recombines and reshuffles these bits for new and possible unique productions.

Support for such an interpretation comes from a study by Cropley (1972), who used Wallach and Wing's (1969) concept of nonacademic talented accomplishments as a criterion measure in his own longitudinal study retesting seventh-graders as high school seniors. The researchers found that the students' out-of-school achievement in art, drama, literature, and music correlated significantly with earlier creativity tests such as tin can uses, consequences, circles, and hidden figures. An intriguing footnote to the workings of spontaneity from a pool of familiar data is the finding (Porter & Wolfe, 1975) that, in an examination of the utility of the doctoral dissertation, "continuation of research by oneself on the same topic showed the highest correlation of any variable with total scientific publications" (p. 1058). It seems to corroborate my interpretation that spontaneity is not age-bound. On the contrary, it may be that the way in which an individual resists considering it age-inappropriate at later stages of development may give a clue to another dimension of ego strength needed for creative production.

That even within the realm of imagination there is a developmental progression of the element of spontaneity corresponding to experiential background is shown by an introspective account of daydreaming (Singer, 1966) during childhood and adolescence. In middle childhood, there was actual motor activity accompanying a fantasized football game acted out by the hero–subject; this imaginary play situation became translated into cartoon drawings during early adolescence and continued in this graphic medium into high school and adulthood. The sequencing in this fantasy game is a good illustration of age-appropriate progression of imaginary and imaginative behavior. The imaginary or make-believe component changes from kinesthetic-motor of the gross muscles (i.e., actual running and tackling) to the kinesthetic-motor of the fine muscles of drawing, with greater involvement of the cognitive element, leading finally to mental imagery alone. In the imaginative arena, the scenario becomes more complex and differentiated, endowed with the trappings of a professional football team, with accolades for the subject–hero. Other fantasies are recounted and, as Singer himself remarks, "thematic variations" are played out on becoming an influential senator or a renowned composer. It is worth noting that the affect reported as accompanying these fantasies was that of moderate enjoyment and excitement.

Another illustration of the working of spontaneity, both in imagination and creativity, is the description given to me by an artist of the creative process. She explained to me that "she needs time to dream." Continuing, then, to talk specifically about her work in landscape sketching, she talked about trees and of how you have to look at the same, seemingly familiar branch or trunk, or configuration, over and over again to activate the creative process and "to see the tree" in its different shapings. As I was listening, I could not help connecting it with the element of combinatorial play in the creative process, which is triggered by the familiar and known and then gropes for variations. Since I had known this artist when she was a child, I remembered the times when she was coming home from school and would, at intervals, take out time to just stare at the trees, the river, and the mountains that surrounded her path. Was she already then collecting the building stones of her later career? In his discussion that leisure education be already included in childhood, Neulinger (1974) holds that leisuring is an attitude, it involves an awareness of the spontaneity of the action, an unhurriedness. It is only recently that I myself have rediscovered the importance of the element of "pacing" as a necessary ingredient in productive activity. Singer's (1966) pioneering work with daydreaming underlines that, from a developmental and an educational point of view, more "time out" needs to be allowed for this activity, which is, after all, a familiarizing yourself with your own thoughts. The emotional fringe benefits, of course, are that the individual becomes comfortable with his own thinking and aware of his own personality dynamics. It leads again to the psychological distancing that we found to be also a necessary ingredient of sense of humor and points to possible interaction patterns between sense of humor and spontaneity in the playfulness syndrome.

Cognitive Spontaneity

The evidence that comes most readily to mind when we talk about cognitive spontaneity is in the imaginative play of the young child and the combinatorial play of the creative adult. Yet, we have already noted that there is a developmental progression in spontaneity in general, and we may certainly assume that this applies to the spontaneous cognitive processes from the primary grades through graduate school and, hopefully, also outside the structured classroom environment. Hard-nosed evidence is not that easily come by, and, in my presentation of it, I myself had to apply some of the theoretical principles I put forward. In short, studies that were familiar to me before in the context of various research angles had to be viewed from the different perspective of spontaneity.

Focusing on tempo of play, Kagan (1971) detects among infants of 4 to 8 months those who already seem to activate a dense set of cognitive structures in the service of assimilating a new event. There is no clear-cut answer as to whether the resulting dimension of reflectivity–impulsivity is based on differences in the rate of establishing a new satiation level or on differences in richness of reservoir of responses. It is well to bear this in mind in relationship to spontaneity as distinguished from impulsivity. This is illustrated by Messer and Lewis (1972) in their study of "style of play" of 13-month-old infants in a free play situation. In contrast to Kagan's categorization of "hasty, more impulsive processors," they look upon the children who display a high number of changes of toys as possessing a superior cognitive ability. The question suggests itself: Is this age-appropriate and indicative of a quicker and more facile familiarization of the objects around them rather than of a short attention span? Kagan's thesis of emerging consistencies, or *Anlagen*, needs to be modified by a developmental framework. Kagan finds the reflective 3-year-old to be a thoughtful child, checking the validity of each solution hypothesis before responding. The impulsive child, by sharp contrast, acts on his first hypothesis and then turns his attention from the problem to other affairs. As an illustration, he cites the case of one child breaking a ball of clay into 15 small pieces, then feeding them to a doll as if they were cookies, while the second breaks the ball into three pieces, drops the clay, and pounces on the blocks. What the child knows, or the assimilative cognitive structures as posited by Piaget and adopted by Kagan, may give additional clues. In support of this interpretation, it is worth noting that Fein (1975), in analyzing the pretend-play of 2-year-olds, remarked that "children imitate that which they can already understand" (p. 295). If we wanted to look at the two examples by Kagan in terms of playfulness in the young child, we would be justified in considering the transformation of the ball of clay into cookies an example of cognitive spontaneity and imagination, and if the frequency count of this transformation within the particular group, or a representative reference group, were available, it might be possible to draw some conclusions about the uniqueness or originality of the behavior. Style of thinking would then emerge as an orderly age variation of earlier play behavior and support the proposed thesis of a connection between play and type of thinking, which underlies Kagan's approach.

Observations of children at play with blocks or in the housekeeping corner, which I carried out as part of establishing criteria for playfulness, give further evidence that boys and girls transform one given thing, say a block, into a brick or become consecutively mother, daughter, or visiting nurse. In short, their pretend approach changes one given into something else that is known or familiar to them. It is in this sense that the deprived child operates under a handicap, and intervention programs such as Headstart or "Sesame Street" and "The Electric Company" provide an opportunity for gathering more facts and a setting in which the child is allowed to play with them. Smilansky (1968) used sociodramatic play with disadvantaged children in Israel to increase both their cognitive competence and their enjoyment of the activities. Similar results were reported by Lovinger (1974) with preschoolers and by Hartshorn and Brantley (1973) with lower-class second- and third-graders in this country.

Studies assessing spontaneity or any other cognitive–affective dimension shown during manipulation of toys must take into account the type of toy and its familiarity to the child. Allowances must be made for different expectations from playing with a gun or with a jigsaw puzzle, or using paper and a box of crayon. The choice of toy interacting with age will contribute to the constructiveness with which it is used. The influence of familiarity of objects and persons in young children's play is demonstrated by older infants showing less decrease in play activities, speech, and movement after the mother's departure (Cox &

Campbell, 1968; Eckerman & Rheingold, 1974). A strange room and absence of mother did, on the other hand, produce performance decrements in speech, movement, and play measures of both younger and older children, ranging in age from 13 to 15 months.

The effects of play on association fluency (Dansky & Silverman, 1973, 1975) in preschool children also underline the role of familiarity in spontaneous productions measuring creativity. Children who were permitted to play freely with paper towels, a screwdriver, a wooden board, and paper clips made significantly more nonstandard responses about the use of these objects than those who just watched an adult working with them. In the follow-up study, the familiarity engendered by the use of play objects as such generalized from one set of toys such as wooden spools, pipe cleaners, and clothes pins to another set consisting of a paper towel, a plastic cup, and even a coat hanger.

Another avenue of examining cognitive spontaneity is the longitudinal study. Kogan and Pankove (1972) followed a sample of fifth-grade middle-class children, whose levels of associative creativity had been assessed with the Wallach and Kogan (1965) tasks, on identical and similar tasks into the tenth grade. Substantial stability in ideational productivity and uniqueness scores over a 5-year period was noted for boys when the setting was that of a group administration, and for girls in the context of individual testing. Since creativity was also assessed by looking at the type of extracurricular activities that the tenth-graders pursued, it was interesting to note that the prediction of such involvement from fifth-grade scores was much better for youngsters attending a smaller school system. In the larger school system, validation of creative ability measures against out-of-classroom criteria of activity and accomplishment was obtained when anxiety (fear of failure) was not present as a disruptive element. Again, we must note the influence of environmental variables as a powerful determinant. One might conjecture even that the smaller system affords a better chance for the youngsters to familiarize themselves with the setting.

Denny, Starks, and Feldhusen (1967), who used the Wallach and Kogan tests with junior high school students in a longitudinal study of divergent thinking and creative performance and tested the students again as seniors in high school, did not employ a game-like setting, but did include in their directions for the Consequences Test the sentence, "The Consequences Test can be fun to take." Their findings were clear-cut: The means for the divergent thinking scores were all significantly greater in high school than they were 4 years earlier. Ideational fluency and flexibility showed the highest increases. It may point to a greater ease in producing ideas and in shifting from one focus to another, qualities which might be linked to the element of spontaneity in playfulness.

Inasmuch as ideational productivity, as measured by the Wallach and Kogan measures of line meanings and pattern meanings, can be labeled spontaneous fantasy production, the higher mean scores of college women (Wallach & Wing,

1969) point to what may be a significant differentiation in young adults. While Wallach and Wing did not pursue further this sex bias in favor of women, the fact remains that, in these verbal measures, women excel. Yet, their actual output in plays, fiction, and poetry does not reflect this higher potential, or at least not as of this writing. I am saying this advisedly because sex barriers are coming down in these fields. However, the data also show that output rather than uniqueness of idea related to the nonacademic accomplishments in music, art, writing, and drama, so that there would still be the need to assess the quality of the ideas for more conclusive answers. One might even conjecture that there is a spontaneous element in the quantity production of ideas. There is no indica-tion, however, on the affect accompanying the activity. That and a scoring for sense of humor might have been further clues to an underlying creativity dimension.

That there may even be a predictive relationship between spontaneity in early play activities and later creative productivity is illustrated by Helson (1967) when she examined the developmental history of 22 creative college women. In childhood, the creative girls showed more imaginary—artistic activities, such as creating complex imaginary situations and acting in them. In follow-up data 5 years after leaving college, those rated creative were engaged in more activity that could be called creative, such as writing children's stories. The stability shown here may be considered as covering both process and product and is noteworthy for this fact. At the same time, the creative subjects were rated higher on ability to change, and this was most pronounced in such dimensions as being perceptive, alert, and spontaneous, as well as welcoming challenges in disorder and complexity.

Similar findings indicative of cognitive spontaneity were reported by Schaefer (1969), whose creative young adolescents scored higher on adjective checklist scales relating to openness to both external and internal experience, while scoring low on scales pertaining to inhibition of impulses and social acceptance. Schaefer also found these traits to be fairly stable after a lapse of 5 years (Schaefer, 1973).

A special category of studies involving spontaneity in play are those dealing with imitative behavior. These either direct, limit, or altogether preclude the show of spontaneity. To the extent that a familiar response is carried over into a different situation, some form of spontaneity may, however, be claimed. This would apply to Altman's (1971) finding that a learned cooperative response was carried over from a laboratory situation of dyadic teams, ranging in age from 3½ to 6 years, to a spontaneous play situation. In a different experimental manipu-lation (Durrell & Weisberg, 1973), high and low probability associations were stimulated in 32 kindergartners through a story reading that influenced both the affect and the information provided in the subsequent play of the boys and girls. Spontaneity was found to be restricted by a model high in distinctiveness and one involved in prior imitative training. There was no age difference between the younger children (average age 4.8 years) and the older ones (average age of 7.5 years). No opportunity was afforded to the children to structure the play materials according to their own fancy. While imitation certainly has its place in learning, at best, it provides material for later imaginative and creative activities, and, at worst, it may stifle these altogether.

Social Spontaneity

To be comfortable in a group setting and move freely in and out of such a social structure was considered the hallmark of social spontaneity in both kindergartners and adolescents in assessing their playfulness (Lieberman, 1964, 1967). The play setting, involving more than one individual in most instances, lends itself admirably to observing and analyzing such behavior. Seagoe (1970) used children's play as a measure of their socialization. Based on the Sullivanian concepts of emotional–social development, she sees play as moving from infor-mal–individual involvement at the preschool stage to competitive–cooperative interaction at preadolescence. Her norming study was based on a middle-class, geographically representative sample of 620 boys and 625 girls aged 5 to 11 years. From the vantage point of social spontaneity, it is interesting to note that individual play seems to persist at a much higher rate for girls through preadoles-cence, while boys prefer socially more complex forms of play. If we speculate about a possible connection to imagination and creativity, it might indicate that boys experience more opportunities to handle social relations, thereby increasing the variety of their role playing, fantasizing, and creative output. Helson's (1968) findings of special techniques used by creative women to stay with their work may add support to our speculation. She found an accentuation of inner orientation, a defensive attitude toward the environment, and a narrowing of interests differentiating creative women from creative men, even though they may have the same creative style, that is the Jungian matriarchial approach.

Social spontaneity is also influenced by historical time and cultural setting. Data on the social aspect of play which give a clue about change over time are provided by Barnes (1971), who replicated Parten's (1932) study on preschool play norms. His findings on 42 preschoolers, aged from 3 to 5 years, suggest that their play behavior is significantly less social than 30 years ago. He offers as two possible explanations the number of hours spent with mass media and the reduction in family size. In the light of Piaget's (1945) observation that both language and thought need to progress from the egocentric to the socialized stage, it raises the question of whether or not spectator type of information gathering may have a limiting effect on cognition, in the sense that the individual does not have an opportunity to bat ideas around with others. That playing with ideas in a group setting may aid the creative process is the underlying rationale of synectics. Gordon (1961) reports considerable success with this tactic in integrating diverse individuals into a problem-stating and problem-solving group.

It is also interesting to note here that the accompanying affect is called the "hedonic response," which would indicate a joyful climate. The brainstorming sessions carried out under the direction of Parnes and his associates at the University of Buffalo and by the Center for Creative Leadership in Greensboro, North Carolina, attest to the value of limbering up cognitive processes through a manipulation of a socially accepting atmosphere.

An interesting sidelight on possible cultural impact on social spontaneity is provided by Seagoe's (1971) investigation of children's play in six modern cultures. The informal aspect is more dominant in democratic countries such as the United States, Great Britain, and Norway, while the competitive element enters much earlier and remains the dominant mode in Spain, Greece, and Egypt. Even subculture was found to be a differentiating factor in play socialization in Seagoe's (1971) study of three subcultures in the United States. While Mexican-American girls had the same degree of play socialization as did Caucasian girls, Black girls showed a markedly lower degree in late childhood than did their Caucasian counterparts. Further supportive evidence of similarities between Mexican-American and Caucasian children comes from a replication of Lieberman's study with kindergartners by Durrett and Huffman (1968) with Mexican-American 5-year-olds. There were no differences between their social spontaneity scores on the playfulness scales with the predominantly white middle-class sample of the earlier study. That age may be a factor in the kind of spontaneity that is related to divergent thinking is suggested in Sitkei and Meyers' (1969) findings that Black 4-year-olds of both lower-class and middle-class background scored equally well on divergent semantic and figure tests, as did their white peers.

That there needs to be a balance between the social and cognitive aspects of spontaneity, and that age is a variable as well, is shown in the more playful behavior of preschoolers when they were paired in a task with friends rather than with unfamiliar peers (Rosenfeld & Gunnell, 1973). In this instance, the play orientation, however, is at the expense of task completion, which was a "Gibson match-to-sample" performance. It allows for some interesting speculations. From the samples of dialogue accompanying the performance, there were more positive and joyful comments in the familiar setting, which would again underline the importance of the baseline of the knowns. What might be worthwhile to follow up is the question regarding what age children can handle social spontaneity for cognitive productivity.

Physical Spontaneity

Physical spontaneity is most readily associated with unstructured play activities, such as jumping rope, or the more structured games, such as Hopscotch, Farmer in the Dell, Simple Simon, and the like, emphasizing again the familiar element in the activity.

In the kindergarten study of playfulness, it was the youngster who hopped, skipped, and jumped with obvious enjoyment who rated high on the physical spontaneity subscale of the playfulness instrument. I already referred to the soothing and goodness of rhythm experienced by infants (Zern & Taylor, 1973) and the suggestion that this may later express itself in dance rhythms. Recently, I found myself for the first time in a discotheque. There were other middle-aged couples like my husband and myself, but the majority of the audience were, of course, in their late teens or early twenties. As I am recalling the scene, I could see the possibility of rating these young men and women on a continuum of playfulness expressed in physical spontaneity. There was a range of facial expressions and body movements from relaxed enjoyment to tense self-observation. The steps and movements themselves were quite repetitious—or familiar, in my terms—and by this token should have brought out the play element. However, the interplay of one's own feeling about the competence of one's body and the social—emotional elements of heterosexual and other affective influences was instrumental in the variation of physical spontaneity demonstrated.

In any discussion of spontaneity, it is very important to differentiate it from impulsivity. This becomes even more imperative when we focus on the physical aspect of spontaneity.

The definition of impulsivity used by Sutton-Smith and Rosenberg (1959) covers many facets of behavior, such as horseplay, restlessness, loss of control, and overly vigorous activities. It is, therefore, not surprising that some of the studies using the scale for identification of behavior problems reported by Sutton-Smith and Rosenberg do not show significant relationships with measures of anxiety or rated impulsivity by staff workers in a residential treatment center. There seems to be a suggestion in two studies (Halverson & Waldrop, 1973; Victor, Halverson, Inoff, & Busakowski, 1973) that vigor of play, which seemed to be equated with hyperactivity, should relate to higher scores on the behavior problem checklist. The danger of confusing spontaneity with hyperactive or impulsive behavior is very real. One of the variables that must be kept in mind is age; another is setting; yet another is outcome of the activity. Considering that the subjects were first- and second-grade boys during their free play period at school, the finding of no relationship between vigor of play as measured by an activity recorder and behavior problem checklist should not be surprising. Teacher ratings did, however, correlate with objective measures of activity. But again, it must be remembered that vigorous activity might have been quite appropriate in the school yard during break and that those considered "hyperactive" in the classroom might also engage in more vigorous free play, without necessarily manifesting behavior problems.

Setting may be an important variable in the consideration of impulsive behavior as either acceptable or unacceptable; the testing of the various ego—psychological postulates about impulse control that this impulsivity scale and the activity recorder sought to accomplish may have been contaminated by the different valences and settings. Haan (1963) describes various modes of impulse diversion when she tries to draw a distinction between coping and defense mechanism in her proposed model of ego functioning, and this is helpful in tying the behavior to consequences.

Another facet that enters any discussion of physical spontaneity is a possible differential expression in vigor by boys and girls. Early sex differences are already noted by Maccoby and Jacklin (1973), and what these may portend for later imagination and creativity is open to speculation. This linkage becomes even more perplexing in the light of an investigation by Bates and Bentler (1973), whose major interest was in understanding changes in gender-typed game play occurring with normal development. They labeled the spontaneous games of early childhood as "feminine" and the more rule-dominated games of middle childhood as "masculine," and found their more effeminate 10-year-old boys more interested in spontaneous games.

In addition to the developmental aspect, a historical footnote should be appended. As mentioned earlier, a 60-year review of children's games (Sutton-Smith & Rosenberg, 1971) found a general trend to more spontaneous games in our day and age and interpreted this as a reflection of the zeitgeist.

INDIVIDUAL DIFFERENCES IN SALIENT CHARACTERISTICS OF PLAY AS A RESULT OF SEX, LEVEL OF INTELLIGENCE, CHILDREARING PRACTICES, AND SCHOOLING

Play as a setting and play viewed through the prism of the special ingredients of sense of humor, manifest joy, and spontaneity gave us a perspective on what may be universal qualities in play or its quintessence. There are other variables that influence play patterns or the expression of the salient qualities of play. These are sex, brightness, and the environmental influences coming from the home and school. Some reference has already been made to one or the other in my earlier discussions, and certainly their interaction with the expression of humor, joy, and spontaneity is self-evident. In singling them out for special treatment here, I hope to highlight and supplement previously cited findings.

Play Patterns of Boys and Girls: Their Relationship to the Salient Characteristics of Play and to Imagination and Creativity

In his pioneer studies on the characteristics of the gifted, Terman (1922, 1925) and his co-workers were already interested in the relationship of play activities to their M—F index. They found their gifted boys from age 8 to 12 to be more masculine than the control sample but to exhibit no difference after-ward. Gifted girls, however, did not differ in their interests from control girls up to age 10, after which their play interests tended to be more masculine. At midlife, the leading hobbies of these men and women (Terman & Oden, 1959) were, in descending order, sports, music, and gardening for males, and music, gardening, and sports for females. To this must be added the information that, at the average age of 44, about half the gifted females were housewives.

The update on the career and life satisfaction among Terman's gifted women carried out by Sears and Barbee (1975) provides us with the additional findings that head-of-household women, which are those that are single, divorced, or widowed, are more likely to find great satisfaction in life, and especially in their work. While most of those who are homemakers with children also found their style of life generally satisfying, many of them would—in 1972—opt for a career, except when actually raising a family. Of interest here is also that personality profiles of gifted women psychologists (Bachtold & Werner, 1970) found women to be more aloof and less dominant than their male colleagues, but high on assertiveness and self-assurance compared with the general female population.

These hard facts provide an illuminating backdrop to the examination of current studies in this area and may also help to provide direction to our inquiry. Without necessarily giving the data a sexist interpretation, it becomes clear that the sex-typing of play interests is already ingrained in the elementary school child and that gifted girls are more likely to buck the stereotype, but the price to pay may be high. In today's literature, we are beginning to see a labeling of "opposite sex" or "cross-sex" toy play side by side with "sex-inappropriate" toy play (Bary, 1974) and, as in so many instances, language reflects changing attitudes to changing roles. This particular study found that, if parents approve or if the children feel parents approve, these kindergartners displayed a signifi-cantly greater amount of cross-sex toy play. Of interest, also, is that with this sanction came a show of greater enjoyment and that the boys' enjoyment was higher than the girls' after social approval was obtained.

It might help to add here a historical footnote for our better understanding of the interaction of play and games with historical and developmental time. In their review of 60 years of historical change in game preferences of American children, Sutton-Smith and Rosenberg (1971) come to the conclusion that singing games, dialogue games, team guessing and acting games, cooperative parlor games, couple and kissing games, all of which they classify as predomi-nantly girls' games, have declined in importance. Of the boys' games, the only ones that have been abandoned are team games without role differentiation. In an effort to establish a revised conception of masculine—feminine differences in play activities, Rosenberg and Sutton-Smith (1960), taking the Terman model as their point of reference, found fourth-, fifth-, and sixth-grade girls of today substantially more like boys in their game preferences than they were 30 years ago.

Another intriguing speculation that grows out of a later analysis of historical change (Sutton-Smith & Rosenberg, 1971) is that formal games may themselves become anachronistic in our time and that, in line with the loosening of the social structure in general, the spontaneous rather than the rule-dominated element in play may become prevalent.

If we are indeed entering an era in which sex stereotyping in play—and later on in work—may be deliberately countered, then the studies testing sex-appropriate versus sex-inappropriate toys and play interests should be viewed from a different perspective. To talk about sex differences per se does not introduce a cultural bias, and we may be able to get less contaminated data from such investigations. Therefore, the behavioral sex differences found by Moss (1967) at ages of as early as 3 weeks may be less adulterated by the environment and based to a greater extent on innate motility patterns. At 6 months, Goldberg and Lewis (1969) observed that mothers already respond differentially to boys and girls, and reinforce sex-appropriate behavior. We need to keep in mind, however, that Maccoby and Jacklin (1973) postulate greater excitability in male infants, and the gross motor involvement as well as vigor of handling toys shown by the 13-month-old infants in the Goldberg and Lewis study would bear this out. However, exploratory behavior, measured in motor performance of number of squares traversed away from mother, was more prevalent among girls in the Finlay and Layne (1971) sample of 1- to 3-year-olds; this held for both Mexican Mayan Indians and New England children. There are further paradoxes and refutations of hypotheses found in Jacklin and Maccoby (1973) and Maccoby, Jacklin, and Dick (1973). Faced with a choice of masculine-typed toys (large and small robot, play school, workbench) and female-labeled toys, such as a ferris wheel with pink ribbons and two stuffed animals, mothers of 13- and 14-month-old boys and girls showed no sex-typed preference in offering toys. These infants also did not differ in their own preference for either a cuddly toy or one with a facelike feature. Based on their conjecture of higher motility patterns of boys, these investigators, however, found that, contrary to their expectations, boys showed less arousal and less readiness "to flee" when faced with a fear stimulus. My own comment would be that this behavior may indeed be culturally sex-stereotyped in the sense that boys are supposed to be less afraid—but already at 13 months old! To paraphrase Gardner Murphy (1958), the cultural mold has indeed descended too soon. Messer and Lewis (1972), focusing on style of play as measured by number of toy changes, found no sex differences in either middle-class or lower-class infants. It is legitimate to ask whether these inconsistencies are the signs of changing times or methodologies that bias the outcome. The investigation by Wolf (1973), while not a definitive answer to this question, may provide a clue about some of the external influences, since it underlines the importance of situational variables in the performance of sex-typed behaviors. His 9-year-old subjects, exposed to a live same-sexed peer model who played with a sexually inappropriate toy, imitated that model more than an opposite sex model or no model. The author relates this with Mischel's (1966) social learning theory of sex typing. This would suggest that there is constant flux and reevaluation of the appropriateness of social roles, including sex-appropriate play interests.

Some support for differential development of sex role and creative potential comes from Biller, Singer, and Fullerton (1969), who broke down the concept of masculinity into sex-role orientation, sex-role preference, and sex-role adoption. While the total creativity index failed to show significant correlation with either sex-role orientation or sex-role preference, there was a highly significant relationship between sex-role pattern and creative potential in their kindergarten boys. It was the 5-year-olds with mixed sex-role patterns (high orientation—low preference; low orientation—high preference) that manifested high performance on Ward's adaptation of Wallach and Kogan's verbal measures of creativity. The authors go on to speculate that because of the found inverse correlation in adolescent and adult males, with social pressure, low-orientation—high-preference produced low creativity at later developmental levels. This could be interpreted as an early manifestation of the crossover or mix between traditional female and male traits found in creative adults (Barron, 1972). We must raise the question, also, of whether involvement in male, rule-dominated games is an orderly age variation that may reverse itself in adolescence and adulthood, or are already personality traits that will maintain a continuity into later years, based on gender identity. In his review of game choices as an index of sex-typed standards for behavior, Kagan (1964) notes that, while boys show an increasing preference for sex-appropriate games with age, the "wall separating male and female recreational activities is cracking" (p. 142), and we should be alert to possible changes. Such changes also affect the fantasy content accompanying the games, especially those with role interpretations, and, if we follow through fantasy play into the vocational choice patterns of adolescence, it may well influence the proportion of women translating their creativity into science and mathematics or, in larger proportions, into the arts (Helson, 1970). In his discussion of sex-role identification and intellectual mastery, Kagan also suggests that, if teachers believed that girls can do as well as boys in science and mathematics, and if female teachers become more confident themselves about their own abilities in these areas, they might be seen as desirable role models by young girls. At an earlier age, Rosenberg (1972) points an accusing finger at the mother as the agent of limitation for a girl's fantasy aspirations and reality-translated creative products. Recent studies (Fox, 1975; Fox & Stanley, 1973) support these statements, especially as they relate to academically gifted girls in mathematics. The influence of parents and teachers as counselors and models is underlined.

A study on intrinsic motivation (Harter, 1975) finds "mastery fun" in problem solving, which involved a game of marbles to be more openly expressed by older boys, aged 10, and young children without sex difference. I would interpret this, again, as a significant indicator of social learning of sex-appropriate behavior.

While the initial study (Horner, 1972) and a replication with a variation by Hoffman (1974) documenting the trend in female college students to exhibit the "fear of success" underlined an important variable influencing the achievement of women, a recent study (Romer, 1975) of school-age males and females from the fifth to the eleventh grades points to the situational variable of competition as an important determinant in showing "avoidance of success." While, overall, no sex differences or clear-cut age trend in motive-to-avoid-success imagery were found, ninth- and eleventh-grade females with motive to avoid success performed better in noncompetitive situations, while older females without motive to avoid success performed better in noncompetitive conditions. Since males in the eleventh grade who also showed no motive to avoid success performed better in a noncompetitive situation, it is legitimate to raise the question of whether or not the socialization of achievement motivation is undergoing a change as a result of historical time. If this involves tension reduction, it might point to more playfulness in the show of humor and joy. A social-class variable interacting with sex at both the elementary and the high school level was found by Butler and Nisan (1975) in disadvantaged Israeli boys, who showed similar fear of success as did advantaged high school girls. Studies from the 1930s, cited by Pollio, Mers, and Lucchesi (1972) in their discussion of humor, laughter, and smiling, found that within a 24-hour period, on the average, women estimated that they laughed 13 times a day, while male college students did so 19 times per day, and Vassar college students in the mid-1920s recorded only an average of between 4 or 5 laughs a day over a period of a week. More recently, Prentice and Fathman (1975), who had used a structured setting involving joking riddles with aggressive and dependent content, aimed at tapping sex differences in comprehension and enjoyment of humor in boys and girls from Grades 1 through 5, found no major sex differences. However, a study (Damico & Purkey, 1976) focusing specifically on the production of humor in eighth-grade students found that only 16 out of 134 peer-nominated class clowns were female. In the category of "superclowns," only one out of nine was a girl.

In the light of the common-sense view that the female sex is guided by the emotions to a greater extent than the male, this is a surprising finding. There are two possible explanations. One is that the acting out of both negative and positive affect is more accepted in boys. This seems plausible when we recall Watson's (1957) findings and the Fels study (Baldwin, Kalhorn, & Breese, 1945) that children from a democratic home are both more cruel and more curious and ready to express affect more openly at both ends of the continuum. The second is that because of sex stereotyping, females are more constrained in their manifestation of affect and use displacement to a greater extent for both hostility and joy. That this influences cognitive mastery and playing with ideas is more than a speculation. The factual evidence of the dearth of creative writers, musicians, and painters, as well as of scientists, would bear out this contention, though the actual causal link has not been proved.

Level of Intelligence as a Variable in Play Patterns, Use of Imagination, and Potential Creativity

Studies of exploratory behavior (Berlyne, 1963; Fowler, 1965; Hutt, 1966; Maw & Maw, 1970; Switzky, Haywood, & Isett, 1974) illustrate that curiosity leads to the seeking of novelty; information gained through novelty seeking becomes incorporated into the existing schemata making for familiarity; familiarity, in turn, triggers the kind of activity called play, with the individual in charge of direction and selection of activities. Elkind (1969) suggested that three major learning abilities, namely, stimulus-seeking, stimulus-storing, and stimulus-exploitation, operate at all developmental levels, as does the dictum "after mastery, you play." Rearranging of known connections and relationships through imagination either concretely or in the abstract may lead to a unique and original product, one of the hallmarks of creativity.

Even this brief outline indicates how much what we call intelligence is operating in the sequences spelled out above. Developmental age and level of intelligence have been known to influence the creation of imaginary companions (Jersild, 1933). Inhelder and Piaget (1958) postulate that viewing himself vis-à-vis an imaginary audience is part of developmental sequencing of logical thinking in the adolescent. Today (Barnes, 1971), not only social aspects but also cognitive aspects of play may be changed, and there seems to be a good basis for speculation that one of the variables would be the child's new technological companion, the TV set. While this may encourage more passive interaction, including information seeking and imagining, the very real contribution of such programs as Sesame Street and Electric Company to intellectual development must be acknowledged. An adult model or guide emphasizing make-believe activities in combination with a television program (Singer & Singer, 1974) brought about increased concentration—a definite intellectual ability—in subsequent play sequences of 4-year-olds. However, use of the information offered will depend on what Kagan (1971) has labeled the density of existing cognitive structures, resulting in differences in richness of reservoir of responses. Conceptual style, in turn, may influence the rate of emission of such response behavior. Gray (1974), using Kagan's conceptual framework, found, for example, that fifth-graders using a flexible style—that is, categorial, descriptive, or relational as it may best apply—obtained higher performances on school learning measures than those using a consistent style. Since reading scores are increasingly used by school systems to indicate intellectual level of functioning, a study by Wolfgang (1974) relating cognitive aspects of reading with selected developmental aspects of first-grade boys is of interest. It indicated that developmentally advanced readers attained high levels of complex symbolic and dramatic play, though they used fewer toys than developmentally retarded readers. It would indicate possibly richer associations with fewer props and a longer staying power with what has become familiar. When children are confronted with the solution of riddles (Shultz, 1974; Sutton-Smith, 1975) or the interpretation of cartoons (Zigler *et al.*, 1966, 1967; McGhee, 1971), we are, also, dealing with functions of intelligence. If any support for our argument is needed, we need only to refer to that section of the WISC (Wechsler, 1974), and, for that matter, also the WAIS (Wechsler, 1950), which uses cartoons to assess logical reasoning. In a broader sense, we may ask whether riddles, cartoons, and puzzles are not part of play. And as we go further up the developmental ladder, it is not unreasonable to suggest that the problem solving of the adult is akin to solving puzzles. To the extent that the creative individual sets up his own problems and thus is in control of familiar components of the puzzle, it can be likened to a play situation. The amount of spontaneity shown and the psychological distancing afforded by not taking oneself too seriously while taking the work seriously would provide conditions conducive to creative productivity.

Parents and Teachers as Encouragers or Inhibitors of the Quintessence of Play

Parents and teachers are more than just individuals interacting with children and young people. As cultural surrogates, they represent also the environment at large, and it is in this sense that I shall examine their influence on some of the qualities of play that may aid or hinder imagination and creative potential.

Feitelson and Ross (1973) are very emphatic about the need for adequate space in order for play activities to develop and refer to evidence from early studies in that area illustrating that lower-class children in crowded metropolitan areas did not develop play behavior. Social class of parents also influences the availability of play materials, another factor cited by Feitelson from her own studies and those of other investigators dealing with children in Egypt and Oriental immigrant children in Israel. However, American and British studies (Kniveton & Pike, 1972; Messer & Lewis, 1972) do not find social class affecting play patterns in young children. It may, therefore, be due more to cultural or subcultural differences and the zeitgeist of today vis-à-vis play that is of decisive importance. We do know that in order for play patterns to develop, mothers need to let go of children (Corter, Rheingold, & Eckerman, 1972; Ross, Rhein-gold, & Eckerman, 1972) and degree of punishment needs to be of a moderate nature for normal play to continue (Cheyne, 1969). These could be interpreted as types of control less likely to be found in lower-class than in middle-class childrearing practices (Collard, 1971). Another variable, much investigated of late and cited above (Bary, 1974; Fagot, 1974), is the inclination of boys and girls to play with sex-inappropriate—now more often called "cross-sex"—toys. As already pointed out, attitude of parent or model (Fagot, 1973b) is known to influence enjoyment of that activity as well as frequency of occurrence. Again, to the extent that we know lower-class parents to hold fast to the more traditional sex stereotypes, we can extrapolate that it would affect the play of their children as a restriction of their choices. When we remember that creative individuals show a crossover of the traditional masculine and feminine traits, which are acquired in earlier role-playing activities, it points to some significant consequences for creative potential. Indeed, one of the items of a playfulness questionnaire completed by mothers and fathers of nursery-age children (Bishop & Chace, 1971) addressed itself directly to that problem by stating, "Boys (girls) should be discouraged from playing with girls' (boys') toys and games," to which the criterion answer was "never." It was also found that mothers with a more abstract conceptual style created a more playful home play environment and the children, in turn, showed evidence of greater creative potential on measures of complexity and flexibility. However, some note needs to be made of findings (Fagot, 1974; Fein, Johnson, Kosson, Stork, & Wasserman, 1975) that show parents giving girls more praise and more criticism than boys during play, joining boys' play more than girls, and that toddlers' play matched adult sex stereotypes in choice of toys. Perhaps what it does suggest about parental handling of play activities is that there is, at the same time, a continuation of orienting the boy and girl toward a sex preference, while being more accepting of cross-sex choices in toys. What is rather surprising—and this indicates a continuation of a stereo-type—is that cross-sex stereotypes are less likely to appear in boys than in girls. It would indicate that the male toy is still more highly valued and is perhaps a clue also to one interpretation of being a liberated woman, namely, adopting the traditional male characteristics of dominance and aggression. It would be well to remember that there is a crossover of characteristics in creative adults and, thus, being a liberated woman does not necessarily equate with being a creative individual.

While play as an environment may not be so readily envisaged as influenced by teachers, we may find some worthwhile pointers to the encouragement of spontaneity, joy, and sense of humor in an examination of classroom manage-ment. We shall certainly find no arguments about the role of nursery and kindergarten teachers in play and play-related activities. When I assessed playfulness in kindergartners, I was made very much aware that, in follow-up investigations, the playfulness of the teacher also needs to be considered as a variable. It may be indicative already of the influence of the teacher in the preschool setting on future creativity that Fagot (1973a) found consistent differences in teacher directiveness to boys and girls, with girls getting more instructions, more answers to questions, and more favorable comments. The first two elements, especially, may encourage cognitive conformity, while the third may lead to social conformity. If we now recall Singer and Rummo's (1973) findings that male kindergartners were both more playful and more creative, we can at least speculate on a connection here. If sex typing of behavior by teachers may result in constriction of playing with ideas as a function of expected dependency behavior in females and assertiveness in males (Etaugh & Hughes, 1975), then we have good reason to look at teachers as encouragers or inhibitors of imagination and creativity. Fox (1975) also emphasizes, on the basis of her work with academically gifted girls, that teachers need to encourage them to become better risk takers. Even more important than the attitude of the preschool teacher is that of the elementary and high school teacher in not only tolerating but also encouraging playfulness in their classrooms. Using play and games as part of the instructional process (De Vries & Edwards, 1974a; McKinney & Golden, 1973; Nesbitt, 1970) was found to influence both types of learning and accompanying affect. Second-graders using dramatic play as an approach to social studies increased their scores on ideational fluency and spontaneous flexibility tests (Hartshorn & Brantley, 1973). Supervisors of student-teachers at the junior high school and high school levels (Berger, 1975; Klein, 1975) have found not only that learning increased on that level, but that the college-age student-teachers who practiced simulation games themselves enjoyed them so much that they were reluctant to return to the role of teacher. Similar evidence comes from the Teams–Games–Tournament structure for classroom learning developed by De Vries and his colleagues (De Vries & Edwards, 1974b) at the Johns Hopkins Center for Social Organization of Schools. Using expectancy theory as a mediating variable and choosing the groups on the basis of equal ability, they found not only increased achievement but also heightened positive affect in the learning process. Their own studies were mainly in the area of mathematics, which seemed to produce more clear-cut results than social studies. A paper submitted to me by a teacher trainee in mathematics (Goldberg, 1976) listing as aids and devices to be used in the teaching of mathematics at the secondary level such ingenious methods as the "percent game," the "geoboard," and "Ripley's Believe It or Not" augurs well for future approaches to a subject that is low on enjoyment in the classroom setting. Here we might also mention again the "games" approach to writing skills used at the college level (Troyka & Nudelman, 1975), which proved very effective. What it suggests is that the playful attitude can create an effective climate for learning at all age levels.

Some mention needs to be made also of the role of television. Perhaps we should even have included it in our caption with the same weighting as parents and teachers. Certainly, television is an extension of the parenting function as a model and as a representative of cultural norms and standards. Because it is labeled "entertainment," the approach used in such programs as "Sesame Street," "Mr. Rogers' Neighborhood," and "The Electric Company" is very much imbued with the play spirit. Yet, evaluative studies (Lesser, 1974) have come up with a good score card for the programs in terms of promoting learning. Admittedly, the appeal seemed to be more to the middle-class child rather than to the disadvantaged youngster, for whom the programs were originally planned. But then again, I found in my examination of parental attitudes that the playful approach is more likely to be found in middle-class parents who can be more relaxed and comfortable on the basis of feeling competent in their childrearing practices. That the teaching should not be left entirely to the television set is demonstrated by Singer and Singer (1974). Their technique of using an adult model in conjunction with television viewing, and their findings that this not only increased learning but the enjoyment of learning, may be a worthwhile pointer to the further use of the above-mentioned programs with disadvantaged children. The availability and reinforcement of an adult as an information dispenser is again underlined as an important variable in at-home teaching.

If we introduce the variable of amount of time as a possible influence on playfulness, a study by Gadberry (1974) suggests some interesting ramifications. Using a middle-class sample of male preschoolers, she found those whom she called "low TV viewers" to "self-stimulate" more and shift attention less in playtime, either before or after viewing TV. One of the characteristic features of any TV program is the frequent interruption by commercials which would, of course, encourage attention-shifting regardless of age. Since playfulness is more likely to thrive in a familiar setting, we could make the inference that an overexposure to TV might undercut the development of spontaneity, sense of humor, and manifest joy in play and other activities.

Subcultural and Cross-cultural Influences on Play Patterns

In considering subcultural and cross-cultural differences in play, we are widening the influence of environment, which we started to examine by looking first at the cultural surrogates, namely parents and teachers. It should, therefore, be no surprise that social control as evidenced by distance from mother (Finley & Layne, 1971) was a differentiating variable between American and Mexican children, aged 1 through 3 years. While that study found Mexican children more social and visual in exploration in comparison to American youngsters, Seagoe (1971) found groups of Mexican-American and Black American youngsters, aged 6 through 11, scoring lower on her play socialization measure. That developmental age may be a critical variable is suggested by a replication of Lieberman's

(1965) original study with Mexican-American kindergartners by Durrett and Huffman (1968). In their study, disadvantaged boys and girls from a subcultural group in the United States showed the same patterns in playfulness and divergent thinking as the middle-class and predominantly white kindergartners. That spontaneity, show of joy, and glint-in-the-eye behavior may not be subculturally determined in young children is further supported by a study of Black kindergartners (Sitkei & Meyers, 1969), who scored higher than their white peers on divergent thinking scores.

More intriguing—and also more speculative—are the possible consequences of the more structured nursery and kindergarten play periods described in reports from child development experts visiting the Soviet Union and China (Bronfenbrenner, 1970; Kessen, 1974). The recent work by Baltes and Schaie (1973) and Nesselroade and Baltes (1974), with its emphasis on cohorts, would suggest follow-ups that might probe the questions of whether or not individuals growing up in certain social and political climates at a crucial period in their development might be differentially influenced in their show of spontaneity, sense of humor, and joy. Some indication of this comes from Seagoe's (1971) previously cited data comparing children's play in six modern cultures, which finds the more informal aspect of play prevailing in countries such as the United States, Great Britain, and Norway.

SUMMARY STATEMENT AND RECOMMENDATIONS

The Relationship of Playfulness to Studies of Humor, Manifest Joy, and Spontaneity

The preceding sections have attempted to show that, during the last decade, there has been increasing interest to study humor, joy or pleasure, and, to some extent, spontaneity as a by-product of cognitive and affective behavior. Some of the impetus to investigate these concepts and their operational manifestations came from a growing focus on prosocial behavior. It is now time to ask ourselves what, if anything, playfulness as a concept and its behavioral correlates have contributed to this *nouvelle vague* and what its role in the future might be.

Playfulness in Relation to Existing Research

By stipulating that there is a behavior syndrome that encompasses humor, joy, and spontaneity, the natural linkings of these three dimensions are underlined. Psychological distancing in humor, the focus on the producer of humor in natural settings, the relationship of humor to cognitive mastery, and the existence of friendly wit would be specific findings in support of my conceptualization of playfulness. The emphasis on joy as part of humor, of liking as measurable behavior, and the need to take into account physiological correlates of pleasure also tie in with the playfulness concept. Finally, spontaneity, to be differentiated from both flexibility and impulsivity, touched upon obliquely in some studies, was identified as evidence in support of playfulness and as a clue to cognitive style.

Playfulness in Relation to Future Directions in Research

The major question is whether or not playfulness, as a composite, is useful enough to supplement studies specifically geared to the separate dimensions subsumed under it. I was careful not to suggest a supplanting, since I believe that there is need for both approaches. What we may lose in precision by using the composite of playfulness, we gain in meaningfulness. Using the umbrella concept, while constantly checking out the validity of its component parts, would be one way of applying playfulness to future research studies. Another reason, perhaps of even greater importance, is the use of the composite for further investigations of cognitive style, especially creativity. Not to be overlooked is the use of playfulness in probing different types of imaginative processes. Imagination, like play, has many uses, and the functional differences have been well documented. Playfulness could be helpful in a further exploration of the qualitative differences of fantasy. A good deal is already known about the use of aggression in fantasy. More needs to be known about humor, joy, and spontaneity, in short, the degree of playfulness in imagination. This qualitative difference in the silent partner of the triad play—imagination—creativity may lead to further pinpointing of the type of fantasy that nurtures creativity.

Sex, Brightness, Parents, and Society:
Their Impact on Playfulness

As a logical sequence to the findings on affect and more joyful expression of it in boys, I am forced to conclude that the playfulness that leads to creativity is more readily found in males. However, as we have seen, parental and societal norms in encouraging brightness are not independent of sex. Expectations for intellectual expression of playfulness may not be conveyed to girls in the same way as they are to boys. Any change in these areas would be, to no small extent, also a function of historical time.

Exploratory Behavior and Play:
Their Impact on Playfulness

My examination of the studies of playfulness in play as they relate to imagination and creativity further underlined the distinction between exploration and play. Using a Piagetian framework, one might want to compare it to the alternation of assimilation and accommodation with the state of equilibrium, the latter being the play period. Play can be considered a period when the environment is in equilibrium and is known. Exploration is a period of flux, with unknown quantities abounding. In this conceptual schema, playfulness may either be considered a catalyst between the two or as triggering the reassembling of known factors into new combinations.

Developmental and Historical Time:
Their Impact on Play and Playfulness

One of the major insights that emerged from my review of age-related studies of play is that they cannot be regarded in isolation from the time in which they were conducted. The degree of structure permitted, the freedom with which affect may be expressed, including glint-in-the-eye behavior, is a reflection of the Zeitgeist, which, in turn, becomes part of the underlying philosophy of child-rearing and educational practices. Looking at the past decade from this vantage point, I feel justified in assessing the climate as moving toward looser structure and more tolerance for expression of affect. Theoretically, there would, there-fore, be a more receptive frame of mind for playfulness not only as part of play behavior but also as a personality trait of the individual.

V

The Role of Playfulness
in a Theoretical Framework
for a Relationship among Play,
Imagination, and Creativity

"When in doubt, diagram it out" might be appropriate advice when there is a profusion of ideas and a diffusion of hard data. Accordingly, in Figure 5.1, I am offering a schematic presentation of the possible relationship between play, imagination, and creativity as first-order elements, and playfulness, divided into sense of humor, manifest joy, and spontaneity, as second-order elements. The labeling has no statistical connotation but is to be considered figurative. It is meant to indicate the differential weightings given to the component factors. Put differently, we might look at playfulness as the factor common to play, imagination, and creativity. Playfulness, itself, however, may not be a unitary trait, and this can be caused either developmentally or situationally, as illustrated in my studies.

The task in this chapter is to construct or, better still, to sift out from the research findings the theoretical underpinnings that would afford a clearer understanding of existing relationships and point to possible future ramifications of the proposed matrix. My intention is more realistically to set up a working model of relationships, bearing in mind Bass's (1974) caution that early closure on theory may be counterproductive to relating specific variables to real-life characteristics. In order to achieve this, the approach to the examination of the theoretical basis will be along the major areas of functioning in the individual, namely, through the cognitive, affective, and social processes.

107

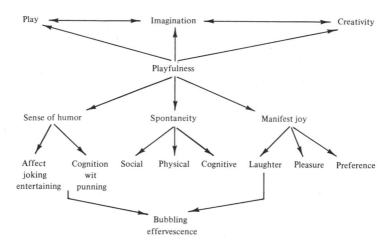

Figure 5.1   Model of relationships among play, imagination, and creativity, and playfulness.

CLUES TO PLAYFULNESS IN A COGNITIVE LINKAGE BETWEEN PLAY, IMAGINATION, AND CREATIVITY

The impetus to my own research came from the observation that playfulness is an ingredient of the creative individual's cognitive style. At the time when I postulated this relationship, I had not been aware of Dewey's (1933) formulation of playfulness, which he described as follows: "Playfulness is an attitude of mind; [play] a passing outward manifestation of this attitude" (p. 210). Earlier, Dewey (1913) gave this definition of playfulness: "[It is] the capacity to draw satisfaction from the immediate intellectual development of a topic, irrespective of any ulterior motive" (p. 727). As a social philosopher and educator interested in the broadest possible application of his theories, Dewey did not limit the characteristic of playfulness to a particular cognitive style, such as divergent thinking. In the light of current research on creativity (Guilford, 1968; Torrance, Bruch, & Morse, 1973), which points to a continuum of creative potential and productivity, rather than to an all or nothing trait, his approach would still be acceptable to contemporary thought. That my conceptualization of playfulness was arrived at independently some 50 years later may be cited in support of the validity of the concept and the reliability of its manifestation in play. However, it had gathered dust as a definition all these years and needed to be tested experimentally, as I did in the playfulness studies. Now it invites further research for theoretical model building and description and prediction of behavior. As Klinger (1971) sums it up: "In the course of fantasy, a person works over, recombines, and sometimes reorganizes the information, often creatively" (p. 356). Singer (1973), too, refers to the mounting evidence that fantasy and imaginativeness can be a useful, cognitive skill. Focusing on this utilitarian aspect, I might venture to say that here again the element of familiarity would spark the cognitive spontaneity that is part of playfulness. When we fantasize, more often than not, we start from what we know and the embellishments we add to make it something different also may come from a pool of knowledge already there. This is not to say that the novel and original must be left out of a consideration of imagination, but the humble known is sometimes given short shrift in theoretical discussions. It needs to be underlined because it is the foundation on which we build the practical applications. The latter will be illustrated in greater detail in the following chapter. Here, I want to point to some of the theoretical links. For one, stream of consciousness associations may also be viewed from the angle of familiarity, and spark the play element in imagination. If, as we shall see later, positive affect accompanies the "replay of old reels," then playfulness can operate and become a link to the creative product.

A word needs to be said also about the neurological underpinning of the paradigm. My own view of seeing playfulness as part of an intrinsic motivational force was greatly influenced by Hebb's (1949, 1955) thinking, especially when he ascribes the variability in the mammalian responsiveness to the environment to an intrinsic element in the organization of cerebral activity. Cell assemblies can be likened to familiar material; phase sequences may encompass recombinations of familiar material and, to that extent, trigger "insights" and unique new combinations. In other words, thist might be a neurological approach to understanding the creative process.

The Familiar versus the Novel

One of the major pointers in understanding the relationship between play, imagination, and creativity on a cognitive basis is the differentiation between exploratory behavior and play. If we note what has become an accepted differentiation between play and exploratory behavior, demonstrated by Hutt (1966) and restated recently by Switzky, Haywood, and Isett (1974), namely, that familiarity, clarity, simplicity, and congruity are stimulus characteristics eliciting play, while novelty, ambiguity, incongruity, surprise, and complexity spark exploratory behavior, we may look at exploratory studies as preparing the ground for play. It may be that when the child feels that he is in control of the environment or that he feels competent to deal with the environment, the "function pleasure" first referred to by Buehler (1918/1930), and later used again by Piaget (1945), becomes part of his approach. In my analysis, it is at this point that the playfulness element enters into play. That a picture is sometimes worth a thousand words is illustrated by the two photographs accompanying the write-up of the Hutt study (as cited in Herron & Sutton-Smith, 1971). They are captioned "characteristic patterns of exploration" and "the characteristic pattern of play," respectively. Both facial expressions and body postures indicate the transition from arousal to relaxation, from concentrated attention to smiling enjoyment. One may conjecture that both show evidence of the presence of a hedonic element, but the evidence is more concrete in the pattern of play.

If we pursue the argument that, as a result of continued exploration, the individual becomes more familiar with an increasing quantity of factual information, we can establish the connection of playfulness in play as a link to imaginative creativity. According to Berlyne (1963), novelty–familiarity operates in exploratory behavior as a collative variable. My review of the studies would suggest that, once the novel becomes familiar—and this may be as a result of exploratory behavior—the playful attitude or playfulness can set in. This interpretation can also be applied to Piaget's model of assimilation and accommodation. The existing, assimilated structures are the basis for recombinations not only in the preoperational stages but also in the concrete and formal stages of intellectual development and make up the content of imagination that leads to creative production.

The 4-year-old's definition of "butterfly" as a fly on the butter is an example of this type of creative thinking. That it does not stop at the preoperational stage was demonstrated to me by one of my students, a college junior, who, in reply to the question of what is "homeostasis," answered "liking to stay at home." I have always felt that, although she could not get credit for the answer in the usual sense, she should have been credited with ingenuity or at least demonstrating assimilation at work in the thought processes of the young adult. Since both replies, because of their incongruity, have humorous overtones, it brings to mind McGhee's (1972) formulation of the role of fantasy assimilation in sense of humor. While these were unplanned and fortuitous productions, they serve the purpose of illustrating that particular process in the natural situation and in a developmental framework. Viewed in this light, it might even be possible to gather data either by the ethological method or by experiments that would present the individual with novel objects or concepts and ask him to solve problems in the context of present assimilative structures.

Looking at the clues of the play–imagination–creativity linkage from the creativity end, we can cite references (Dewey, 1958; Wallas, 1921) to the incubation period as a prerequisite to coming up with a new or unique solution to a problem. Again, we can postulate that fact gathering preceded the emergence of the creative product. It is at this point that combinatorial play enters, aided by the powers of imagination. In the psychoanalytic term, it is that type of fantasy that frees itself from the restrictions of reality and thus combines with regression "in the service of the ego" (Hartmann, 1958; Kris, 1952). Viewing it within a philosophical framework, Langer (1951) expresses the creative process as "one influenced by the power of conception, the wealth of formulative notions with which the mind meets experiences" and goes on to say that "most new discoveries are suddenly-seen things that were always there" (p. 8). This is a type of thinking very different from the one Henle (1975) criticizes as the associationist point of view of creativity. It would come closer to a new configuration based on material already in the cognitive structures. To give a concrete example, it would be the kind of approach that made Scarlett O'Hara cut up the velvet portieres and fashion a ballgown from them. She thus saw the piece of velvet—familiar enough to her—in a new light. It also suggests an intriguing interpretation to the clause that would supposedly make Faust lose his soul to the devil. As Goethe puts it, "Verweile doch, du bist so schoen" ('Linger for awhile, you are so beautiful') could be seen as that element that would bring satisfaction and joy arising from the familiar. Conversely, no longer would Faust merely collect new experiences, but he might have the time to ingest them, recombine them, and become creative in his own right. Was that the danger that Mefistofeles saw? Returning to the psychological literature, the collective unconscious posited by Jung (1959) can be viewed as something that is common and, to a certain extent, familiar to all of us. Being able to communicate with this pool of data would, therefore, constitute another source for combinatorial play with knowns.

Some mention needs to be made about the difference between spontaneity and flexibility in thought processes. Within my theoretical framework, based on current research and empirical observations, cognitive spontaneity is more likely to be triggered by intrinsic stimuli that are part of the existing cognitive structures. Cognitive flexibility may be a reaction to either intrinsic or extrinsic stimuli, but, whichever they are, the differentiating element would be the novelty of the stimulus. Hutt's (1970) presentation of the characteristics of investigation and play, which she connected in a more general framework with specific versus diversive exploration, would support my thesis. At another time, Hutt (1971) uses the word "nonchalant" to describe the transformation from exploratory to play behavior. It is a delightful, nontechnical way of capturing that ease of movement, not only in cognitive, but also in social and physical spontaneity, that I have found to be a major component of playfulness.

Developmental and Historical Aspects in the Cognitive Linkage

We also need to look at the intertwining of play, imagination, and creativity in a developmental framework and ask ourselves what is species-specific about

Homo ludens—playing man—that is inextricably bound up with *Homo sapiens* and *Homo faber*—man the thinker, and man the producer. We know that play itself is not species-specific to the human infant. Therefore, the crucial question does not concern play itself, but the role of play in human development. One indication of this role is spelled out by Bruner (1972) in his discussion of the nature and uses of immaturity applied to the human infant. His suggestion that "in order for tool using to develop, it was essential to have a long period of optional, pressure-free opportunity for combinatorial activity" (p. 693) supports my thesis of the importance of playfulness as well as of the situational or ecological determinants for its development. While Dolhinow and Bishop's (1970) comments refer to the play of primates in general, they, too, note that play and playful activity "occurs only in an atmosphere of familiarity, . . . emotional reassurance, and lack of tension or danger" (p. 142). If we connect these observations with those put forward by Kagan (1971) about individual differences in richness of reservoir of responses and those found by Singer (1973) in degrees of fantasy production in children and adults, we might use these cognitive clues as support for an interface between play, imagination, and creativity. Playfulness as a personality trait would be an important variable contributing to the effectiveness of the linkup. To use an anatomical analogy, play, imagination, and creativity are the vertebrae of the model; playfulness is the connecting tissue and in this way affects and interacts with each component part separately. Looking at our diagram, it might, therefore, help to turn it 90° and thus increase the pictorial likeness to the spinal column. And, again, reversing the flow of the diagram, we can look upon spontaneity, manifest joy, and sense of humor as the ennervating fibers of playfulness itself. Going one step further, we can tease out the cognitive elements in sense of humor as wit and punning, the way one might find it and use it in a riddle; similarly, we have a cognitive component of spontaneity, as illustrated by new combinations and recombinations of familiar facts and structures; and even manifest joy in its dimension of preference and liking has an evaluative ingredient.

Historical examination of the riddle in the broader spectrum of playing and knowing (Huizinga, 1955) brings out yet another facet of the relationship between play, imagination, and creativity. Huizinga emphasizes the riddle's play quality and calls it a sacred game, a bridge between the serious and the nonserious. In a phylogenetic sense, he considers the riddle to be connected not only with the sacred but also with the mysterious. Experimental studies previously cited used the riddle because, by its very construction, resolution of incongruity and sense of mastery could be tapped. Was it left to the priests of old to resolve the incongruities of life and master its mysteries? One is tempted to extrapolate that playing imaginatively with the riddles of nature and finding a solution would be one way of describing the creative process, and if indeed there is nothing new in the world, then this very familiarity of the components triggers the play element. Admittedly, these are almost metaphysical speculations. Yet, the riddle is very much a part of the everyday routine of children in their attempts at mastery and resolution of incongruities. Sutton-Smith (1975) formulated a developmental structural account of riddles indicating the growth of information, language, and reasoning through seven different types, ranging from preriddles to multiple classifications. Similarly, slips of the tongue (Freud, 1938a) occurring in natural settings sometimes involve transgression against taboos and sacred cows and possibly aid in mastery of conflicts.

It is also pertinent to look at imitation from the vantage point of a cognitive linkage between play, imagination, and creativity. A look at games in relation to play might be helpful. Avedon and Sutton-Smith (1971), in trying to draw a dividing line between play and games, look upon play as unique, individual, and ephemeral, whereas they consider a game to be sufficiently systematic for a replication by others in other places. In addition, they find, in their study of games, that these are more likely to have predictable outcomes, while play remains open-ended. There are two qualitative ingredients mentioned that have a direct bearing on creativity, and these are the open-ended process and the unique outcome, both of which are used by Guilford and his associates (1951) in the assessment of divergent thinking and divergent production. Another element that is implicit in this formulation of play versus games is a change-with-age component. Young children play; older children play games, suggesting that, with age, a certain restrictive element enters the play situation. The young child's play, by dint of his preoperational (symbolic) approach, would have more unique elements that could be labeled "creative" at that time. When we come to consider the middle-childhood child, already occupied with reversibility of concrete operations and fact finding, we can understand how he is more accepting of the real world, willing to abide by rule-dominated games, and possibly uncomfortable with the ephemeral quality of early childhood play. Thus, play in its pure form can be depicted on a decelerating curve, but playfulness may increase. The basic tenets and philosophy of transactional analysis (Kambly, 1975) would be applicable here, inasmuch as they describe the "free child" as "the spontaneous, playful, . . . creative part of us" (p. 253) and explain that this part of the ego state also realizes that what constitutes fun or play changes as we grow older. If the psychological basis of rule-governed behavior is not a direct stimulus–response imprinting, as suggested by Segal and Stacy (1975), but a learning of rules as part of the individual's cognitive structure, then we may posit that there is leeway for cognitive spontaneity in games as well. Just as we recombine and reshuffle individual bits of information, we can apply the same process to rules. It is interesting to note that the original thesis by Segal and Stacy was suggested in connection with linguistic rules. What more concrete example of rearranging rules in language can be given as those seen in poetic license? The violation of rules is part and parcel of the creative process, but rules have to be known first before they can be discarded.

CLUES TO PLAYFULNESS IN AFFECTIVE STATES
COMMON TO PLAY, IMAGINATION, AND CREATIVITY

Play as a mode of behavior with obvious enjoyment, happy daydreamers, positive excitement as part of the creative process, psychological distancing in the appreciation of humor—these were some of the major findings that emerged from the review of studies in the areas of sense of humor, manifest joy, and spontaneity. To paraphrase Shakespeare, "Is this the stuff that playfulness is made of?" and more specifically, are these the kind of pointers we can use to put together a theoretical model in which the role of playfulness will become evident as a catalyst between play and imagination, play and creativity, and imagination and creativity? At this point, it will also be well to remember Rest's (1974) warning to developmental psychologists to stay away from transitory affective states such as joy and spontaneity. Since I am not going to heed his warning, I need to make an especially strong case for affect as expressed in playfulness as a link in the play—imagination—creativity triad.

In my very first attempt to extend playfulness as a quality of play in the young child into playfulness as a personality trait in the adolescent and adult, I had hypothesized that its physical expression might be eliminated as we go up the developmental ladder but that it would still figure strongly in the social—emotional and cognitive domain. Perhaps I should have been alerted by the tentative interpretation of the hand-rotated factors in the kindergarten study, which suggested that joyful spontaneity, brightness and sparkle, and maturation might be considered separate dimensions. The "bubbling effervescence" syndrome in the adolescent might be cited as further evidence that a strong affective variance is surfacing. In other words, joyful spontaneity might have a cognitive strain but is subordinated to affect.

The Familiar versus the Novel

A promising start in looking at the role of affect in our model building will be the suggested dichotomy between the familiar and novel as it relates to play and exploration. Waelder's (1933) psychoanalytic formulation commenting on the place of repetition compulsion and function pleasure as major dynamics in play can be interpreted as repeating some activity to the point of mastery, to the point where it is familiar and one can be comfortable with it. The subsequent enjoyment can lead to fantasy play and creative products using known factors.

It is commonplace knowledge, attested to by personal statements from creative individuals in the past and present, that there is both joy and anguish in the creative process. Psychological research and theory might give further support to these speculations. Berlyne (1960) talks about a curvilinear relationship between amount of arousal increment and positive and negative affect. If we recall the research findings suggesting that familiarity leads to play and that novelty leads to exploration, we might posit the following process. There is a point of transition between the known and the unknown. When the creative individual uses the familiar facts in his repertory, we can postulate a joy of recognition similar to that of seeing old acquaintances. But this is only a way station. There is the urge to create something new, the drive to disturb the equilibrium of assimilative structures in the Piagetian sense. Would it not be justified to assume that, at this time, negative affects would arise? It must be considered to be a crucial point and may, indeed, be accompanied by considerable anguish. What, then, makes the creative individual go out into the unknown? Perhaps the concept of fantasy assimiliation put forward by McGhee (1972) may enter the process at this juncture. Known elements are rearranged into new constellations; there still may be considerable negative affect in overcoming the obstacles to the solution of the problem, but there is a concurrent flow, possibly increasing, of positive excitement in seeing closure leading to the creative product. I am suggesting that this may be one way of looking at the psychological undercurrents of the agony and the ecstasy that accompany creative production. The explanation offered is plausible to the extent that it rests on the theoretical framework underlying recent studies of play, imagination, and creativity. A philosophical footnote is provided by Tomkins (1965), who cites Whitehead as the principal representative of the proposition for creative synthesis, in which loyalty to tradition must be combined with willingness to experiment. When we recall, also, that psychological distancing aids humor appreciation (Goldstein, 1972) and that Helson (1967) found her female creative subjects more defensive, it may allow us to speculate on possible causes of sex differences. The greater field dependency of women (Witkin, Dyk, Faterson, Goodenough, Karp, 1962) may provide further clues for greater constraints in perception and, thus, less ability or inclination to play the field and receive the impressions without trying to fit them into a preconceived structure. I may be skating on thin ice if I apply the thesis that familiarity makes for ease in perception and recombination of facts. A possible explanation might be that women do not even allow themselves to see what is known in any given environment because of greater tension and threat from the unknown. This is not a question that can be answered by speculation; it must be tested experimentally or observed empirically.

Whether locus of control also has an affective dimension is another aspect worth exploring. It is easy to conjecture that if an individual is confident that he is master or she is mistress of any given situation, there should be satisfaction, if not joy, accompanying these perceptions. In my theoretical framework, internal-control persons who would be more likely to operate with known variables would also be more likely to show playfulness in a situation in which they are asked to perform a task. Again, experimental data would need to be obtained to confirm such a hypothesis.

The tenets of behavior modification, with their avowed aim at working for satisfied and happy customers, also need to be examined in the light of whether or not this type of positive affect allows an individual to let his imagination roam and come up with creative and unique products.

Another useful conceptualization (Tomkins, 1962) sees joy as a reward from the reduction of excitement, which helps create familiar objects and long-term commitments. At the same time, new learning has to go on and become old learning, thus establishing the basis for the degree of creativity, namely, the ratio of new learning to old learning.

Developmental and Historical Aspects

In her historical introduction to *The Psychology of Play*, Millar (1968) refers to play as an attitude of throwing off restraint, to which pleasure and enjoyment are essential. In support, she cites Sully (1902), who, in his *Essay on Laughter*, speaks of the play mood, or playful attitude, in which laughter is an element. If we relate this to Dewey's (1913, 1933) definitions of the playful attitude, we realize that playfulness needs to encompass more than the cognitive element. In fact, affective states such as joy, laughter, and sense of humor are subsumed under playfulness not only in my conceptualization, but also in everyday usage of the word. That "bubbling effervescence" enters the creative process is borne out in the theoretical writings of Tomkins (1962), Berlyne (1960), and Schachtel (1959), who deal with expressions of positive affect as part of the creative process, of curiosity, and of heightened cognitive awareness. Tomkins speaks of this type of excitement as a positive affect that, coupled with the courage to resist competing negative affects, is a necessary condition for revolutionary intellectual activity. If we supplement this statement with one of the items in his polarity scale (Tomkins, 1965), we have a developmental foundation for the survival of play affect beyond early childhood days. The item in question, Number 59, reads, "Play is important for all human beings. No one is too old to enjoy the excitement of play" (p. 88). Yet, a strange thing happens to the element of joy on the way to growing up. It becomes differentially valenced for boys and girls and, ultimately, for women and men.

While, theoretically, the work of Freud (1938a), and later of Parsons and Bales (1955), would suggest that instrumental and expressive modes characteristic of male and female behavior should be reflected in the early play activities of boys and girls, a closer scrutiny of the affective needs expressed through play does not support this dichotomy. We find greater amounts and freer expression of enjoyment in the play of the male child, and this holds for both free play and structured games. Indeed, in the interaction of historical and developmental time, it was found (Sutton-Smith & Rosenberg, 1971) that we are moving toward a predominance of spontaneous, masculine play activities and games. Thus, there seems to be no end to paradoxes. At this point, I should like to introduce Emmerich's (1973) proposition that, in order to get a more accurate picture of sex differences in development, we need to look at *age-specific* sex differences. For my purposes, this narrower focus allows me to posit that cultural role expectations assert an increasing influence on the expressive behavior of boys and girls, so that the affect of joy is more accepted as an accompaniment to intellectual achievement in boys and to personal relationships in girls as they reach adolescence. At present, and very likely in the future, historical time may counteract what used to be the influences of developmental change. By the time girls reached adolescence, their world had become more circumscribed. Figuratively, the playground of the mind had become restricted. Imagination, now developmentally influenced to engage in fantasy roles for the future, focused on the roles of wife and mother. Creativity was thus confined to the locus of the home. Today, with expanded options available to women, we can expect changes both in their fantasy content during adolescence and in their creative productivity. I shall return to this point in my consideration of the social aspects in the linkage of play—imagination—creativity. Within the affective focus, we may conclude that we need to revise our thinking not only about characteristically feminine and masculine feeling states, but also about the feelings that characteristically accompany the play, imagination, and creativity of boys and girls. We need to ask ourselves how much models of patriarchial and matriarchal consciousness, cited by Helson (1968), are applicable and, if so, how helpful they are in understanding differential affect in male and female creativity. Helson found that the patriarchal approach, which is purposeful, assertive, and objective, was not restricted to the male creative individual, and she noted that the main resource of creative women was their patriarchal ability to direct and order their cognitive processes. This finding was contrary to an earlier study of creative women mathematicians, who showed an intensified, yet directed, matriarchal pattern characterized by brooding and inner-directed reflection. In testing the generality of this assumption, creative males with a matriarchial approach of receiving and nurturing creative content were identified. It is, therefore, oversimplified to equate patriarchial consciousness with creative men and matriarchial consciousness with creative women. Helson herself found an interaction between field and creativity in men, but not in women. This would point very strongly to the influence of situational variables, including historical time in the life-span sense used by Baltes and Schaie (1973). The special techniques cited by Helson as being used by women would support such an interpretation. Since they are more likely to use a defensive attitude toward the environment, they feel the need to narrow their interests and accentuate their inner orientation in order to function as creative individuals. The question suggests itself of whether or not women are less capable of the "activity joy" that is gained from current involvements and may be more prone to magic joy, which is based on passive anticipation and expectation (Schachtel, 1959, p. 43).

It is also commonly held that women lack a sense of humor, or at least show less of it than men. Empirically speaking, there are certainly fewer female than male comedians. Both theory and research indicate the important role of humor in at least two of the behavior dimensions under discussion, namely, play and creativity. Humor also enters fantasy, but, of course, in a more covert manner. The studies I examined and the model I diagrammed suggest that there is an affective dimension to sense of humor. It is interesting to note that none of the humor studies deals explicitly with sex differences. The theoretical underpinnings allow us some speculations about possible causes, however. Do women feel more defensive about enjoyment of mastery, which Zigler et al. (1966, 1967) found to be a prerequisite to humor appreciation? Tomkins (1962) looks at the relationship of creativity and humor and the degree of enjoyment as expressed in laughter as a function of the relationship between anticipatory and payoff affect. Are, as Horner (1972) and others (Bachtold & Werner, 1970; Helson, 1967, 1968; McClelland, 1975; Oden, 1968) have found, women afraid of success?

I have noted in the review of studies dealing with humor and manifest joy that there can be problem-solving activity manifested in a cooperative setting, which does not have the variable of besting an opponent as part of an incentive for achievement. It has also been suggested that a certain degree of psychological distance is necessary to appreciate humor at one's own expense. I want to add another variable, or perhaps it is already part of some of the behavior mentioned, but never labeled as such, and that is altruism and generosity. Here, I challenge Huizinga's contention that the agonistic element in play is a civilizing factor. I found Caillois' (1961) introduction of the element of *paidia*, as the tumultuous agitated opposite to *ludus* as the regulated competitive ingredient of games, a worthwhile addition to the conventional classification. The way in which Piaget and others use ludic does not imply a structured, competitive type of activity. On the contrary, there is more of *paidia* than *ludus* in Piaget's use of "ludic." My mentioning the two terms is not for semantic but for behavioral reasons and links up with my interest in the prosocial and altruistic ingredient in play, which may more readily grow out of a spontaneous climate rather than a tight, rule-dominated setting. It brings to mind the nonevaluative, free-wheeling atmosphere advocated for brainstorming sessions that use the group setting for the production of creative ideas (Gordon, 1961; Osborn, 1963; Parnes & Meadow, 1959).

CLUES TO PLAYFULNESS IN SOCIAL EXPECTATIONS
RELATED TO PLAY, IMAGINATION, AND CREATIVITY

It was possible—and I thought helpful—to examine cognitive and affective clues to playfulness in play, imagination, and creativity along two major themes, namely, the familiar versus the novel, and the interaction of developmental with historical time. In the social arena, such a division would be an artifact without paying dividends in greater clarity of presentation. Therefore, the interaction of known versus unknown in developmental and historical time is considered.

To paraphrase or to extend Ecclesiastes, there is a time to play and a time to work, a time to dream and a time to face reality, a time to produce new things and a time to be content with the old. In other words, social expectations will guide an individual's manifestation of play, imagination, and creativity. We can see this from comparative, developmental, and cross-cultural data. Bruner (1972) holds that the more productive the adult of a species, the earlier we can find mastery play in the immature organism. A comparison between Koehler's (1925) and Dolhinow's (1972) chimpanzees and Piaget's (1966) three subjects would bear out this contention. A needed clarification is the differentiation between mastery and play. The young chimps achieve mastery over a more limited amount of skills in a shorter play time; the human infant achieves mastery over a larger number of skills but needs a much longer play time to accomplish this. Looking at the comparison in this fashion also gives us further insight into the developmental model of play in the human social group. When I introduce playfulness into the theoretical model, I stress the role of spontaneity, manifest joy, and sense of humor in play. The next question follows quite logically: How much of playfulness in play and in the player does our society allow during an individual's life span? It is interesting to recall here Gardner Murphy's (1958) observation that the cultural mold descends too soon on the child. In other words, rigidity sets in before a full exploration of, or playing with, further options is given an opportunity. We have already found evidence of the workings of this mold in elementary school and, to an even greater detriment, in the high school classroom. There is some reason for hope, though. This comes from an application of Baltes and Schaie's (1973) concept of the cohort in the life span of the individual, or what we prefer to call the interaction of historical with developmental time. If I am reading the indicators right, then the greater spontaneity and freedom enjoyed by children today in their play and imagination may very well have an influence on creative productivity in the next generation.

The crucial element in my assumptions is the social climate, be this expressed in the small group setting or in the larger societal structure. Referring again to Gardner Murphy's thesis, we find that he talks about creative eras in history. While he sees wealth and leisure as important ingredients, he holds that challenge and response leading into progressive mastery are the sparks that produce creativeness. When we examine the thrust of McClelland's (1953, 1955) work about achievement motivation, we recall that high achievement, expressed in n-Ach scores, is more often shown in the entrepreneur than in the academician. On the other hand, prosperity is found in nations with societal reinforcement of high-achieving individuals. It becomes evident, therefore, that the individuals who provide for wealth and leisure in the society may not be the same as those who are the creative producers. However, they prepare the ground for creativity to flourish.

The Sullivanian approach underlying Seagoe's (1970) analysis of children's play as an index of degree of socialization also throws light on the spontaneous, informal setting and its impact not only on the individual but also on national societies. Play is seen to move on a hierarchical ladder from informal–individual at the preschool level to competitive–cooperative by early adolescence. Seagoe's (1971a) comparison of children's play in six modern societies, which included the USA, England, Norway, Spain, Greece, and Egypt, suggests that, in individualistic–democratic countries, there is earlier and prolonged individual–informal play, whereas in monolithic–authoritarian countries, the direction points to individual–competitive play. Since I look upon playfulness in play as a forerunner to the combinatorial play in the creative process, it would be legitimate to assume that it is more likely that the social structure in a democracy will encourage divergent thinking. We have seen in our own time how authoritarian governments prescribe acceptable modes of creative expression in art, literature, and music. While we have few hard data on the childrearing practices in countries like the Soviet Union or China, Bronfenbrenner's (1970) comparison of Soviet and American educational systems and a recent report by a delegation from the Society of Research in Child Development (Kessen, 1974) give us some inkling of the objectives stressed in these cultures. In citing the stated objectives of aesthetic culture in Russia, for both ages 7–11 and 16–18, Bronfenbrenner reproduces a table with an entry reading "artistic creativity." Under "responsible attitude toward learning," we note "perseverance and initiative in learning" for the adolescent. Yet, the anecdotal material in the book indicates that expectations are for the "right" answer, even in the case of a TAT-type storytelling session. Similarly, the child development experts visiting China were indeed impressed by the courtesy and motivation in the classrooms at all levels, but noted the lack of critical evaluation or playing with ideas. Recalling my own educational experience in Austria under successive authoritarian regimes ranging from Christian Socialist to National Socialist, I know the stress that was placed on convergent thinking. As a matter of fact, in a humanistic gymnasium, we were taught shorthand so that we could take down the lectures of our high school teachers *verbatim*. To argue a point with the teacher was unheard of, and ours was considered a progressive school! This difference in social expectations as mediated by the educational system became even more apparent to me when I observed the type of schooling that my sister was getting at a well-known English public school for girls. Classroom discussion thrived on controversy, and the interpretation and challenge of even factual information was a regular practice.

Social expectations affecting play and creativity are not too difficult to document. We meet a thornier problem when we try to tackle the way imagination yields to group pressures. Of course, we know that every male preschooler in the United States, at one time or another, imagines that he will grow up to be a fireman or policeman, and, until recently, every young girl fantasized herself as a nurse or a mother. One of my students, a liberated woman herself, was upset when her 5-year-old daughter rejected the notion of becoming a pilot as "not for a girl."

Imaginary companions are rarer and may already indicate a richer fantasy life, triggered by being an only child with few friends. Another source for fantasy productions would be protocols of therapy sessions dealing with daydreams. If we added the unconscious content of our dreams, we might do well to examine the Jungian archetypes as representatives of social stereotypes. Would the degree of a reconciliation by the two sexes of their persona with the its unconscious opposite-sexed anima be a criterion or a clue to creative potential? Empirically, trait studies have shown that creative individuals successfully combine masculine and feminine traits (Barron, 1972). Can one posit that our unconscious helps us in accepting the contradictions within ourselves? In his pioneering treatment of imagery and daydream methods in psychotherapy and behavior modification, Singer (1974) suggests that one of the major tools available to the practioner and patient is a heightened sensitivity to ongoing fantasy processes. He further illustrates that such fantasy production can come about by means of training, and that positive affect to accompany therapeutic imagery can be encouraged. Such an approach can have far-reaching social consequences. Even orthodox Freudianism has backed away from the claim of a culture-free or universal-value-guided therapeutic environment. If we use fantasy for new learning and better functioning in the social group, then both the therapist and the patient need to keep the social referent group in mind as they work on the healing process. The stress of positive affect would allow the hope that joy may enter the fantasy productions, that spontaneity may grow, and that sense of humor may emerge on occasion. This would be a hopeful sign that the imagery may not only lead to good health but to creative production.

What about the commonly held notion that most of the fantasy productions of creative individuals are bizarre, that, in fact, it is a sick mind that correlates with genius? Some of the drug-induced imagery reported by individuals who either voluntarily or in an experimental situation took the so-called mind-expanding drugs might throw further light on this problem. The distorted perceptions, or even the claimed heightened awareness, did not produce great contributions to works of science or of art. As a matter of fact, one painter who took it on an experimental basis to see what type of art he would produce under the influence of mescaline, promptly destroyed his paintings when he examined them after the "trip." Based on the theoretical model suggested here, I would say that affective spontaneity without cognitive awareness or control would not produce the kind of playfulness that is germane to creativity.

THE ROLE OF PLAYFULNESS IN AESTHETICS

Cognitive manifestations, affective needs, and social expectations can thus be seen to influence the way we play, the way we allow our imagination to roam, and what we offer as creative products. Can all this perhaps be linked to a sense for the aesthetic? Berlyne (1971) seems to think that art grows out of some fundamental characteristic of the human nervous system. He sees a work of art as transmitting four types of information, namely, semantic, expressive, social and syntactic, and suggests that the psychological processes dominating the expressive content of a work of art are "thought, perceptual, emotional, and imaginative" (p. 253). Perhaps we have come full circle in our search for the connecting link between play, imagination, and creativity, and the role of playfulness in that model. Among the personality characteristics of his art-wise subjects, Child (1965) found a capacity to escape momentarily from the usual logical restraints of adulthood and the ability to take an interest in playful, imaginative, and unusual aspects of things. This formulation separates the playful from the imaginative and the unusual. The model here would suggest that, to the extent that the playful enters imagination and originality, it creates that suspense of tension, that psychological distancing required for the idea to form and to be produced. In a way, it is more than what Gordon (1961) suggests in his synectic approach to the development of creative capacity. It is not only suspension of evaluation but suspension of ego involvement as well. Those of us who have experienced it, even only fleetingly, will agree that the task on hand takes over; that, physiologically, one experiences a supercharge of adrenalin; that there may be a sense of well-being that could best be described as cosmic floating, a loss of boundary of self, and a merging with the universe.

VI

Practical Implications: The Place of Playfulness in Everyday Living

Translating both research and theory into practical applications of everyday activities has often been shunned by behavioral scientists, but it may become the touchstone of our usefulness in the long run. What seems to emerge from my own research, and from the majority of studies that I reviewed here, is that the first consideration in choosing the problem to be investigated is not necessarily to find a solution to some actual difficulties encountered in the real world. In my own case, I was intrigued by a behavioral ingredient of creativity, hardly tangible, for which I had to develop a conceptualization and operational definitions. Practical implications were a secondary consideration. This experience is not an isolated instance. On a different level, Piaget, Einstein, and Marx are examples of theoreticians whose esoteric investigations have yielded fallout of social significance. Indeed, they provide a convincing argument that the most fruitful approach is from playing with what might seem to be idle and far-fetched notions, and that the greatest practical benefits may come from way-out ideas.

In this chapter, I want to elaborate, therefore, on some of the immediate fringe benefits to everyday living that come from my investigations into playfulness and from related research on play. I shall limit my discussion to five areas which are of particular interest to the developmental psychologist. These are, in order of appearance in the life cycle: *(1)* the home; *(2)* the classroom; *(3)* career choices; *(4)* on-the-job satisfaction; and *(5)* the use of leisure.

THE HOME ENVIRONMENT: CAN PARENTING
HAVE A LIGHTER VEIN?

Whether our allegiance in theoretical outlook is to Freud or to Watson, or is eclectic, there is little disagreement among psychologists that the first 5 years in an individual's life are crucial to later development. It is, therefore, very relevant to look at childrearing practices and how they might influence playfulness. The average person picturing the mother–child dyad will more likely than not see a happy mother holding a smiling child. As professionals, we must admit that this is an ideal situation. Ideal in two ways: that it is desirable and that it is not the typical interaction. We know from previously cited studies on smiling (Wilson, 1963; Wolff, 1963) that the human face produces this response in the infant. We know also from empirical observation that mothers do not usually spend the greater part of their day in face-to-face contact with the infant. When and how, then, can we expect a playful parent to interact with a playful child?

In practical considerations of childrearing, the element of consistency is of paramount importance. Even when I am asked in an informal setting by a casual acquaintance whether or not it is best to allow a child freedom of choice in activities, my usual preamble is: "more often than not" or "more likely than not" indicating that the mother's or father's behavior needs to correspond with what the parent usually does and, thus, also what the child has come to expect. In other words, even in a social situation, some indication of expected routines must be the baseline of information. If changes are suggested, they should be a gradual modification of the familiar situation.

Let me now suggest how playfulness, with its component parts of spontaneity, manifest joy, and sense of humor, can be used in the ecological setting of the home and in the parent–child relationship in particular. Play is the dominant behavior mode of the first 5 years of life. Play occurs when both setting and materials have been assimilated as part of the child's cognitive structure. Playfulness in play—the spontaneous recombination of elements, the joy of mastery, and the glint-in-the-eye joviality—would be an indication that the play element is at work. What are some of the practical implications of such an approach? An example might help to illustrate and clarify further the behavioral correlates of playfulness in play.

Johnny is told to go play with his blocks. They are well used. He makes a face: "I played with them when Diane was here." Mother: "That was yesterday, and there were two of you making things. What do you think you might want to do on your own? Something that you did not get around to yesterday?" If Johnny accepts his mother's suggestion, picks up the blocks, makes some tower or aeroplane or a house with a slight variation, is delighted with his product, and even good-naturedly jokes about how Diane's tower always collapsed yesterday, the mother has succeeded in stimulating the play element in play.

The episode might have taken another turn. Johnny could not be persuaded to play with "those old blocks again." His desire was to try something new and different—in our theoretical terms, he was interested in exploratory behavior. It is these subtle cues that need to be picked up by mother or caretaker. For, as we have seen, exploration of the novel often precedes play and, in the everyday situation, a delicate balance between play and exploration is called for. Some of the factors determining whether it will be one or the other may lie with the child's physical condition. A tired child, a sick child, may be more content with the familiar. We all know the function of the security blanket. This example shows the difficulty of separating the physical from the emotional factors. Feeling good about the known, and the need for such a boost, is another indicator of when to encourage play rather than exploration. There is also a very important cognitive element in going over familiar materials and situations. The other day the local TV station featured five upstate New York teenagers who had made the Guinness Book of Records by jumping continuously on a trampoline for some 580 hours. When asked why they did it, they said "they were bored in the summer." This particular news item tells us a number of things in relation to the play element in everyday life. First of all, in order to get away from the boredom of everyday life, they chose an activity that called upon them to do the same thing for over 3 weeks. There were only a few shots of the youngsters jumping, and it was not possible to assess the affect from their facial expressions. It is a good hunch, though, to presume that at the end it was all smiles. Taking a cue from Singer's (1966, 1973) research, it might have been interesting to ask them if they had daydreamed during the jumping and what the content of any such fantasies were. A film might also have shown different patterns of jumping, thus making for a recombination of givens. Here, the contributing factors to the spontaneous in playfulness would be physical and cognitive.

The incident also reflects on some of the variables in the home environment that led to the activity and the reasons it took place. Today we live in a physically, socially, and cognitively contracting world. The frontiers of today's knowledge may lie in outer space, but most of our children will spend their lives within the confines of the planet Earth. Some of the exploration may continue to be directed to inner space and, as a psychologist, I would hope that this is going to be the case. On the other hand, we need to raise the children of today to take delight in familiar surroundings and known facts.

As a relaxation and change of pace from working on this manuscript and as a kind of marking of the bicentennial in my own fashion, I have taken up reading American history in various guises. These range from Washington Irving's *Knickerbocker Miscellanies* to Daniel Boorstin's *The Americans.* The recurrent theme in these and other books is the opportunities for expansion and exploration that shaped the habits and expectations of the individual American and the nation as a whole. Concomitant with this approach was a restlessness, an inability, even of the leisure class, to be idle. We might paraphrase here and say that there was very little room for play in that kind of world and, consequently, little evidence of the playful approach to living. As we are moving into the third century of independence, a very different Zeitgeist prevails. There is more time for play; more tolerance for idle fantasy; more appreciation for those individual differences that lead to original thinking and products.

Parents are cultural surrogates. The rub here is that we also have to reckon with cultural lag between generations. In other words, we need to ask ourselves whether or not today's parents are playful enough to prepare their children for living in the twenty-first century. The research study by Bishop and Chace (1971), about home environment and its influence on creativity in 3- and 4-year-olds, may point the direction to future work. An application of their findings would suggest that mothers who are more comfortable with their child playing with opposite-sex toys may encourage creativity in the child. They see flexibility as part of playfulness in adults. In my assessment, the spontaneous rather than the flexible element would be crucial. It is, again, the rearrangement of the familiar, the psychological distancing, that frees the individual from being bound by social stereotypes, and the individual may even see humor in such a situation. The ingredient that I consider important in PF comes to the fore when these investigators measure actual playfulness in the child's play through such questions as "Does the child sing or dance along with music?" Here you have a behavioral manifestation of joy, and it is by such indices that we can both recognize and encourage playfulness in young children. In my earlier discussion of this study, I already referred to the influence of abstract thinking by mothers on the playfulness and creativity of their children.

Less obvious, but, in my view, of equal importance, are joy and sense of humor as part of parenting. Admittedly, taking care of young children is not one continuous experience of happiness. Feelings of elatedness are peak experiences, but their runoff should lead to contentment with the role. Seeing an 18-month-old rearrange familiar toys into new combinations or use a familiar toy in a new way are moments of joy, and may make up for some of the drudgery involved in cleaning up after the toddler has strewn everything around the floor. It is in this way that Piaget, Bruner, Freud, and the host of other developmental psychologists really make an impact on everyday living. In this way, we can give the element of "function pleasure" experienced by the child a reciprocal dimension in fostering parental joy. Naturally, this involves both observational skills and factual knowledge on the part of the parent, and is certainly in the direction of "giving psychology away" to the lay person, a process that needs to be started as early as in the elementary school.

What about sense of humor as part of the childrearing process and the home environment? One of my colleagues told me recently that his teenage children chide him for his joking approach in his discussions with them. The question of time and place is, of course, a crucial one when making light of any matter. But what we know of psychological distancing in the appreciation of humor may give us an important clue. If, in the early part of parenting, there are times when both father and mother can step back and look at their role in perspective, they may find it much easier not to take themselves and the problems connected with parenting so seriously all the time. They may more often find the wry humor in the situation of an adamant 2-year-old insisting on lacing up his own sneakers or the 5-year-old telling your Aunt Millie verbatim that you said "she was a fusspot and not to go on climbing all over her." The *Daily News* at one time gave $5.00 for such incidents. But does it take a newspaper and money to see something as funny? Could a parent see the humor at the time, even if it is at his or her expense? The learning derived from such incidents would be beneficial for both adult and child. The adult would be more sensitive to her or his own remarks and the child would not need to learn double standards of evaluation.

Are these pie-in-the-sky expectations? I would think we would find they are not, if we look realistically at some of the ongoing changes that might have an impact on playfulness in parent and child. I have already pointed out that a better-educated parent population will tend to be more spontaneous, more accepting of diverse interpretations, and more resourceful in working with the givens of the home setting. We certainly have concrete evidence that more individuals are spending more time in school. It would, of course, be deceiving ourselves if schooling per se were regarded as developing a playful approach to living; we need to ask ourselves what type of schooling will produce the desired results. I shall do this at some length in the next section. Here, it is sufficient to note that the opportunity or, if you will, the ecological setting for such a development exists. Another recent trend that may also work in the direction for a more relaxed attitude toward parenting is the greater involvement of the father in bringing up the children. We need only to recall the findings from the studies on manifest anxiety in children (Sarason, Davidson, Lighthall, Waite, & Ruebush, 1960): that fathers, who are concretely more removed from the childrearing activities, had a more accurate picture of their children's degree of anxiety. A shared undertaking would, no doubt, undercut the feelings of defensiveness on the part of the mother and allow for more of the joy to emerge. This, in turn, will create the climate for less anxious children. The prescription may almost appear to be simple-minded, but this should not put us off from the underlying soundness of the argument.

THE CLASSROOM: CAN FUN BE PART
OF THE LEARNING PROCESS?

When I first approached kindergarten and nursery school teachers to help me identify playfulness, in the early 1960s, there seemed to be not only willingness to cooperate, but also a genuine surprise to be asked to look for such behavior. As one of the teachers put it: "It's so nice to look for something positive for a change." These were the days before prosocial behavior moved to center stage and I was, in this respect, not in tune with the Zeitgeist; as it turned out, I was ahead of it. So much for my investigations within historical time. What about developmental time? As I indicated earlier, my theoretical model-building suggested the adolescent period as the next stage for the investigation of playfulness, and I therefore moved into the junior high school and high school classrooms. My reception, as mentioned before, was decidedly different. The principal of one prestigious high school expressed some of the feelings aroused when he informed me that, if I am interested in playfulness, I had better concentrate on the junior high schools, since, in his school, the students were serious and college oriented. I had also mentioned that, in the content analysis of teacher conceptualization of playfulness in the high school student, there was a higher percentage of negatively valenced behavior than there was when asked to describe playfulness in the adolescent in general. Obviously, setting or the ecological factor influenced their answers. My own conceptualization of playfulness and that of fellow psychologists was decidedly more positive. There arises the question of whether or not one can be more tolerant of behavior if one is not personally involved in its effects. At this point, I want to offer spectator—observer data and data from graduate students who were teaching at different levels in the public school system. Sense of humor, joy, and spontaneity added a ferment to the classroom climate; however, it was observed more often in high ability classes. This was confirmed by comments from my students who, when asked about their own use of sense of humor, exhibition of joy, and spontaneity in presenting material, stipulated that one must take into account the level of intellectual functioning of the class for the degree in which any of these traits may be used as part of the teaching methodology. Although I personally have not taught below the college level, these remarks became more meaningful to me when I, on occasion, made a joking comment or pun to a class or an individual and, because of cognitive difficulty, this was not taken the way it was meant, and it produced resentment because of noncomprehension. What becomes apparent is the necessary interaction between playfulness in the student and playfulness in the teacher.

Some of the studies dealing with play suggest an approach that could be translated to the classroom. There is ample evidence that working with the familiar sparks the spontaneous element of play. In a learning situation, it is an accepted stratagem of teaching to start the students with material that is known. The playful element would enter in the rearrangement of known facts, which would lead to the learning of new combinations. Admittedly, there must be a baseline of knowledge in order for combinatorial play to take place. My contention is that, within the existing repertory of the class or, better still, of the individual student, this baseline can be identified and used as the starting point for new knowledge. If we look at it in this way, we can apply this approach at different levels of development (i.e., preoperational, concrete operations, formal operations) and at different levels of competence (i.e., average, bright, and even slow learners). A few examples may be helpful here.

The Preschooler

Let us imagine a nursery school setting:

It is story time. The teacher asks whether anyone wants to have their favorite story read. Susan pipes up and makes her choice known. A chorus of voices saying: Yes, yes, let's have the story of the little red locomotive. Rapt attention as the now familiar story unravels.—But, lo and behold, the teacher changes the ending. Groans of disappointment. "No, no. That's not right. The little red locomotive is not going to the museum. It's going to run again and the children will use it." When the story is read with its expected ending, general expressions of glee and delight.

Should we fault the teacher for trying a different ending, for introducing change and encouraging flexibility in her young audience? By no means. Again, as in the case of the mother urging the child to play with his usual playthings, the teacher needs to be responsive to the cues from the children. If, at that point, they are not ready for the exploratory phase in their thinking, it may indicate that they need more preparation. Or, better still, the children themselves may want to try their hand at different endings. This might generate another dimension of joy—that of recombining the familiar with the new. It might also stimulate good-natured ribbing by the other boys and girls, and allow the storytelling child to defend his ending. A playful teacher may also be willing to accept the usefulness of going over the familiar and possibly, herself, to see new overtones in what seemed the same situation. The sometimes frantic search for the new might, at times, be alternated with the comfortable feeling of the known.

The Elementary School Child

Does the known and familiar always presuppose the one and only or convergent answer to a problem? The way I see the application of playfulness as the quintessence of play to classroom learning does not necessarily circumscribe the outcome in this fashion.

An individualized remedial reading session is in progress. The teacher is using the phonics system and is working with the sounding of "-at" in three-letter words. Starting with the familiar and known, which happens to be the child's name "Pat," she starts by substituting consecutive letters of the alphabet. The first example is "bat"; the pupil gleefully continues with "cat." While the "game" of substituting letters may in itself be fun for the primary school child, the learning can be extended by having the pupil construct sentences with the different words; writing them down; finding definitions for some of the words and discovering, for instance, that "bat" has more than one meaning.

The Junior High School Student

Let us look now at a junior high school class in social studies:

> The subject matter is Jefferson's role in the move toward independence of the colonies from England. Various known facts of his participation are presented. Somebody recounts the way these facts are connected in the text. Another student questions both the sequencing and logical inferences drawn from the factual information. He comes up with a different interpretation of the same facts—a reshuffling of knowns. The teacher appreciates the different angle. Both student and teacher show their feelings by smiling. Another student is moved to make a facetious interpretation, without malice. This, too, is taken in stride by the teacher, who acts as a model for the class, and there is general good humor about some of the cold historical fact. Playfulness has generated a good-natured revisionism.

The High School Student

The high school is, if anything, an even more appropriate setting for the manifestation of playfulness in the treatment of subject matter. The ability of "as if" thinking has developed further and, with proper encouragement, propositional thinking can be used in English literature, history, biology, and even mathematics. The assumption is, of course, a solid and common pool of knowledge, which can then be played with for recombinations. Psychological distancing, which would allow emphasis on task orientation rather than on ego orientation, would again provide the climate for joy in mastery and humor in near misses or outright goofs.

The College Student

To an even greater extent, what has been mapped for the high school should be part and parcel of the college classroom. Ego identity, in terms of knowing one's own strengths and weaknesses, should be more firmly established by now. Yet one of the great frustrations of college teaching is the student who wants to find out to the last iota not only how you want a paper to be written, but what topic he should choose and how many pages he needs to write to get an A. It is distressing to see young people who do not seem to have obtained a sense of mastery of what they already know and on which they can build additional understanding. At the other extreme is the student who believes that what he knows is all there is to know and his own subjective experience should be able to explain all relevant happenings in the world around him. Neither of these students is open to playfulness, that is, drawing upon previous knowledge, playing with existing ideas, and relating them to new facts. The first wants to be led by the hand; the second thumbs his nose at you and tells you in so many words that you cannot teach him anything because you do not share his experience and he does not share yours.

Playfulness in the Teacher

Having faced this situation many a time, and realizing that I shall continue facing it to some extent for the rest of my teaching career, it has become a real problem to me; and in an effort to resolve it, it has made me more aware of certain qualities in myself that are related to playfulness. Informal feedback and more structured evaluation from students have emphasized that I have a ready smile, a sense of humor—not always gentle—but also that I tend to rush over material without, at times, the needed repetition or clarification. I do, however, allow certain associations to lead me from one topic to the other, thus weaving together familiar facts into new configurations. The impact on the learner varies. There are some students who, from previous experience and inclination, respond better to a structured presentation that is one-faceted, with clear-cut answers. I recall the plaintive comment of one student, majoring in accounting, who found it disconcerting that one needs to consider so many variables in any given situation in the classroom or in the home that may influence the behavior of an adolescent in school. On the other hand, there was the music student whose all-encompassing love bordered on naïveté, to the extent that he saw no evidence of prejudice in the way today's young people related to one another. Both cases can be helped by the encouragement of psychological distancing, which leads to greater objectivity and ultimately allows the individual to view himself less seriously. Handled in this manner, sense of humor is more likely to operate both on the giving and on the receiving end. This kind of attitude, which I consider to be within the playfulness syndrome, also is more likely to prepare the ground for cognitive spontaneity and the joy of mastery that is derived from knowing what you are doing, even if it is only for isolated and disconnected incidents in the beginning.

The Setting as a Variable

But, as we all know, playfulness in the student and playfulness in the teacher do not occur in a vacuum. The setting, representing the rules and regulations made by a bureaucracy and working in the service of an almost sacrosanct curriculum, cannot be overlooked. As a matter of fact, it must be made part of our considerations if we want the elements of play to survive in it. Again, it might be helpful to view it within the perspectives of both historical and developmental time. Sutton-Smith and Rosenberg's (1971) 60-year overview of play preferences among children showed an increase in more relaxed, spontaneous games, and it was suggested that this might be a reflection of the Zeitgeist. However, we cannot push developmental time to the side altogether, and we need to remember the heightened meaning of rules and regulations to the middle-childhood child. Educational practices, therefore, must take into account both factors. In this sense, the preschooler and the adolescent are alike. Both are more comfortable with spontaneous happenings and less structured presentation of curriculum. Their joy and sense of humor thrive on ambiguities and incongruities. The difference between them lies in the baseline of factual material available and the greater awareness of the difference between fact and fantasy. The middle-childhood child, with his orientation toward the concrete and tangible, would more likely find delight in rules and regulations that make sense to him. I have, as yet, no hard data on playfulness in the elementary school child, but his delight in riddles, with their concrete referent and the one and only answer that is always part of the riddle, seems to support our thesis. Mathematical rules and the rules of grammar would, therefore, seem naturally to appeal to children in the primary grades. Inductive reasoning could be sources of pleasure in the hunt for clues to the rule. When we talk about open classrooms and alternative schools, the ecological setting and the cognitive content are often confused, and developmental level is not given its rightful place in the planning of the curriculum. It is one thing to have children wander around aimlessly and another to have them choose their activities voluntarily and individually. It also should be borne in mind whether we offer these choices to the 5-year-old, to the 15-year-old, or the 8-year-old. My own theoretical orientation and the research data cited would call for greater similarities in the ecological and curricular planning for the kindergartner and the high school student, but a different setting for the elementary school child. In other words, less structure at an early age and again at puberty and beyond, while more routines and group work would be appropriate for the 6–12-year range. An important element in the process of learning is the differential role of imagination. Being able to accept fantasy assimilation in the young child expands his cognitive horizon and will stimulate original products. The adolescent's ability to suspend reality and operate with fantasy content in abstract recombinations of familiar material will similarly lead to creative products on his level of intellectual functioning. The danger here is that some educators will accept preschool-type fantasy productions from an adolescent and call them creative. By not setting different expectations, we do a great disservice to the adolescent, whose assimilative structures are certainly richer in content than the young child's reservoir of knowledge. What the high school teacher needs to provide is the climate that allows for psychological distancing and, thus, less pressure from ego involvement while the creative process is going on.

Some mention needs to be made here about the influence of sex differences on fun in the classroom. Research findings cited earlier suggest that boys show greater enjoyment over accomplishments and that girls like school better. School has also been described as a feminine environment, partly because of the preponderance of female teachers, especially in the lower grades. It would seem to me that school is not so much either feminine or masculine, but mirrors cultural stereotypes expressed in teacher expectations. "Boys will be boys" is conveyed very subtly to the elementary school child and the male may therefore not be expected to adhere that strictly to the rule-dominated primary grade classroom. Girls, on the other hand, are seen as loving to be neat and dainty, keeping their notebooks clean, and doing what the teacher asks. At the elementary school level, this may be more conducive to learning in girls, and they are known to do better during these years. A different story unfolds itself in the high school classroom. While, developmentally, girls are also capable of abstract thought, of playing with ideas, of "as if" thinking, the sociocultural expectations conveyed by the teachers do not encourage them in these aspirations. Even recent studies (Ginzberg, 1966; Ginzberg & Yohalem, 1966; Horner, 1972; Oden, 1968) still talk about the fear of success in women as opposed to the joy over achievement in men. Now, however, historical time is making its impact and, hopefully, during the next decade, women who enjoy their work will not have to be featured as rarities on the family page of the *New York Times* (Curtis, 1975).

To my question of whether or not the qualities inherent in play behavior—the spontaneous, joyful, glint-in-the-eye aspects—can be beneficial to stimulating imagination and creativity in the classroom, we may give an affirmative reply. The practical difficulty lies in their constructive use. If both teachers and students are aware of their potential benefits, then certainly the effort should be made to incorporate them into the curriculum structure. Some suggestions about how this can be done were made earlier, but these were meant only to encourage others to find their own idiosyncratic ways as long as they believe in the basic soundness of the concept and behavior.

CAREER CHOICE: CAN PLAYING WITH OPTIONS BE PART OF IT?

It may not be immediately obvious how play and playfulness relate to making up one's mind about one's future work plans. Ginzberg, Ginsburg, Axelrod, and Herma (1951) call the period from age 11 to 17, which roughly corresponds to adolescence, the tentative stage of vocational choices. It is preceded by the fantasy stage, in which youngsters want to become policemen, nurses, teachers, firemen. Fantasy also enters the adolescent's vocational planning, but, cognitively, it is different. The 8-year-old uses the concrete props of his immediate environment and imagines himself in these various roles. This concrete fantasy may be called play without reality testing. The fantasy play of the adolescent involves occupational roles that should represent realistic options. The playfulness aspect enters into this process because the imaginative content needs to be based on known facts, which are rearranged in a payoff matrix. Just as in producing a work of art or music or formulating a scientific discovery, this process entails both joy and anguish. But, again, we know from psychological theory that the adolescent needs to rework his feelings of ambivalence. Indeed, one of the criteria of resolving his identity crisis successfully is being able to handle inconsistencies.

The Role of the School

Translated into day-to-day application, it would suggest that the high school student who is carried away by his enthusiasm for sports and sees greatness for himself on the diamond with the likes of Babe Ruth and Joe di Maggio after a weekend of watching ballgames, and in midweek is fired by his success in the science lab and sees himself in the company of Einstein, Fermi, and Bohr, should not be chided or ridiculed for the inconsistencies in his aspirations. Playing with occupational options is an appropriate task for the adolescent boy and girl. In the everyday setting, however, we need to take a closer look at the fantasies open to girls and to lower-class youth. In my discussion of the classroom setting, I already mentioned the differential expectations that might be conveyed by teachers to female high school students. Sense of humor, with overtones of sarcasm, is often applied to scotch a girl's aspirations. I recall an experience of my own when I was described at 17 as the "erudite young woman who wants to acquire even more knowledge" as implying that I could certainly find something better to do with my time. Today, we may still find teachers referring to "young ladies," and this label does not necessarily suggest a happy marriage with physicist, biologist, or doctor, in the semantic sense.

But playing with options is not only done on the cognitive level, it combines and is sometimes overshadowed by affective involvement. I am now referring to the adolescent's proneness to hero worship or "crushes." Using such attachments for lower-class youth may be one way of helping them to a richer fantasy life, a more playful orientation to career choices. Again, the teacher's attitude is crucial. I recall the two recent cases in which junior high school students developed crushes on their college tutors and the different ways in which the two tutors handled the situation. In one case, a young boy made no bones about his strong attachment to the young woman teaching him mathematics. When it happened, she saw it as a problem, since young Tom, who was all of 14, even wanted to take her out on weekends. After a discussion with me, we tried to let his positive feelings for the tutor work in the tutoring situation, part of which was spent in formal instruction, and part in informal discussion of what his future plans were and what hers were, including the mention of her boyfriend and his career plans. It took a while for Tom to accept the situation, and it needed delicate handling on the part of the tutor so as not to put him off in a way that might negatively affect his school learning. She used a mixture of delight over the way he felt for her and gentle ribbing about the way it would not work out in a love relationship; but she still maintained warm affection for him, while, at the same time, not forgetting the task at hand. At the end of the term, she was worried about who would be his next tutor and whether or not this person would take a real interest in the boy.

A different picture emerged from the crush that a young girl had on her male tutor. First of all, the young man never realized, or was reluctant to admit to himself, that Sheila came to the tutoring session because she wanted to impress him and not to learn some computational skills. There was no acknowledgment that the way she dressed and made up was to get his attention focused on her. He continued to do the work for her while she watched him. Even after individual conferences in which we discussed the situation, he still was not able to channel her regard for him constructively. In addition to lack of insight, there was little humor or show of enjoyment in his approach. It was strained and belabored to the very end, although he finally admitted that there might have been some sexual overtones in her interest in him. It is appropriate to raise the question of how a young teacher, male or female, can be relaxed enough in such a situation for a show of playfulness. Developmentally, this brings us back to the need to make adolescents feel comfortable about their sexual urges, so that, when they grow up and become teachers of adolescents, they can handle the threats that are inherent in the setting. If an instructor supervising teacher trainees observes such incidents, as I have on occasion, there is still time to give aid and comfort to the stricken. And, of course, once young teachers are out on their own, there are still sympathetic assistant principals and principals who can help and advise, despite all rumors to the contrary.

The Influence of Developmental Dynamics

Parents, teachers, and guidance counselors would do well to bear in mind another important facet of play in vocational choice, namely, the psychosocial moratorium advocated for adolescents by Erikson. An early foreclosure of opportunities would cut off the playing with options that we consider to be crucial in arriving at a meaningful commitment to work. From my own experience, I know that there are young men and women who, even at the junior year in college, still feel the need to consider alternatives. At one point, not so long ago, I would have been more troubled about this so-called indecision or would have called it psychosocial immaturity. Today, I am more careful and slower in coming to such a conclusion. As a matter of fact, in our day and age, the need to keep options open, as well as the ability to reopen them at a later time for a possible change in midlife, would be an important and constructive tool in reevaluating the givens at consecutive levels of maturity. Again, the ability to rearrange the familiar into new combinations is something that needs to be encouraged throughout the life cycle.

There is yet another element of playfulness that needs to enter career choices to make them an organic outgrowth of one's capabilities. Piaget (1945) talks about the personal fable that characterizes the adolescent's egocentrism, in which the young man or young woman sees himself/herself as being on center stage with all eyes upon him/her. Research on sense of humor gave us the clue that affective psychological distancing needs to precede cognitive appreciation of the joke or the riddle. We might want to apply this to the adolescent caught up in his personal fable. While career choice is indeed a serious matter, it is not helped by taking oneself too seriously. Therefore, he needs to have shed his egocentrism and be task-oriented before he can comfortably consider an array of occupational possibilities. From my recent contacts with young people, it has struck me that some of the young men and women have already arrived at that conclusion before psychologists could offer them the advice formally. Their somewhat casual, often nonchalant, attitude to achievement and "making it" may, in the end, signify greater potential for fulfillment than the single-mindedness of what still may be the accepted prototype for success, namely, the individual whose only aim is to get to the top. Our young people may be on the road to developing that psychological distancing that makes them enjoy the level at which they are operating at any given moment and be unhurried about getting to the next rung of competence. My emphasis is advisedly on competence, which is another word for mastery. As we saw from the literature, mastery brings function pleasure.

Illustrations from the Field

As has been stressed throughout, the matrix for play is familiarity with the materials, which in turn brings about playfulness as an approach. This holds true for playing with career options as well. What are some of the practical ways in which we can make the information about different opportunities more readily available to the adolescent? A promising approach, if handled properly, is the work—study program. Today's societal structure tends to close off the growing boy and girl from concrete involvement in on-the-job training. Yet the feedback from actual experience is still invaluable. True apprenticeship programs are few now and are continually shrinking in our increasingly automated world. An example of what might be done is a program that was initiated in a private high school with a bicultural curriculum in both Jewish and secular studies. There is at the moment a dearth of people wanting to go into community and welfare work. The senior year in high school, as we are all aware, is to a great extent a holding operation, with courses mostly geared to rote revision of previously learned material. Seniors are bored and many of them take advanced credits or opt for one of the early college entrance programs. My real concern here is the rushing into careers without adequate testing of both abilities and inclinations. At my suggestion, an internship program was initiated with communal and social welfare agencies. There was mutual benefit from such contacts with old age and children's homes and libraries. From the adolescent's point of view, the young people's idealism was used; they gained a sense of competency from what they were able to do—and letters to the school attested to that—and, at the same time, they established a realistic frame on which to base their career decisions. Naturally, not everything worked out ideally. There were tardy students and supervisors who just gave them busy work or menial jobs. But these, too, were worthwhile experiences that helped them adjust the reality to the ideal situation they might have imagined. Other programs from the public high schools in New York City have placed high school students in governmental offices, to give them a taste of the opportunities and the frustrations. Work—study programs are, of course, part of vocational high schools and, again, the plan itself is sound on psychological principles. The proviso here is that it will lead to meaningful and gainful employment. What is unpardonable is to set off the young people on a path whose end station is nonproductive.

Perhaps it is pertinent here to mention a point of general observation based on some personal experiences with disadvantaged youngsters. These high school students were reading at between the third- and fifth-grade level. I was in that school supervising college students who were using tutoring as a field setting for the analysis and application of adolescent learning and growth. A group of girls known for their lack of concentration and general disruptiveness had wandered away from their classroom and started to talk to me—this was a mini-school setting and they were not disciplined for leaving the class. I casually inquired about their career plans. One wanted to be an airline stewardess; the other wanted to be a beautician. We then started to talk about the kind of things one needs to know—the competencies, if you will, of their career choices. In that way, I was able to latch on to what they know about the job specifications, expand their factual knowledge by supplying some information I had, and suggest further sources where they might get additional particulars. Part of the discussion centered on the importance of current subject matter, including reading, writing, and arithmetic, for their career preparation. Their parting comment was that they had enjoyed talking to me.

I do not offer this as a panacea for salvaging potential dropouts from high school. What I want to stress is that parents, teachers, and guidance counselors need to serve as information dispensers, as sounding boards for "as if" thinking applied to ongoing situations, regardless of whether these are youngsters in a mini-school for potential dropouts or in a special program for the gifted. To connect with the familiar and to help youngsters expand their options can lead to more joyful anticipation of the world of work.

However, theory and empirical research suggest to me that we wait too long to involve adolescents in activities that can give them concrete feedback on both competencies and deficiencies. Why let Emma find out at a community college for beauty culture that she cannot read sufficiently well to apply the hair dye correctly? Why restrict Susan's testing of herself as an economist to the college classrooms? With the growing sophistication brought about by television and the growing technology in general, we tend to fill our high school curricula with a good deal of busy work that does not help the adolescent in forming an ego identity that is both realistic and productive for his adult years. I am the last person to downgrade the need for intellectual food for the mind during these years, but, through observation of adolescents from the most deprived to the highly privileged, I have also come to the painful conclusion that we provide too few opportunities for testing of skills and make not enough demands on the adolescent to integrate the concrete with the abstract for useful generalizations for his own guidance. It is particularly sad for me to see college students floundering in their senior year for lack of proper grounding in information and skills in their high school years.

Without wishing to be too prescriptive, but moved rather by what I know and what I see of young people today, I have come to realize the importance of playfulness as a formative tool in setting the stage for one's future work. If it sounds like a paradox, then so be it, and perhaps it will be to the advantage of all concerned if we acknowledge the place of paradoxes in everyday living. Learning to live with them may also affect our tolerance of fantasies which take off on paths that are not easily reconcilable with the hard realities around us. Finally, the ability to reconcile what may appear to be paradoxical is at the heart of the creative process and may lead to the creative product.

ON-THE-JOB SATISFACTION: CAN ALL OCCUPATIONS PLAY?

Ideally, as a result of sufficient time and opportunity for playing with different options for careers, a young man or a young woman should have chosen the kind of work that they will enjoy. Even in such a desirable situation, we cannot expect continuous satisfaction from all activities connected with performance on the job. If I pursue the major thesis about the precondition of play, namely, familiar and known elements, I arrive at the concept of competence. When White (1959) reconsidered this concept, he included the element of play as part of the motivational backdrop. His emphasis on the intrinsic reward of the child gaining mastery during play makes him speak of competence in relation to the play of contented children. He describes the child as appearing "to be occupied with the agreeable task of developing an effective familiarity with his environment" (p. 321). Applied to the work setting, competence assumes mastery of the skills required for on-the-job performance. Implicit also in the concept of competence is the pleasure and satisfaction derived from the skills exercised successfully, regardless of the extrinsic reward situation.

Developmental Variables

Developmentally, I can, therefore, see two important variables during the socialization process that would later be of paramount importance for any work situation. One would be the opportunity the young child is given to exercise his skills and the feedback he is given about his skills; the second is the element of playfulness allowed in such play learning. The latter involves behavior related to the expression of enjoyment; the encouragement of spontaneous rearrangement of known objects and skill sequences; and, even in the young child, the beginnings of that psychological distancing that would allow for poking fun at oneself. In short, it is the kind of environment that was described earlier in my discussion of the home as a cradle for playfulness.

But even developmental psychologists are aware that only some children experience this type of setting some of the time, and we also realize that today's work settings reflect our mechanistic and extrinsically oriented life style. However, this does not deter me from asking to what extent we can encourage "combinatorial play" in different occupations, including manual and technical work. My hunch is that, if the playful attitude is introduced into thinking about work imaginatively, it will result in greater creativity on the job. We have numerous examples of bright young people rejecting the so-called sterility of college learning and seeking satisfaction by working with their hands, be it in leather, metal, or the soil itself. The search is for the joy derived from the process and product of creating and not the monetary value received. The significance of this life style is not so much its anti-intellectualism as it is its desire for a meaningful occupation. There is no question that it is a sad reflection on the way the mind may not be stimulated in college classrooms. What it does underline at the same time is the fact that you may get joy, satisfaction, and an outlet for creativity in manual work. But then the assembly line is not your little arts-and-crafts endeavor subsidized by parents who may not even get satisfaction from their own work. Recently, newspaper reports have shown that what autoworkers want is more involvement in the product, so that they can get a sense of satisfaction from their work. Some attempts have been made to vary their particular assignments or to have them work on more than one step in the assembly line, in order to concretize the product for them. It is doubtful that this approach will provide the kind of satisfaction today's workers demand. A more cynical or perhaps a more realistic approach is the admission that, in a technological society, with its high degree of bureaucratization, there is very little room for on-the-job satisfaction. This point of view underlies the compensatory hypothesis for the use of leisure, to which I shall refer in greater deal in the next section.

A Hypothetical Case

On the basis of my work with playfulness and the qualities other researchers have found inherent in play, let us sketch for ourselves the type of individual who might have experienced a playful attitude from parents, met teachers who allowed for the joy to develop that comes from mastery of the known, associated with peers who were able to accept a joke and be on the receiving end of ribbing, and who, as a result of unhurried pacing, was able to play with career options as an adolescent. Such a young adult might have decided to become a salesperson for an insurance company. Today, this could be either a young man or a young woman. We shall flesh out the prototype as a young woman. One of the underlying criteria for selection of insurance personnel is that the candidate must like people and like the social context in which one mixes with people. Another important qualification is a sense of humor; and, certainly, after some exposure to a number of model situations, the candidate must become aware that the tailoring of insurance policies will depend on the type of spontaneity that produces the individually appropriate policy from familiar givens. Therefore, a playful young woman should make a very good insurance salesperson. Part of her socialization may have included options to choose either dolls or trucks, doctor's or nurse's kits as a preschooler at home and in nursery school. Singing and dancing as an accompaniment or as part of play activity would have been encouraged through either modeling by parents or imitating the more constructive TV commercials. It may not be so outrageous or odd if a young housewife takes out the laundry basket in a waltzing step as part of expressing her exuberance inspired by sunshine and a blue sky. It is also not unusual for men and women to whistle while they work at household chores. Perhaps this kind of approach would make "chores" a misnomer. Even before I sketch out some later happenings in our young woman's life, I want to make it clear that I do not expect waltzing and whistling parents as a constant accompaniment of a young child's growing up. The emphasis is on the ambience of the home, on things being more often joyous than gloomy. Even when tragedy strikes, as it does in everyone's life, there has been the balancing experience of joy and the realization that it can again be part of life. Such a youngster will come to school and, while exploring the novel, be helped by the ability to make analogies with the known in his or her environment, such as some of the things that the teacher asks of her that would be the same as those asked by her mother or father. Moreover, things the teacher mentions—buildings, parks, subways, buses—may be familiar and thus aid in cognitive spontaneity. If the teacher is the kind of person who not only is playful but knows how to apply playfulness, she will indicate that she enjoys teaching by a smiling countenance, by gladly repeating some of the processes in addition and subtraction that were not understood right away, and so on. Her sense of humor would indicate to her class that she is not perfect and that, when she makes mistakes, she is able to laugh about them; in this way, she is able to help the boys and girls in her care see mastery not as an all-or-nothing concept but as a progression by degrees, in oneself and others. Let us follow our young woman now through junior high school, to high school, and to conferences with her subject matter teachers and guidance counselors. She has, at this point, shown better than average ability in mathematics; shown a good grasp of relationships in historical events and economic developments, and a moderate interest in literature and in music; she performed below average in science and says "she hates it." When asked what she wants to be, she shrugs her shoulders, throws back her head, and almost defiantly states "an actress." Her guidance counselor sympathizes with her ambitions, looks at her acne-scarred face and chubby build, and gives her some factual information about the training needed to become an actress. She also mentions casually a number of internship programs that are at present being tried out in their high school, such as interning in city government, health professions in hospitals, and even some placements in insurance companies "just to get the feel of things." "Next year when you are a senior," the guidance counselor suggests, "you might want to try one or the other of the programs." With the summer to think things over and an opportunity to see summer stock and get some backstage chat, as well as talking to her father who was an accountant, our young friend had gathered enough material to make a preliminary (tentative) choice and it was to take an internship program in an insurance company. Fade out. Happy ending? Not in real life.

Real-Life Illustrations

Perhaps a few vignettes of how people function in their various occupations would supply data to compare the ideal with the real situation. Let me introduce you to four men and women in their occupational settings. These are individuals I have met and observed (although some of their personal data have been changed in order to protect their privacy).

Mr. A. L. is an assistant principal in a junior high school. He freely tells both the boys and girls and his colleagues that he is there because he's having fun doing his job. He is one of a small group of senior staff members who, in his almost 20 years of service, have seen the school change from a predominantly white Jewish middle-class enrollment to a mix of black, Hispanic, Oriental, and white multi-ethnic population of students. He still wears impeccably tailored clothes, though they reflect the more colorful men's fashion of today, but his ways with the youngsters are open, friendly, jocular, and bantering. Interestingly enough, his type of humor did not go down well with some of the college students to whom he talked. The feedback I received was that he was uppity, too sarcastic, almost flippant in his approach to students and subject matter. I was present during his talk, and my perception of his presentation was considerably different from that of my students. While there were times when he was somewhat abrasive, I found these comments to be balanced by a free-flowing fund of information and a general receptiveness to questions. Another group of students had a totally different reaction. There was a good deal of laughter, friendly bantering, and good-humored questioning of some of the statements. Mr. L.'s own playful attitude was reciprocated at that time. What was different other than the student body? To the first-mentioned group he talked mostly about the special program of the gifted and also brought some of the gifted students with him, letting them talk and poking fun at them also. The second group heard him speak about his duties as grade adviser and his special relationships to disadvantaged youngsters. It is my hunch that talking about programs for the gifted was a threat to the first group of college students, especially since he talked about the qualities of the teacher of the gifted, and they may certainly have felt a lack of competence if faced with such a student body. The atmosphere was, therefore, not conducive to the type of psychological distancing that makes for the give and take of banter. Yet, Mr. L.'s reaction to both groups was positive and he obviously enjoyed himself in both situations. He certainly was capable of handling both; although with more exposure, he might have changed his tactics with the first group.

Mrs. M. P. runs one of those general gift merchandizing stores in a small upstate New York country town where you can find anything from old cut glass decanters to the latest in silver jewelry and, in between, piled up collectibles from depression glass to Japan-made salt and pepper shakers. When I first met her, she had just taken over the store from a friend. She was very enthusiastic about how she loved the merchandise and how she enjoyed rearranging things to reflect her particular tastes. The next time I saw her, she was down in the mouth and complaining that business was slow, that people came to look and not to buy. At the same time, she was trying to reassure herself about how much she liked people and about the wares she offered in her store.

H. B. is a creative artist who is promotion director for a book club and a magazine, and has to fit her painting into what so-called spare time she has from the job that pays her rent. She is extremely competent at doing what she has to do and is considered to be jolly by her associates, who think she has a good sense of humor. She recounts this assessment with some bitterness, because inside she is anguished about the time she has to give up from her real commitment, art.

N. M. is another creative artist, who combines teaching with his painting and print making. His adult education classes are conducted in a relaxed manner without giving up standards. He gets his points across with a dash of humor and seems to derive satisfaction from the achievements of his students. His major frustration comes from limited recognition of his own work, but there is within him a stubborn conviction that time is on his side, that in the long run, his paintings will find their way out into the world and carry his message to others. Even in ordinary social context, his conversation is often peppered with puns and gentle wit.

An interesting footnote is also provided by the citation awarded to Frank A. Geldard in 1974 by the American Psychological Association for excellence in teaching. It reads as follows: "Under his care have flourished integrity, compassion, and humor in the elementary and advanced studies of Psychology as science and technology."

As we compare the ideal with what is happening to real people, there are several tentative conclusions that we might draw. The first one is that there are individuals who can be playful in a work setting. The second one is that the playful attitude cannot be applied indiscriminately. The third one is that, in an occupational setting, women may find it more difficult to be playful than do men. As I was writing these profiles, I let the data speak, but now that I am looking back at them, I realize that they fit both into the findings from current studies and into the theoretical framework proposed. In a way, it is a validation of my thesis through empirical observation. This is encouraging in view of the importance of the ecological setting in all behavior.

What does it tell us about the influence of playfulness on imagination and creativity in a work setting? I would hold that, from a psychological point of view, we can claim that both imagination and creativity can become part of any given occupation, provided that one is at ease and, at times, able to step back and not take oneself too seriously. Inasmuch as creativity is not an everyday ingredient, we need not look for this type of approach to be part of every one of the 300-odd workdays that we put in on the job. But the playful approach would guarantee the kind of highlights or "peak experiences" that make the difference between a humdrum performance and real productivity.

USE OF LEISURE: CAN ALL AGES PLAY?

In my short historical review of the role of play, I raised the question of adult-oriented and child-oriented play. I suggested that, during the Middle Ages, the Renaissance, and even the Age of Enlightenment, child's play not only was minimal within the individual's life span, but was accorded little importance in human development as such. If play was emphasized—and written and sung about—it was the play of the adult, and I have to modify this again by adding the play of the adult in the leisure class.

Qualitative and Quantitative Aspects of Leisure

Today, both developmental time and historical time make us view play and leisure in a different relationship. Child's play is too often seen as his work, and the adult is hard at work learning how to play in his leisure. If what has been argued and elaborated about play and playfulness in the preceding sections can be considered to be sound and convincing, then it should help us see leisure as an ongoing process at all stages of development. In short, I suggest that the encouragement of playfulness, first in the play of the child and later as part of an individual's personality dynamics as he progresses from classroom learning to career choice and occupational setting, will facilitate its application to leisure. This is especially important today when, as adults, so many more individuals have so much more leisure.

Current research views leisure both in the conventional sense, as time at one's disposal, and as an attitude (Neulinger, 1971, 1974). My own focus is on that particular, qualitative aspect that flavors leisure with the ingredients of spontaneity, manifest joy, and sense of humor.

There is also an element of quantity that we must consider in the discussion of the use of leisure. Riesman (1950) once suggested that, in the days before the industrial revolution, and even during the industrial revolution, the many worked for the benefit of the few. Today, in the postindustrial age, the few may be called upon to work for the benefit of the many. When we translate this observation into the amount of leisure available to individuals, we come up with more time for leisure for more people. The crux of the matter here is that the educational level and the financial means of the majority of people with leisure on hand are less than those traditionally associated with the leisure class. As a result of economic constraints, the mid-1970s have provided data on the increase of hobbies, as well as on renewed interest in the theatre, museums, and zoos (Shabecoff, 1975). What we have learned from the review of play and studies on playfulness can give us both a clue for the present and a pointer to the future. Play and playful behavior occurs when the setting is familiar, not overly charged with tension, and not ego threatening. We can therefore analyze the trends to entertainment in and near the home as helpful to increased enjoyment in the use of leisure. One's own backyard, basement playroom, or even community center is a more familiar ecological setting than the Costa de Sol, the Swiss Alps, or the Norwegian fjords. Our reference group now is not the jet-setting leisure class who may have homes or rent villas in these places, but the once-a-lifetime participant in a group tour or some other packaged leisure fare. To the extent, then, that our average individual is thrust back into familiar surroundings for his leisure pursuits, to that extent will there be more opportunity for the play element to emerge. Against this, of course, we may need to weigh the equally valid evidence that, in order to relax, one needs a change of venue. Based on current happenings, however, we could say that, if one can psychologically shut the playroom door tight, then the precondition for a change in familiar settings is created. Geographical distance does not necessarily mean psychological distance, and we are all familiar with the type of person who takes his work problems with him on vacation, whether it is 50 or 5000 miles away.

Illustrations from Life

A closer look at how some individuals spend time on hand may tell us a good deal about the place of playfulness in leisure. There was an interesting news item on the CBS newscast reported by George Herman on July 29, 1975, about tennis replacing frisbees among college youth. The newscaster interpreted this as a change from the noncompetitive, relaxed handling of the frisbee to the hard-hitting, out-to-beat-the-other approach with the tennis racket. Two things struck me about both the factual information and the editorial comment. If the facts are as reported, is the Zeitgeist changing again and my hypothesis of the increase of prosocial behavior proven wrong? Certainly, one indicator cannot be taken as proof for one side or the other, but it is something to be watched for on college campuses. The other fact to which I reacted was frisbee-playing itself, since I had only recently become a frisbee player. But it is not only that. During a recent visit of my sister's, I taught her the game, and I was surprised at the affective change in our behavior during the game. Here were two middle-aged females, laughing and gamboling on a lawn, who had only minutes before been uptight about their respective professional concerns. It does suggest that there are activities during leisure that will allow for the playful element to enter; there are others whose grim competitiveness precludes any such ambience. Without making a case that only the former be encouraged as true leisure activities, it is important for us to realize that doing things during leisure does not necessarily mean enjoyment and lack of tension. If we refer back to what Neulinger (1974) calls the attitudinal element in leisure, we see the need for playfulness. In this connection, it should be mentioned that studies (Neulinger & Raps, 1972) comparing an average with a high ability group's approach to leisure found the latter to be more comfortable with having more vacation time, being less structured, and being more on their own.

Another aspect of leisure, which may not be readily admitted as belonging to it, is the practice of religion, or, in more general terms, an individual's search for a relationship to the universe. What I am trying to suggest is that the time spent in the practice of organized religion or different expressions of spiritual cosmic relatedness is time spent voluntarily away from one's occupation and business. If it includes the psychological distancing necessary to separate everyday concerns from the day of rest or the hours of contemplation, then we may have the basis for enjoyment and spontaneity that are part of playfulness. To illustrate the point, let us look at some current expressions of religious experience. In the Jewish tradition, the Oneg Shabbat—the joy of the Sabbath—is an integral part of this celebration. It includes the family gathering around for the festive meal and singing table hymns of joy. In the synagogue, the Sabbath is welcomed like a bride, a greeting that is full of joyous anticipation. Another more mundane memory of my own childhood, which carries within it the psychological distancing necessary for spontaneity and enjoyment, is my father's reference to his handing over of his daily worries and concerns to a "worry-carrier" for the 24 hours from Friday night to Saturday night. Today's observance may be expressed by college students meeting on Friday night through sundown on Saturday for a Shabbat marathon. Part of the time is spent in study; the other part is spent in song and dance. If one looks at ritual laws more in terms of familiarity than restrictions, then we can even apply our thesis that such familiarity may provide the basis for the play spirit in religious observance. The relationship between leisure and religious experiences is, however, not restricted to the old-time religions. The search for meaningful expressions of cosmic relatedness has been going on through the ages and is very much part of our current scene. The practice of yoga, the course on transcendental meditation, and even drug-induced states of altered consciousness can all be viewed as religious activities. Whether or not they qualify as inducing playfulness must be judged from the approach of its prophets and practitioners. It may sound sacrilegious to some to think of the play element in religion, but need we go further than to quote from Christmas carols proclaiming "joy to the world" and Sabbath hymns indicating "this day is to Israel a day of rest and rejoicing"? There certainly is the element of familiar practices in the ritual and, if viewed as I do, there is also leeway for recombination of the familiar without rejecting all proscriptions. What really saddens me is that so many individuals use the exercise of religion as a vehicle for hostile feeling and actions. More often the observance is a punishment for themselves, with their focus on all of the "don'ts," and a weapon against others who fall short of their own degree of interpretation of concepts and practices. Religion can be seen in Kohlberg's (1963) model of the different stages of moral judgment. There is room for the naive hedonism of the infant and the good-boy, good-girl conformity of Level II, but the most highly regarded level and, therefore, the one to be striven for is Stage 6 of Level III, which allows for individual interpretation of moral guidelines. My point is that this need not be accompanied by anguish, but can be a joyous exercise of one's thoughts and feelings, hopefully translated into actions as well.

In the case of leisure activities, it is not difficult to make a case for imagination and creativity as being part of the way we approach them. However, two major preconditions need to be present: familiarity with the setting and materials and unhurried pace. One element that needs to be removed from the situation is hostile competitiveness. One of the important differences to be drawn is that between achievement and creativity. You may do things, you may even get things done, but the end product is not necessarily creative. An interesting clue to this subtle difference is in one of McClelland's studies (1955, 1961) of the high n-Ach type that turns out to be the entrepreneur and not the intellectual. This does not mean that we do not find entrepreneurs in academe, but they have a different function and contribute along different dimensions to a college community. On today's campus, we certainly need both types, but the difference should be acknowledged.

An interesting and pertinent illustration of life and leisure in academe is the custom of the sabbatical year. Not only is it much maligned today, but there are strong efforts afoot to have it abolished. As we all know, the practice stems from the biblical obligation to let fields lie fallow every seventh year. In my interpretation, even in the most literal sense, it allows for a regrouping of extant nutrients and ingredients in the earth into different and more productive combinations. As I look back on my own sabbatical term, I can readily apply this "method" to the field of the mind. As a first step in the writing of this book, I drew on some of the material that was familiar, but I had to have time for the regrouping of data, for playing with different combinations of the findings; in short, I had to give myself the opportunity of lying "fallow" before any true creative process could begin. It was only after I felt less constrained about deadlines and allowed the task to take over that the joy of creating emerged.

A Leisurely Approach to Imagination and Creativity

What about imagination and creativity for the average consumer of leisure? According to the guidelines I developed, these would be most readily sparked in long-time hobbies rather than in competitive sports; this does not preclude group efforts, but in such instances, there should be a basis of cooperation and a relaxed social climate. I could see imagination and creativity operate during a quilting bee, but not during a bridge game. Building furniture, refinishing antique objects, and making sculpture of found objects are other group activities in which playfulness could aid in imaginative productivity. Games like checkers and chess would ordinarily not be conducive to playfulness. Their value as leisure activity would, on the positive side, lie in complete concentration and, particularly in chess, in the excitement that comes from planning one's own moves and the anticipation of those of your opponent. The negative aspects would be a focus on beating the opponent. From this, it becomes obvious that in my books, "winning" is not an integral part of leisure enjoyment.

It may seem that my emphasis is too much on the cognitive approach to leisure. I am certainly aware that what comes to mind when we talk about leisure is the aspect of enjoyment or, in more general terms, the affective element. While it may not be immediately obvious, the coping mechanism of "regression in the service of the ego" in Haan's (1963) model of ego functioning will give us some practical guidelines for managing and enjoying our leisure. To the extent that regression is the going back to an earlier mode of coping, this would imply a more familiar way of handling a situation. Familiarity, as I have emphasized throughout my discussion, is the ecological setting in which play occurs. In the psychoanalytic sense, it is also one of the processes conducive to creativity. Certainly, the joy attendant to producing something unique or original is not misplaced in leisure.

SUMMARY STATEMENT ON THE ROLE OF PLAYFULNESS IN AN INDIVIDUAL'S LIFE SPAN

Just recently, I witnessed reactions by various individuals to an extremely stressful situation affecting their livelihoods. It was interesting to see the mood swing from Pollyanna to panic on the part of some, while others kept their cool. I asked myself what might be the determinants that help some people to maintain a balanced view of a situation. I would rate the following ingredients high: being comfortable with yourself; being able to look at a situation with a grain of salt; having, basically, a *joie de vivre* approach. If I were to translate this into the three component traits of playfulness, I would label the behavior as spontaneity, sense of humor, and manifest joy.

I certainly do not advocate that a threat to one's economic existence be taken lightly. What I am suggesting is that realistic planning, especially in a stressful situation, is aided by the ability to maintain perspective, or, in other words, psychological distancing. It is because of this all-pervasive element, which playfulness represents in our optimal functioning, that it has to be nurtured from infancy to old age. Once we accept this in our philosophy as developmental and educational psychologists, we will have performed an important service to the next generation.

VII

Epilogue: The "Now" and "Future" Scene

The proper function of an epilogue is that of a conclusion. It is an appropriate place, therefore, to review for the reader the questions asked, the answers found, and the problems still left unsolved. The balance sheet will show the present state of affairs and will also take a look at possibilities in the future.

ANSWERS TO QUESTIONS ASKED

Q: Is *play* a legitimate concern in a work-oriented society?

A: Playfulness, derived from play, is carried over into work and aids in lifting the sharp dividing line between work and play.

Because of playfulness, the playing child and the playing adult may become more alike.

Psychological ramifications of using playfulness to establish a continuum between work and play are of special importance at a time when leisure activities are going to take up more of the individual's pattern of living.

Q: What case can be made for *imagination* beyond idle passing of time?

A: Imagination, being a more subjective thought process, can help in strengthening a person's sense of individuality and uniqueness.

Encouraging subjective perception of events and ideas may add to a person's enjoyment of his own cognitive functioning and expand his interpretation of the environment.

Practicing introspection as part of the imaginative process also aids an individual to be in touch, and become familiar, with his or her own thinking.

149

Incorporating the element of playfulness into imagination can lead to unique
and creative products.

"Combinatorial play" would appear to be an important ingredient in imagination for rearranging known facts and a necessary condition for producing unique solutions to existing problems.

Q: Does *creativity*, in the sense of originality and uniqueness, have a place in a
democratically conceived societal structure?

A: Since play is universally available to all children today, the element of
playfulness can be encouraged in everybody.

Application of playfulness or "combinatorial play" in the production of
unique ideas will also be a function of other interacting variables.

The resulting "elite" of creative individuals can still be a true reflection of
the freedom within a democracy.

The importance of considering creativity as a multifaceted dimension (i.e.,
different individuals are "at the top" of different heaps) again reinforces a
democratically conceived structure.

POINTERS TO QUESTIONS STILL TO BE EXPLORED

While the suggested answers to the broader questions asked are encouraging,
there are specific problems related to the conceptualization of playfulness that
call for further investigations. By focusing on such positive behavior as spontaneity, manifest joy, and sense of humor, I see an impetus to observe these
traits more closely in natural settings and to determine more precisely both the
antecedents and consequences of these traits. At a time when we are all more
responsive to child advocacy as a legitimate area of concern for psychologists, a
closer look at positive behavior and clues to when, and under what circum-
stances, it occurs will also provide us with tools to encourage and, if necessary,
to train those involved in childrearing, both at home and in the schools, in using
spontaneity, joy, and sense of humor in their everyday interaction with the
growing individual. Such training should benefit not only the young but also
those who show these traits, conterbalancing the pressures and anxieties of
today's life space, and, at the same time, preparing the citizens of tomorrow to
exercise the type of prosocial behavior that will be necessary for them to fulfill
their potential and teach their young to survive. Man certainly does not live by
bread alone, and developmental and educational psychologists, in particular,
need to recognize their responsibility in that area and to shoulder it willingly. In
doing so, we, too, should make spontaneity, manifest joy, and sense of humor
part of our professional equipment. Indeed, if we consider ourselves competent,
then there is every reason for us to play with the givens, look at familiar sights,
allow ourselves the psychological distancing that makes for a wry look at

ourselves, and, at the same time, let ourselves enjoy what we are creating for the future. The new look at familiar patterns will even give replication of studies a greater respectability, and spark an in-depth approach and a slower pace in the interpretation of findings, all of which will give us true educational benefits, for we shall learn new things from the old.

PERSPECTIVE ON THE TWENTY-FIRST CENTURY

I sometimes look at my own students wistfully—and at the same time hopefully—because, whether they will become teachers in a professional sense or cultural surrogates to children as parents or caretakers, they will be taking some of what we, as psychologists, collectively say into the next century. Also, looking at them keeps my optimism intact, because, basically, they give out good vibes for prosocial behavior to develop and survive. Admittedly, they are still motivated by grades and are anxious to find out what the instructor wants, but, at the same time, they are receptive to working for intrinsic rewards; they suggest, by their attire and actions, that to "get a piece of the pie" is not the most important thing and, certainly, it is not worth doing at all costs.

Going beyond personal observations, I was intrigued by an interpretation offered by Commager (1950) as part of his analysis of the American character. While, as he admitted, there were no American theoreticians expounding the principles of the Enlightenment, eighteenth-century American history is a translation of these principles into practical philosophy, which, at that time, included economics. Perhaps a similar case can be made for the social sciences in this bicentennial year. Again, while we have produced no outstanding theoreticians, we may, at present, see a translation into everyday sociology and psychology of the lofty principle of the "pursuit of happiness." Indeed, *Walden Two*, a contemporary utopia by a well-known psychologist, ends on a note that would agree with my thesis of joy. A somewhat fearful Professor Burris is depicted as glancing upward and then finding himself comforted in the following way.

> But I saw the familiar features of Walden Two stretched before me just as I had recalled them, again and again, on my journey back, and I drew a deep breath of satisfaction. [Skinner, 1948, p. 320]

I hold no brief for *Walden Two* except as an illustration of a point. Equally influential to our thinking of today have been the writings of Maslow (1968) and Berne (1964/1972), two social scientists who see the human being and his or her future in a very different light. It ties in also with Bennis' (1970) observation, that he sees a shift from valuing independence to valuing interdependence, from the endurance of stress to a capacity for joy, from the desire for full employment to a demand for full lives.

Appendix A

Playfulness Scale (Form K)

RATING INSTRUCTIONS

As a teacher, you know that children differ in many ways—some are shy, some are friendly, some grab what they want, others ask, or wait, for it.

In this study, we are interested in finding out how children differ in the way they go about their play activities—how spontaneous, how cheerful, how "full of the devil" they are—and we hope to have your cooperation in this work.

Attached you will find, therefore, a rating measure made up of five scales that refer directly to a child's behavior during play. You will note that each of the five scales or questions has two parts. Part A of the question aims to get at the frequency or quantity of the trait; Part B tries to assess the quality of the trait shown. For example, "how often does the child show joy" would be the quantity of the trait, and "with what freedom of expression" would be the quality of the trait.

We hope you will find it possible and worthwhile to look at the children in your group along the traits suggested in the rating scales and give us your evaluation of them.

We are also interested in finding out what your impression is of the child's intelligence and physical attractiveness, and we would like you to give us your estimate of these as well.

When you rate the children, you will, of course, want to compare them with one another as well as keep in mind a general standard for these traits in kindergartners.

It is easier and better to rate all children first on one trait (or question) and then do the same for each of the six other questions. The sheets for marking down your ratings have, therefore, been set up for the different traits.

There will be 12 ratings for each child. Please put down the figure that best indicates your evaluation of the child's present standing. Descriptive terms are also given to help you in making your rating.

Any comments about the content or form of the questions, or about any difficulties that you may have in answering them, will be welcomed.

RATING SCALES

I. A. *How often does the child engage in spontaneous physical movement and activity during play?*
This behavior would include skipping, hopping, jumping, and other rhythmic

153

movements of the whole body or parts of the body, like arms, legs or head, that could be judged as a fairly clear indication of exuberance.

Very often	Often	Occasionally	Rarely	Very rarely
5	4	3	2	1

B. *How is his/her motor coordination during physical activity?*

Excellent	Very good	Good	Fair	Poor
5	4	3	2	1

II. A. *How often does the child show joy in or during his/her play activities?*
This may be judged by facial expression, such as smiling, by verbal expressions, such as saying "I like this," or "This is fun," or by more indirect vocalizing, such as singing as an accompaniment of the activity, for example, "choo, choo, train, go along." Other behavioral indicators would be repetition of activity or resumption of activity with clear evidence of enjoyment.

Very often	Often	Occasionally	Rarely	Very rarely
5	4	3	2	1

B. *With what freedom of expression does he/she show joy?*
This may be judged by the intensity or loudness of a chuckle or a sing-song, as well as by the child's ability to repeat or resume his/her activity by his/her own choice.

Very high	High	Moderate	Some	Little
5	4	3	2	1

III. A. *How often does the child show a sense of humor during play?*
By "sense of humor" is meant rhyming, gentle teasing—a "glint-in-the-eye" behavior—as well as an ability to see a situation as funny as it pertains to himself/herself or others.

Very often	Often	Occasionally	Rarely	Very rarely
5	4	3	2	1

B. *With what degree of consistency is humor shown?*
This may be judged by its occurrence across situations and from day to day.

Very high	High	Moderate	Some	Little
5	4	3	2	1

IV. A. *While playing, how often does the child show flexibility in his interaction with the surrounding group structure?*
This may be judged by the child joining different groups at any one play period, and becoming part of them and their play activity, and by being able to move in and out of these groups by his/her own choice or by suggestion from the group members without aggressive intent on their part.

Very often	Often	Occasionally	Rarely	Very rarely
5	4	3	2	1

B. *With what degree of ease does the child move?*
This may be judged by ready acceptance of the new situation, lack of distress shown over the change, including an ability also to amuse himself/herself if left solitary after peer interaction.

Very high	High	Moderate	Some	Little
5	4	3	2	1

V. A. *How often does the child show spontaneity during expressive and dramatic play?*
Instances of such behavior would be labeling the play products in clay, sand, or paints as they grow and/or changing them as a result of, for example, a personal whim, an accidental shape, or a suggestion from the peer group; similarly, in dramatic play, a labeling of play roles as the group structure develops and changes, for example, extending or shrinking a "family" as playmates come or go.

Very often	Often	Occasionally	Rarely	Very rarely
5	4	3	2	1

B. *What degree of imagination does the child show in his/her expressive dramatic play?*
Instances of imagination would be labeling and using inanimate or animate objects for other than the accepted usage, as well as incorporating nonexistent objects into the play situation.

Very high	High	Moderate	Some	Very low
5	4	3	2	1

VI. *How bright is the child?*
This is your estimate of the child's intelligence based on observed behavior or inferred potential.

Extremely bright	Bright	Average	Moderately bright	Not too bright
5	4	3	2	1

VII.   *How attractive is the child?*
         This is your evaluation of the child's physical appeal.

Beautiful	Very attractive	Nice-looking	Passable in looks and appearance	Somewhat homely and unattractive
5	4	3	2	1

Appendix B

Playfulness-Nonplayfulness Scale (Form A)

RATING INSTRUCTIONS

As you look at adolescents in a classroom setting, you realize that they differ in the way they move about, address themselves to their tasks, and interact with peers and teachers.

In this study we are trying to assess how much spontaneity can be found in the behavior of high school students in the classroom. Also, how cheerful and how "full of the devil" these youngsters are.

Attached you will find a rating measure made up of five scales that refer to a student's behavior in class. You will note that each of the five scales or questions has two parts. Part A of the question aims at measuring the frequency or quantity of the trait; Part B tries to assess the quality of the trait shown. For example, "How consistently does the student show a sense of fun?" would be the quantity of the trait, and "How much is wit and subtlety a part of his sense of humor?" would be the quality of the trait.

We hope that we shall have your cooperation in this work and that you will find it possible and worthwhile to look at the students in your classroom along the traits suggested in the rating scales and give us your evaluation of them.

We are also interested in finding out what your impression is of the student's achievement orientation and physical attractiveness and would like you to give us your estimate of these as well.

When you rate the students, you will, of course, want to compare them with one another as well as keep in mind a general standard for these traits in adolescents in the high school setting.

It is easier and better to rate all students first on one trait or question and then do the same for each of the six other questions. The rating scales have, therefore, been set up for one trait per page.

PLEASE PUT DOWN THE FIGURE THAT BEST INDICATES YOUR EVALUATION OF THE STUDENT'S PRESENT STANDING.

A PROFILE IS GIVEN AT THE EXTREME ENDS OF EACH SCALE AS AN AID IN MAKING YOUR RATING. THE SCALE IS TO BE REGARDED AS A CONTINUUM AND THE IN-BETWEEN NUMBERS SHOULD BE USED TO INDICATE DEGREES IN FREQUENCY AND INTENSITY.

Any comments about the content or form of the questions, or about any difficulties that you may have in answering them, will be welcomed.

Thank you for your help in this study.

RATING SCALES

Name of student:
Grade (or level):
Subject:
Teacher:
School:

SCALE IA. *How consistently does the student show spontaneous physical movement and activity in class?*

Physically on the move				Physically rigid
5	4	3	2	1

This is the student who moves around a lot, likes to change his/her seat, has trouble settling down, fidgets with things, mischievously throws objects.

This is the student who sits stiffly, with a tense facial expression and a rigid manner.

SCALE IB. *What degree of energy does the student show in physical activity?*

Physically alert				Physically apathetic
5	4	3	2	1

This is the student who has an animated and alert facial expression, waves his/her hand to be recognized, uses gestures freely to underline a point, nods in response to teacher's points.

This is the student who slumps in his/her seat, looks sluggish and sleepy, yawns, and stares into space.

SCALE IIA. *How consistently does the student show enthusiasm during classroom activities?*

Enthusiastic				Discouraged
5	4	3	2	1

This is the student who is eager and enthusiastic in his/her approach to work and optimistic and high-spirited.

This is the student who needs reassurance, is unhappy and sullen, gets easily discouraged, and is unsure of himself/herself.

SCALE IIB. *With what ease (freedom) does the student show joy?*

Relaxed (spontaneous)				Tense (constricted)
5	4	3	2	1
This is the student who is relaxed and boisterous, chuckles and laughs, can express feelings freely, sometimes unpredictably.				This is the student who is tense and quiet, rarely laughs, lacks spontaneity, stereotype in reactions (you just know what he/she is or is not going to do next).

SCALE IIIA. *How consistently does the student show a sense of fun (humor) in class?*

Fun-loving				Humorless
5	4	3	2	1
This is the student who is the entertainer, who constantly makes jokes, enjoys horseplay, clowns engages in cross-sex teasing.				This is the student who becomes irritable in a fun situation, who is anxious to get back to the "real business"—the lesson— who fails to see the funny side of situations.

SCALE IIIB. *How much is wit and subtlety a part of his/her sense of humor in class?*

Accepting in wit				Hostile in wit
5	4	3	2	1
This is the student who recognizes and searches for the humor in situations, can take teasing and teases others, including the teacher, who uses wit in puns, off-beat comparisons, and sometimes slightly off-color remarks.				This is the student who laughs at the discomfort of others, gets angry when he/she is the butt of a joke, hits back with insults when teased.

SCALE IVA. *How consistently is the student engaged in interaction with peers in class?*

Group-oriented				Self-oriented
5	4	3	2	1
This is the student who is busy passing notes, talking to neighbors, and seeking attention also by pushing and shoving, and calling out in class.				This is the student who keeps to himself/herself, is "a loner" does not respond to classmates, and does not, on his/her own, seek association with them.

SCALE IVB. *What is the tone or quality of the involvement with peers in class?*

Friendly				Rejecting
5	4	3	2	1

This is the student who is outgoing, friendly, able to move from one group to another.			This is the student who gets easily hurt, is on the defensive with others, wants to hurt others, and is uncooperative.

SCALE VA. *How consistently does the student show spontaneity in intellectual tasks in class?*

Intellectually alive				Intellectually stagnant
5	4	3	2	1

This is the student who is curious, inventive, volunteers frequently, introduces relevant and sometimes far-out material in questions and answers.			This is the student who approaches work in a routine and mechanical way, does not volunteer in class, and, when called upon, does not respond, sometimes daydreaming or appearing bored.

SCALE VB. *What is the quality of the student's work involvement in class?*

Erratic				Conscientious
5	4	3	2	1

This is the student who is more concerned with play than work, is bored with the regular classroom atmosphere, and is off in his/her own world, sometimes asking questions to disrupt the lesson.			This is the student who is conscientious, completes his/her assignments, and takes his/her work seriously— sometimes too seriously.

SCALE VI. *How achievement-oriented is the student?*

Ambitious				Indifferent
5	4	3	2	1

This is the student whose whole attention is on excellence as shown by grades and tests.			This is the student who cares little or nothing about his/her academic standing in class.

SCALE VII. *How attractive is the student physically?*

Beautiful (handsome)				Plain (unattractive)
5	4	3	2	1
This is the student who is exceptionally good-looking.				This is the student who is homely and unattractive.

References

Achenbach, T. M., & Weisz, J. R. Impulsivity–reflectivity and cognitive development in preschoolers: A longitudinal analysis of developmental and trait variance. *Developmental Psychology*, 1975, *11*, 413–414.

Aldis, O. *Play fighting*. New York: Academic Press, 1975.

Altman, K. Effects of cooperative response acquisition in social behavior during free play. *Journal of Experimental Child Psychology*, 1971, *12*, 387–395.

Aronfreed, J., & Paskal, V. Altruism, empathy, and the conditioning of positive affect. Unpublished manuscript, University of Pennsylvania, 1965.

Avedon, E. M., & Sutton-Smith, B. *The study of games*. New York: Wiley, 1971.

Bachtold, L. M., & Werner, E. E. Personality profiles of gifted women: Psychologists. *American Psychologist*, 1970, *25*, 234–243.

Baldwin, A. L., Kalhorn, J., & Breese, F. H. Patterns of parent behavior. *Psychological Monographs*, 1945, *58*(3).

Baltes, P. B., & Schaie, K. W. (Eds.). *Life-span developmental psychology: Personality and socialization*. New York: Academic Press, 1973.

Barnes, K. E. Preschool play norms: A replication. *Developmental Psychology*, 1971, *5*, 99–103.

Barron, F. *Creative person and creative process*. New York: Holt, 1969.

Barron, F. *Artists in the making*. New York: Seminar Press, 1972.

Bary, B. B. The effect of reinforcement and modeling of opposite-sex toy play on subsequent toy preferences. Paper presented at the meeting of the Eastern Psychological Association, Philadelphia, April 1974.

Bass, B. M. The substance and the shadow. *American Psychologist*, 1974, *29*, 870–886.

Bates, J. E., & Bentler, P. M. Play activities of normal and effeminate boys. *Developmental Psychology*, 1973, *9*, 20–27.

Bayley, N. Behaviorial correlates of mental growth: Birth to 36 years. *American Psychologist*, 1968, *1*, 1–17.

Beach, F. A. Current concepts of play in animals. *American Naturalist*, 1945, *79*, 523–541.

Bennis, W. A funny thing happened on the way to the future. *American Psychologist*, 1970, *25*, 595–608.

Berger, G. Personal communication, May 1975.

Berkowitz, L. Aggressive humor as a stimulus to aggressive responses. *Journal of Personality and Social Psychology*, 1970, *16*, 710–717.

Berlyne, D. E. *Conflict, arousal, and curiosity*. New York: McGraw-Hill, 1960.

Berlyne, D. E. Exploratory and epistemic behavior. In S. Koch (Ed.), *Psychology as a science* (Vol. 5). New York: McGraw-Hill, 1963.

Berlyne, D. E. Laughter, humor, and play. In G. Lindzey & E. Aronson (Eds.), *The handbook of social psychology* (Vol. 3, 2nd ed.). Reading, Mass.: Addison Wesley, 1969.

Berlyne, D. E. *Aesthetics and psychobiology.* New York: Appleton, 1971.

Berlyne, D. E. Humor and its kin. In J. H. Goldstein & P. E. McGhee (Eds.), *The psychology of humor.* New York: Academic Press, 1972.

Berlyne, D. E. The vicissitudes of aplopathematic and thelematoscopic pneumatology (or The hydography of hedonism). In D. E. Berlyne & K. B. Madsen (Eds.), *Pleasure, reward, preference: Their nature, determinants, and role in behavior.* New York: Academic Press, 1973.

Berne, E. *Games people play: The psychology of human relationships.* New York: Grove Press, 1972. (Originally published 1964.)

Biller, H. B., Singer, D. L., & Fullerton, M. Sex-role development and creative potential in kindergarten-age boys. *Developmental Psychology,* 1969, *1,* 291–296.

Bishop, D. W., & Chace, C. E. Parental conceptual systems, home play environment, and potential creativity in children. *Journal of Experimental Child Psychology,* 1971, *12,* 318–338.

Bowlby, J. A. *Maternal care and mental health.* Geneva: World Health Organization, 1951.

Boyd, W. *The educational theories of Jean Jacques Rousseau.* New York: Russell & Russell, 1963.

Bridges, K. M. B. *The social and emotional development of the pre-school child.* London: Routledge, 1931.

Bronfenbrenner, U. *The two worlds of childhood: U.S. and U.S.S.R.* New York: Russell Sage Foundation, 1970.

Bruner, J. S. Nature and uses of immaturity. *American Psychologist,* 1972, *27,* 687–708.

Buehler, K. *Die geistige Entwicklung des Kindes.* Jena: Fischer, 1918. (*The mental development of the child.* New York: Harcourt Brace, 1930.)

Butler, R., & Nisan, M. Who is afraid of success and why? *Journal of Youth and Adolescence,* 1975, *4,* 259–270.

Caillois, R. [*Man, play, and games*] (M. Barash, trans.). New York: Fress Press, 1961.

Cellini, B. *The autobiography of Benvenuto Cellini.* New York: Modern Library, undated.

Chadwick, B., & Day, R. Systematic reinforcement: Academic performance of underachieving students. *Journal of Applied Behavior Analysis,* 1971, *4,* 311–319.

Cheyne, J. A., Goyeche, J. R. M., & Walters, R. H. Attention, anxiety, and rules in resistance-to-deviation in children. *Journal of Experimental Child Psychology,* 1969, *8,* 127–139.

Child, I. L. Personality correlates of esthetic judgment in college students. *Journal of Personality,* 1965, *33,* 476–511.

Claparede, E. Sur la nature et la fonction du jeu. *Archives Psychologiques, Geneve,* 1934, *24,* 350–369.

Collard, R. R. Social and play responses of first-born and later-born infants in an unfamiliar situation. *Child Development,* 1968, *39,* 325–334.

Collard, R. R. Exploratory and play behaviors of infants reared in an institution and in lower- and middle-class homes. *Child Development,* 1971, *42,* 1003–1017.

Commager, H. S. *The American mind.* New Haven, Conn.: Yale University Press, 1950.

Cook, H., & Stingle, S. Cooperative behavior in children. *Psychological Bulletin,* 1974, *81,* 918–933.

Cooper, S. Personal communication, December 1974.

Corter, C. M., Rheingold, H. L., & Eckerman, C. O. Toys delay the infant's following of his mother. *Developmental Psychology,* 1972, *6,* 138–145.

Cox, F. N., & Campbell, D. Young children in a new situation with and without their mothers. *Child Development,* 1968, *39,* 123–131.

Crockenberg, S. B., Bryant, B. K., & Wilce, L. S. The effects of cooperatively and competitively structured learning environments on inter- and intrapersonal behavior. *Child Development,* 1976, *47,* 386–396.

Cropley, A. J. A five-year longitudinal study of the validity of creativity tests. *Developmental Psychology,* 1972, *6,* 119–124.

Curtis, C. They can't be "workaholics"—They're having too much fun. *New York Times,* Sunday, March 30, 1975, p. 38.

Damico, S., & Purkey, W. The class clown phenomenon among middle school students. Paper presented at the annual meeting of the American Educational Research Association, San Francisco, April 1976.

Dansky, J. L., & Silverman, I. W. Effects of play on associative fluency in preschool-aged children. *Developmental Psychology,* 1973, *9,* 44–54.

Dansky, J. L., & Silverman, I. W. Play: A general facilitator of associative fluency. *Developmental Psychology,* 1975, *11,* 104.

Davie, C., Forrest, B., Hutt, C., Mason, M., Vincent, E., & Ward, T. Play at home and in school. Paper presented at the biennial meeting of the International Society for the Study of Behavioral Development, Guilford, England, 1975.

Denney, D. R. Reflection and impulsivity as determinants of conceptual strategy. *Child Development,* 1973, *44,* 614–623.

Denny, T., Starks, D., & Feldhusen, J. Predictions of divergent thinking and creative performance over a four-year period: A longitudinal study. Paper presented at the meeting of the American Psychological Association, Washington, D. C., September 1967.

Deutsch, K. *Creativity in a scientific civilization.* New York: Proceedings of Bank Street College of Education Conference, 1958.

De Vries, D. L., & Edwards, K. J. Expectancy theory and cooperation—competition in the classroom. Paper presented at the meeting of the American Psychological Association, New Orleans, August 1974. (a)

De Vries, D. L., & Edwards, K. J. *Teams–games–tournament: A technique using small groups in the classroom.* Baltimore, Md.: Center for Social Organization of Schools, Johns Hopkins University, 1974. (b)

Dewey, J. Play. In P. Monroe (Ed.), *A cyclopedia of education.* New York: Macmillan, 1913.

Dewey, J. *How we think* (2nd ed.). Boston: Heath, 1933.

Dewey, J. *Art as experience.* New York: G. P. Putnam, 1958. (Originally published 1934.)

Dolhinow, P. *Primate patterns.* New York: Holt, 1972.

Dolhinow, R. J., & Bishop, N. The development of motor skills and social relationships among primates through play. *Minnesota Symposia on Child Psychology,* 1970, *4,* 191–198.

Dreman, S. B., & Greenbaum, C. W. Altruism or reciprocity: Sharing behavior in Israeli kindergarten children. *Child Development,* 1973, *44,* 61–68.

Durrell, D. E., & Weisberg, P. Imitative play behavior of children: The importance of model distinction and prior imitative training. *Journal of Experimental Child Psychology,* 1973, *16,* 23–31.

Durrett, E., & Huffman, W. Playfulness and divergent thinking among Mexican–American children. *Journal of Home Economics,* 1968, *60,* 355–358.

Dworkin, M. S. (Ed.). *Dewey on education.* New York: Teachers College, Columbia University, 1959.

Eckerman, C. O., & Rheingold, H. L. Infants' exploratory responses to toys and people. *Developmental Psychology*, 1974, *10*, 255–259.

Eifermann, R. *School children's games.* Final Report to the Office of Education, Health, Education, and Welfare, June 1968.

Eifermann, R. *Determinants of children's game styles.* Jerusalem: Israel Academy of Sciences and Humanities, 1971.

Einstein, A. [*Mozart: His character, his work*] (A. Mendel & N. Broda, trans.). London: Oxford University Press, 1945.

Elkind, D. Piagetian and psychometric conceptions of intelligence. *Harvard Educational Review*, 1969, *39*, 319–337.

Emmerich, W. Personality development and concepts of structure. *Child Development*, 1968, *39*, 671–690.

Emmerich, W. Socialization and sex-role development. In P. B. Baltes & K. W. Schaie (Eds.), *Life-span developmental psychology: Personality and socialization.* New York: Academic Press, 1973.

English, H. B., & English, A. C. *A comprehensive dictionary of psychological terms: A guide to usage.* New York: Longmans, Green, 1958.

Erikson, E. H. Studies in the interpretation of play. I. Clinical observation of play disruption in young children. *Genetic Psychology Monographs*, 1940, *22*, 557–671.

Erikson, E. H. *Childhood and society.* New York: Norton, 1950.

Etaugh, C., & Hughes, V. Teachers' evaluations of sex-typed behaviors in children: The role of teacher sex and school setting. *Developmental Psychology*, 1975, *11*, 394–395.

Eysenck, H. J. The appreciation of humor: An experimental and theoretical study. *British Journal of Psychology*, 1942, *32*, 295–309.

Eysenck, H. J. Foreword. In J. H. Goldstein & P. E. McGhee (Eds.), *The psychology of humor.* New York: Academic Press, 1972.

Fagot, B. I. Influence of teacher behavior in the preschool. *Developmental Psychology*, 1973, *9*, 198–206. (a)

Fagot, B. I. Sex-related stereotyping of toddlers' behavior. *Developmental Psychology*, 1973, *9*, 429. (b)

Fagot, B. I. Sex differences in toddlers' behavior and parental reaction. *Developmental Psychology*, 1974, *10*, 554–558.

Fein, G. A transformational analysis of pretending. *Developmental Psychology*, 1975, *11*, 291–296.

Fein, G., Johnson, D., Kosson, N., Stork, L., & Wasserman, L. Sex stereotypes and preferences in the toy choices of 20-month-old boys and girls. *Developmental Psychology*, 1975, *11*, 527–528.

Feitelson, D., & Ross, G. S. Neglected factor: Play. *Human Development*, 1973, *16*, 202–223.

Finlay, G. E., & Layne, O. Play behavior in young children: A cross-cultural study. *Journal of Genetic Psychology*, 1971, *119*, 203–210.

Ford, J. D., & Foster, S. L. Extrinsic incentives and token-based programs: A revaluation. *American Psychologist*, 1976, *31*, 87–90.

Fowler, H. *Curiosity and exploratory behavior.* New York: Macmillan, 1965.

Fox, L. H. Sex differences: Implications for program planning for the academically gifted. Paper presented at the Lewis M. Terman Memorial Symposium on Intellectual Talent, Johns Hopkins University, Baltimore, November 1975.

Fox, L. H., & Stanley, J. C. Educational facilitation for mathematically and scientifically precocious youth. Paper presented at the annual meeting of the American Educational Research Association, New Orleans, February 1973.

Freud, S. [*Civilization and its discontents*] (J. Riviere, trans.). New York: Cape & Smith, 1930.

Freud, S. [Psychopathology of everyday life.] In A. A. Brill (Ed. and trans.), *The basic writings of Sigmund Freud.* New York: Random House, 1938. (a)

Freud, S. [Three contributions to the theory of sex.] In A. A. Brill (Ed. and trans.), *The basic writings of Sigmund Freud.* New York: Random House, 1938. (b)

Freud, S. [Wit and its relation to the unconscious.] In A. A. Brill (Ed. and trans.), *The basic writings of Sigmund Freud.* New York: Random House, 1938. (c)

Freud, S. [*Leonardo Da Vinci: A study in psychosexuality*] (A. A. Brill, trans.). New York: Random House, 1955.

Freyberg, J. T. Increasing the imaginative play of urban disadvantaged kindergarten children through systematic training. Chapter in J. L. Singer, *The child's world of make-believe.* New York: Academic Press, 1973.

Froebel, F. *Mother Play Songs.* (S. Blow arrang.) New York: Appleton, Company, 1895. (a)

Froebel, F. [*Pedagogics of the kindergarten*] (J. Jarvis, trans.). New York: Appleton, 1895. (b)

Gadberry, S. Television as baby-sitter: A field comparison of preschoolers' behavior during playtime and during television viewing. *Child Development,* 1974, *45,* 1132–1136.

Getzels, J. W., & Jackson, P. W. *Creativity and intelligence.* New York: Wiley, 1962.

Gewirtz, J. L. The course of infant smiling in four child-rearing environments in Israel. In B. M. Foss (Ed.), *Determinants of infant behavior* (Vol. 3). New York: Wiley, 1965.

Ginzberg, E. *Life styles of educated women.* New York: Columbia University Press, 1966.

Ginzberg, E., Ginsburg, S. W., Axelrad, S., & Herma, J. L. *Occupational choice: An approach to general theory.* New York: Columbia University Press, 1951.

Ginzberg, E., & Yohalem, A. M. *Educated American women: Self-portraits.* New York: Columbia University Press, 1966.

Goldberg, C. Aids and devices that can be used in the teaching of mathematics at the secondary level. Unpublished manuscript, Brooklyn College, 1976.

Goldberg, S., & Lewis, M. Play behavior in the year-old infant: Early sex differences. *Child Development,* 1969, *40,* 21–31.

Goldstein, J. H., & McGhee, P. E. (Eds.). *The psychology of humor.* New York: Academic Press, 1972.

Goodchilds, J. D. Effects of being witty on position in the social structure of a small group. *Sociometry,* 1959, *22,* 261–272.

Goodchilds, J. D. On being witty: Causes, correlates, and consequences. In J. H. Goldstein & P. E. McGhee (Eds.), *The psychology of humor.* New York: Academic Press, 1972.

Goodenough, F. L. *Anger in young children.* Minneapolis: University of Minnesota Press, 1931.

Gordon, W. J. J. *Synectics: The development of creative capacity.* New York: Harper & Row, 1961.

Graham, L. R. The maturational factor in humor. *Journal of Clinical Psychology,* 1958, *14,* 326–328.

Gray, J. L. Stability and generalizability of conceptual style. *Psychology in the Schools,* 1974, *11,* 466–475.

Griffiths, R. *A study of imagination in early childhood.* London: Kegan Paul, 1935.

Groch, A. S. Joking and appreciation of humor in nursery school children. *Child Development,* 1974, *45* (4), 1098–1102.

Groos, K. *The play of animals.* New York: Appleton, 1898.

Groos, K. *The play of man.* New York: Appleton, 1901.

Guilford, J. P. Creativity. *American Psychologist,* 1950, *5,* 444–454.

Guilford, J. P. Structure of intellect. *Psychological Bulletin*, 1956, *53*, 267–293.

Guilford, J. P. *Intelligence, creativity, and their educational implications*. San Diego, Calif.: Robert Knapp, 1968.

Guilford, J. P., Wilson, R. C., & Christensen, P. R. *A factor-analytic study of creative thinking. I. Hypotheses and description of tests.* (Reports of Psychological Laboratory, No. 3.) Los Angeles: University of Southern California, 1951.

Guilford, J. P., Wilson, R. C., & Christensen, P. R. *A factor-analytic study of creative thinking. II. Adminstration of tests and analysis of results.* (Reports of Psychological Laboratory, No. 8.) Los Angeles: University of California, 1952.

Haan, N. Proposed model of ego functioning: Coping and defense mechanisms in relationship to IQ change. *Psychological Monographs*, 1963, No. 8 (Whole No. 571).

Hall, G. S. *Youth.* New York: Appleton, 1906.

Halverson, C. F., & Waldrop, M. F. Relations of mechanically recorded activity level to varieties of preschool play behavior. *Child Development*, 1973, *44*, 678–681.

Harlow, H. F. The nature of love. *American Psychologist*, 1958, *13*, 673–685.

Harter, S. Pleasure derived by children from cognitive challenge and mastery. *Child Development*, 1974, *45*, 661–669.

Harter, S. Developmental differences in the manifestation of mastery motivation on problem-solving tasks. *Child Development*, 1975, *46*, 370–378.

Harter, S., Shultz, T. R., & Blum, B. Smiling in children as a function of their sense of mastery. *Journal of Experimental Child Psychology*, 1971, *12*, 396–404.

Hartley, R. E., Frank, L. K., & Goldenson, R. G. *Understanding children's play.* New York: Columbia University Press, 1952.

Hartmann, H. [*Ego psychology and the problem of adaptation*] (D. Rappaport, trans.). New York: International Universities Press, 1958.

Hartshorn, E., & Brantley, J. C. Effects of dramatic play on classroom problem solving ability. *Journal of Educational Research*, 1973, *66*, 243–246.

Hebb, D. O. *Organization of behavior.* New York: Wiley, 1949.

Hebb, D. O. Drives and the C.N.S. *Psychological Review*, 1955, *62*, 243–254.

Helson, R. Personality characteristics and developmental history of creative college women. *Genetic Psychology Monographs*, 1967, *76*, 205–256.

Helson, R. Generality of sex differences in creative style. *Journal of Personality*, 1968, *36* (1), 33–48.

Helson, R. Sex-specific patterns in creative literary fantasy. *Journal of Personality*, 1970, *38*, 344–363.

Henle, M. Fishing for ideas. *American Psychologist*, 1975, *30*, 795–799.

Herron, R. E., & Sutton-Smith, B. (Eds.). *Child's play.* New York: Wiley, 1971.

Hoffman, L. W. Fear of success in males and females: 1965 and 1971. *Journal of Consulting and Clinical Psychology*, 1974, *42*, 353–358.

Hoffman, M. L. Developmental synthesis of affect and cognition and its implications for altruistic motivation. *Developmental Psychology*, 1975, *11*, 607–622.

Horner, M. S. Toward an understanding of achievement-related conflicts in women. *Journal of Social Issues*, 1972, *28*, 157–175.

Huizinga, J. *Homo ludens.* Boston: Beacon Press, 1955.

Hunt, J. McV. *Intelligence and experience.* New York: Ronald Press, 1961.

Hutt, C. Exploration and play in children. *Symposium of the Zoological Society of London*, 1966, *18*, 61–81.

Hutt, C. Specific and diversive exploration. In H. W. Reese & L. P. Lipsitt (Eds.), *Advances in child development and behavior* (Vol. 5). New York: Academic Press, 1970.

Hutt, C. Exploration and play in children. In R. E. Herron & B. Sutton-Smith (Eds.), *Child's play.* New York: Wiley, 1971.

Inhelder, B., & Piaget, J. *The growth of logical thinking from childhood to adolescence.* New York: Basic Books, 1958.

Jacklin, C. N., Maccoby, E. E., & Dick, A. E. Barrier behavior and toy preference: Sex differences (and their absence) in the year-old child. *Child Development,* 1973, *44,* 196–200.

Jackson, P. W., & Messick, S. The person, the product, and the response: Conceptual problems in the assessment of creativity. *Journal of Personality,* 1965, *33,* 309–329.

Jersild, A. T., & Markey, F. V. Conflicts between preschool children. *Child Development Monographs,* 1935, No. 21.

Jersild, A. T., Markey, F. V., & Jersild, C. L. Children's fears, dreams, wishes, daydreams, likes, dislikes, pleasant and unpleasant memories. *Child Development Monographs,* 1933, No. 12.

Jones, R. M. *Fantasy and feeling in education.* New York: New York University Press, 1968.

Josselyn, I. M. *The happy child: A psychoanalytic guide to emotional and social growth.* New York: Random House, 1955.

Jung, C. [*The basic writings of C. J. Jung*] (Violet S. de Laszlo, Ed.). New York: Random House (Modern Library), 1959.

Kagan, J. Acquisition and significance of sex typing and sex role identity. In M. L. Hoffman & L. W. Hoffman (Eds.), *Review of child development research,* (Vol. 1). New York: Russell Sage Foundation, 1964.

Kagan, J. *Change and continuity in infancy.* New York: Wiley, 1971.

Kambly, A. Transactional analysis: Basic tenets and philosophy. *Psychology in the Schools,* 1975, *12,* 252–263.

Kessen, W. (Ed.). *Childhood in China.* New Haven, Conn.: Yale University Press, 1974.

Klein, D. Personal communication, April 1975.

Klinger, E. *Structure and functions of fantasy.* New York: Wiley, 1971.

Kniveton, B. H., & Pike, C. L. R. Social class, intelligence and the development of children's play interests. *Journal of Child Psychology and Psychiatry,* 1972, *13,* 167–181.

Koehler, W. *The mentality of apes.* New York: Harcourt, Brace, 1925.

Kogan, N., & Pankove, E. Creative ability over a five-year span. *Child Development,* 1972, *43,* 427–442.

Kohlberg, L. The development of children's orientations toward a moral order. I. Sequence in the development of moral thought. *Vita Humana,* 1963, *6,* 11–33.

Kohlberg, L., & Kramer, R. Continuities and discontinuities in childhood and adult moral development. *Human Development,* 1969, *12,* 93–120.

Kris, E. *Psychoanalytic explorations in art.* New York: International Universities Press, 1952.

Kruesi, H. *Pestalozzi: His life, work, and influence.* Cincinnati: Wilson, Hinkle, 1875.

Kruglanski, W. W., Alon, S., & Lewis, T. Retrospective misattribution and task enjoyment. *Journal of Experimental Social Psychology,* 1972, *8,* 493–501.

Lange, K. *Ergaenzungstheorie.* Berlin: Dummler, 1901.

Langer, S. K. *Philosophy in a new key: A study in the symbolism of reason, rite, and art.* Cambridge: Harvard University Press, 1951.

Lazarus, M. *About the attraction of play.* Berlin: Dummler, 1883.

Lefcourt, H. M., Sordoni, C., & Sordoni, C. Locus of control and the expression of humor. *Journal of Personality,* 1974, *42,* 130–143.

Lehman, H. C., & Witty, P. A. *The psychology of play activities.* New York: A. S. Barnes, 1927.

Lepper, M. R., Green, D., & Nisbett, R. E. Undermining children's intrinsic interest with extrinsic rewards: A test of the "overjustification" hypothesis. *Journal of Personality and Social Psychology,* 1973, *28,* 129–137.

Lesser, G. S. *Children and television: Lessons from Sesame Street.* New York: Random House, 1974.

Levine, F. M., & Fasnacht, G. Token rewards may lead to token learning. *American Psychologist,* 1974, 29, 816–820.

Levine, F. M., & Fasnacht, G. Extrinsic incentives and token-based programs: A reply. *American Psychologist,* 1976, *31,* 90–92.

Levine, J. (Ed.). *Motivation in humor.* New York: Atherton Press, 1969.

Levy, A. Personal communication, January 1975.

Lieberman, J. N. Playfulness and divergent thinking: An investigation of their relationship at the kindergarten level. Unpublished doctoral dissertation, Columbia University, 1964.

Lieberman, J. N. The relationship between playfulness and divergent thinking at the kindergarten level. *Journal of Genetic Psychology,* 1965, *107,* 219–224.

Lieberman, J. N. Playfulness: An attempt to conceptualize a quality of play and of the player. *Psychological Reports,* 1966, *19,* 1278.

Lieberman, J. N. A developmental analysis of playfulness as a clue to cognitive style. *The Journal of Creative Behavior,* 1967, *1,* 391–397. (a)

Lieberman, J. N. *Personality traits in adolescents: An investigation of playfulness–nonplayfulness in the high-school setting.* NIMH Terminal Report, December 1967. (ERIC Document Reproduction No. ED 032 584) (b)

Lieberman, J. N. Influence of setting and instrument on a personality trait. Paper presented at the meeting of the Eastern Psychological Association, Philadelphia, April 1969.

Loizos, C. Play behavior in higher primates: A review. In D. Morris (Ed.), *Primate ethology.* London: Weidenfeld & Nicolson, 1967.

Lombroso, C. *The man of genius.* New York: Scribner's Sons, 1895.

Lovinger, S. L. Sociodramatic play and language development in preschool disadvantaged children. *Psychology in the Schools,* 1974, *11*(3), 313–320.

Maccoby, E. E., & Jacklin, C. N. Stress, activity, and proximity seeking: Sex differences in the year-old child. *Child Development,* 1973, *44,* 34–42.

Markey, F. V. Imagination. *Psychological Bulletin,* 1935, *32,* 212–236.

Maslow, A. H. *Toward a psychology of being* (2nd ed.), Princeton, N.J.: Van Nostrand, 1968.

Maw, W. H., & Maw, E. Nature of creativity in high- and low-curiosity boys. *Developmental Psychology,* 1970, *2,* 325–329.

McCall, R. B. Smiling and vocalization in infants as indices of perceptual-cognitive processes. *Merrill–Palmer Quarterly,* 1972, *18,* 341–347.

McClelland, D. C. (Ed.). *Studies in motivation.* New York: Appleton, 1955.

McClelland, D. C. *The achieving society.* Princeton, J.J.: Van Nostrand, 1961.

McClelland, D. C. *Power.* New York: Wiley (Interscience), 1975.

McClelland, D. C., Atkinson, J. W., Clark, R. A., & Lowell, E. L. *The achievement motive.* New York: Appleton, 1953.

McGhee, P. E. Cognitive development and children's comprehension of humor. *Child Development,* 1971, *42,* 123–138.

McGhee, P. E. On the cognitive origins of incongruity humor: Fantasy assimilation versus reality assimilation. In J. H. Goldstein & P. E. McGhee (Eds.), *The psychology of humor.* New York: Academic Press, 1972.

McGhee, P. E. Development of children's ability to create the joking relationship. *Child Development,* 1974, *45,* 425–431. (a)

McGhee, P. E. Moral development and children's appreciation of humor. *Developmental Psychology,* 1974, *10,* 512–525. (b)

McGraw, M. Maturation of behavior. In L. Carmichael (Ed.), *Manual of child psychology.* New York: Wiley, 1946.

McGrew, W. C. *An ethological study of children's behavior.* London and New York: Academic Press, 1972.

McKellar, P. *Imagination and thinking.* New York: Basic Books, 1957.

McKinney, J. D., & Golden, L. Social studies dramatic play with elementary school children. *Journal of Educational Research*, 1973, *67*, 172–176.

Medland, M., & Stachnick, T. Good-behavior game: A replication and systematic analysis. *Journal of Applied Behavior Analysis*, 1972, *5*, 45–51.

Messer, S. B., & Lewis, M. Social class and sex differences in the attachment and play behavior of the year-old infant. *Merrill–Palmer Quarterly*, 1972, *18*, 295–306.

Millar, S. *The psychology of play.* Harmondsworth, Eng.: Penguin Books, 1968.

Mischel, W. A social learning view of sex differences in behavior. In E. E. Maccoby (Ed.), *The development of sex differences.* Stanford, Calif.: Stanford University Press, 1966.

Montessori, M. [*The secret of childhood*] (B. Carter, trans.). New York: Longmans, Green, 1936.

Moss, H. A. Sex-age and state as determinants of mother-infant interaction. *Merrill–Palmer Quarterly*, 1967, *13*, 19–36.

Moustakas, C. E. The frequency and intensity of negative attitudes expressed in play therapy: A comparison of well-adjusted and disturbed young children. *Journal of Genetic Psychology*, 1955, *86*, 309–325.

Munsinger, H., & Kessen, W. Uncertainty, structure, and preference. *Psychological Monographs*, 1964, *78* (Whole No. 586).

Murphy, G. *Human potentialities.* New York: Basic Books, 1958.

Nesbitt, W. *Simulation games for the social studies classroom.* New York: Foreign Policy Association, 1970.

Nesselroade, J. R., & Baltes, P. B. Adolescent personality development and historical change: 1970–1972. *Monographs of the Society for Research in Child Development*, 1974, *39*(1) (Series No. 154).

Neulinger, J. Leisure and mental health. *Pacific Sociological Review*, 1971, *14*, 288–300.

Neulinger, J. *The psychology of leisure: Research approaches to the study of leisure.* Springfield, Ill.: Charles C Thomas, 1974.

Neulinger, J., & Raps, C. S. Leisure attitudes of an intellectual elite. *Journal of Leisure Research*, 1972, *4*, 196–207.

O'Connell, W. E. Creativity in humor. *Journal of Social Psychology*, 1969, *78*, 237–241.

Oden, M. H. The fulfillment of promise: 40-year follow-up of the Terman gifted group. *Genetic Psychology Monographs*, 1968, *77*, 3–93.

O'Leary, K., Poulos, R., & Devine, V. Tangible reinforcers: Bonuses or bribes? *Journal of Consulting and Clinical Psychology*, 1972, *38*, 1–8.

Osborn, A. F. *Applied imagination.* New York: Scribner's Sons, 1963. (Originally published 1953.)

Parnes, S. J., & Meadow, A. Effects of "brainstorming" instructions on creative problem-solving by trained and untrained subjects. *Journal of Educational Psychology*, 1959, *50*, 171–176.

Parsons, T., & Bales, R. F. *Family, socialization and interaction process.* Glencoe, Ill.: Free Press, 1955.

Parten, M. B. Social participation among preschool children. *Journal of Abnormal and Social Psychology*, 1932, *27*, 243–269.

Pestalozzi, J. H. [*How Gertrude teaches her children: An attempt to help mothers teach their own children*] (L. E. Holland & F. C. Turner, trans.). New York: Bardeen, 1898.

Piaget, J. *Play, dreams and imitation in childhood.* London: Routledge, 1945.

Piaget, J. [*The origins of intelligence in children*] (M. Cook, trans.). New York: International Universities Press, 1966. (Originally published 1952.)

Piddington, R. *The psychology of laughter.* New York: Gamut Press, 1963.

Pollio, H. R., Mers, R., & Lucchesi, W. Humor, laughter, and smiling: Some preliminary observations of funny behavior. In J. H. Goldstein & P. E. McGhee (Eds.), *The psychology of humor.* New York: Academic Press, 1972.

Porter, A. L., & Wolfle, D. Utility of the doctoral dissertation. *American Psychologist,* 1975, *30,* 1054–1058.

Prentice, N. M., & Fathman, R. E. Joking-riddles: A developmental index of children's humor. *Developmental Psychology,* 1975, *11,* 210–216.

Pulaski, M. A. Play as a function of toy structure and fantasy predisposition. *Child Development,* 1970, *41,* 531–537.

Rest, J. R. Developmental psychology as a guide to value education: A review of "Kohlbergian programs." *Review of Educational Research,* 1974, *44,* 241–259.

Rheingold, H. L. The modification of social responsiveness in institutional babies. *Monograph of the Society for Research in Child Development,* 1956, *21,* No. 63.

Rheingold, H. L., & Bayley, N. The later effects of an experimental modification of mothering. *Child Development,* 1959, *30,* 363–372.

Riesman, D. *The lonely crowd: A study of the changing American character.* New Haven, Conn.: Yale University Press, 1950.

Roberts, J. M., & Sutton-Smith, B. Child training and game involvement. *Ethnology,* 1962, *1,* 166–185.

Rogers, C. R. Toward a theory of creativity. In H. H. Anderson (Ed.), *Creativity and its cultivation.* New York: Harper & Brothers, 1959.

Romer, R. The motive to avoid success and its effects on performance in school-age males and females. *Developmental Psychology,* 1975, *11,* 689–699.

Rosenberg, B. G. Sex, sex role, and sex role identity: The built-in paradoxes. Sex role learning in childhood and adolescence. Symposium presented at the meeting of the American Association for the Advancement of Science, Washington, D.C., December 1972.

Rosenberg, B. G., & Sutton-Smith, B. A revised conception of masculine–feminine differences in play activities. *Journal of Genetic Psychology,* 1960, *96,* 165–1970.

Rosenfeld, H. M., & Gunnell, P. Effects of peer characteristics on preschool performance of low-income children. *Merrill–Palmer Quarterly,* 1973, *19,* 81–94.

Rosenhan, D. L., Underwood, B., & Moore, B. Affect moderates self-gratification and altruism. *Journal of Personality and Social Psychology,* 1974, *30,* 546–5552.

Rosenwald, G. C. The relation of drive discharge to the enjoyment of humor. *Journal of Personality,* 1964, *32,* 682–698.

Ross, H. S., Rheingold, H. L., & Eckerman, C. O. Approach and exploration of a novel alternative by 12-month-old infants. *Journal of Experimental Child Psychology,* 1972, *13,* 85–93.

Rousseau, J. J. *Emile ou de l'éducation.* Paris: Editions Garnier Frères, 1964.

Sarason, S. B., Davidson, K. S., Lighthall, F. F., Waite, R. R., & Ruebush, B. K. *Anxiety in elementary school children.* New York: Wiley, 1960.

Schachtel, E. G. *Metamorphosis: On the development of affect, perception, attention, and memory.* New York: Basic Books, 1959.

Schaefer, C. E. The self-concept of creative adolescents. *Journal of Psychology*, 1969, *72*, 233–242.

Schaefer, C. E. Five-year follow-up study of the self-concept of creative adolescents. *Journal of Genetic Psychology*, 1973, *123*, 163–170.

Schaller, J. *Das Spiel und die Spiele.* Weimar: Bohlan, 1861.

Seagoe, M. V. Instrument for the analysis of children's play as an index of socialization. *Journal of School Psychology*, 1970, *8*, 139–144.

Seagoe, M. V. A comparison of children's play in six modern cultures. *Journal of School Psychology*, 1971, *9*, 61–72. (a)

Seagoe, M. V. Children's play in three American subcultures. *Journal of School Psychology*, 1971, *9*, 167–172. (b)

Sears, P. S., & Barbee, A. H. Career and life satisfaction among Terman's gifted women. Paper presented at the Lewis M. Terman Memorial Symposium on Intellectual Talent, Johns Hopkins University, Baltimore, November 1975.

Segal, E. W., & Stacy, E. W., Jr. Rule-governed behavior as a psychological process. *American Psychologist*, 1975, *30*, 541–552.

Shabecoff, P. Leisure activities thrive in recession. *New York Times*, May 11, 1975, pp. 1 and 28B.

Sheehan, P. W. (Ed.). *The function and nature of imagery.* New York: Academic Press, 1972.

Sherman, L. W. An ecological study of glee in small groups of preschool children. *Child Development*, 1975, *46*, 53–61.

Shultz, T. R. The role of incongruity and resolution in children's appreciation of cartoon humor. *Journal of Experimental Child Psychology*, 1972, *13*, 456–477.

Shultz, T. R. Development of the appreciation of riddles. *Child Development*, 1974, *45*, 100–105.

Shultz, T. R., & Horibe, F. Development of the appreciation of verbal jokes. *Developmental Psychology*, 1974, *10*, 13–20.

Singer, D. L. Aggression, arousal, hostile humor, catharsis. *Journal of Personality and Social Psychology*, Monograph Supplement, 1968, *8* (1), 1–14.

Singer, D. L., & Rummo, J. Ideational creativity and behavioral style in kindergarten age children. *Developmental Psychology*, 1973, *8*, 154–161.

Singer, J. L. *Daydreaming: An introduction to the experimental study of inner experience.* New York: Random House, 1966.

Singer, J. L. *The child's world of make-believe: Experimental studies of imaginative play.* New York: Academic Press, 1973.

Singer, J. L. *Imagery and daydream methods in psychotherapy and behavior modification.* New York: Academic Press, 1974.

Singer, J. L., & Singer, D. Fostering imaginative play in pre-school children: Effects of television-viewing and direct adult modeling. Paper presented at the meeting of the American Psychological Association, New Orleans, September 1974.

Sitkei, E. G., & Meyers, C. E. Comparative structure of intellect in middle- and lower-class four-year-olds of two ethnic groups. *Developmental Psychology*, 1969, *1*, 592–604.

Skinner, B. F. *Walden two.* New York: Macmillan, 1948.

Smilansky, S. *The effects of socio-dramatic play on disadvantaged preschool children.* New York: Wiley, 1968.

Smith, E. E., & Goodchilds, J. D. Characteristics of the witty group member: The wit as leader. *American Psychologist*, 1959, *14*, 375–376.

Staats, A. W., Brewer, B. A., & Gross, M. C. Learning and cognitive development: Representative samples, cumulative–hierarchical learning, and experimental–longitudinal methods. *Monographs of the Society for Research in Child Development*, 1970, *35* (8) (Series No. 141).

Staub, E. The use of role playing and induction in children's learning of helping and sharing behavior. *Child Development*, 1971, *42*, 805–816.

Sully, J. *Essay on laughter.* New York: Longmans, Green, 1902.

Suls, J. M. A two-stage model for the appreciation of jokes and cartoons: An information-processing analysis. In J. H. Goldstein & P. E. McGhee (Eds.), *The psychology of humor.* New York: Academic Press, 1972.

Sutton-Smith, B., & Roberts, J. M. Studies of an elementary game of strategy. *Genetic Psychology Monographs*, 1967, *75*, 3–42.

Sutton-Smith, B. A developmental structural account of riddles. In B. K. Gimblett (Ed.), *Speech, play, and display.* The Hague: Mouton, 1975.

Sutton-Smith, B., & Rosenberg, B. G. A scale to identify impulsive behavior in children. *Journal of Genetic Psychology*, 1959, *95*, 211–216.

Sutton-Smith, B., & Rosenberg, B. G. Sixty years of historical change in the game preferences of American children. In R. E. Herron & B. Sutton-Smith (Eds.), *Child's play.* New York: Wiley, 1971.

Switzky, H. N., Haywood, H. C., & Isett, R. Exploration, curiosity, and play in young children: Effects of stimulus complexity. *Developmental Psychology*, 1974, *10*, 321–329.

Symonds, P. M. *Adolescent fantasy.* New York: Columbia University Press, 1942.

Terman, L. M. A new approach to the study of genius. *Psychological Review*, 1922, *29*, 310–318.

Terman, L. M. Mental and physical traits of a thousand gifted children. *Genetic studies of genius* (Vol. 1). Stanford, Calif.: Stanford University Press, 1925.

Terman, L. H., & Oden, M. H. *Genetic studies of genius* (Vol. 5). *The gifted group at mid-life.* Stanford, Calif.: Stanford University Press, 1959.

Tomkins, S. S. *Affect, imagery, consciousness* (Vol. 1). *The positive affects.* New York: Springer, 1962.

Tomkins, S. S. Affect and the polarity of knowledge. In S. S. Tomkins & C. Izard (Eds.), *Affect, cognition and personality.* New York: Springer, 1965.

Torrance, E. P. *Assessing the creative thinking abilities of children.* Minneapolis: University of Minnesota Press, 1960.

Torrance, E. P. Priming creative thinking in the primary grades. *Elementary School Journal*, 1961, *62*, 139–145.

Torrance, E. P. *Guiding creative talent.* Englewood Cliffs, N.J.: Prentice-Hall, 1962.

Torrance, E. P. *Torrance tests of creative thinking: Verbal forms A and B.* Princeton, N.J.: Personnel Press, 1966.

Torrance, E. P., Bruch, X. B., & Morse, J. A. Improving predictions of the adult creative achievement of gifted girls by using autobiographical information. *Gifted Child Quarterly*, 1973, *17*, 91–95.

Troyka, L. Q., & Nudelman, J. *Taking action.* Englewood Cliffs, N.J.: Prentice-Hall, 1975.

Victor, J. B., Halverson, C., Jr., Inoff, G., & Buczkowski, H. J. Objective behavior measures of first- and second-grade boys' free play and teachers' ratings on a behavior problem checklist. *Psychology in the Schools*, 1973, *10*, 439–443.

Waelder, R. Psychoanalytic theory of play. *Psychoanalytic Quarterly*, 1933, *2*, 208–224.

Wallach, M. A., & Kogan, N. *Modes of thinking in young children: A study of the creativity–intelligence distinction.* New York: Holt, 1965.

Wallach, M. A., & Wing, C. W. *The talented student.* New York: Holt, 1969.

Wallas, G. *The art of thought.* New York: Harcourt, Brace, 1921.

Ward, W. C. Creativity in young children. *Child Development,* 1968, *39,* 737–754. (a)

Ward, W. C. Reflection–impulsivity in kindergarten children. *Child Development,* 1968, *39,* 367–374. (b)

Watson, G. B. Some personality differences in children related to strict or permissive parental discipline. *Journal of Psychology,* 1957, *44,* 227–249.

Wechsler, D. *The measurement of adult intelligence.* Baltimore: Williams & Wilkins, 1950.

Wechsler, D. *WISC-R manual for the Wechsler Intelligence Scale for Children* (Revised). New York: Psychological Corporation, 1974.

White, R. W. Motivation reconsidered: Concept of competence. *Psychological Review,* 1959, *66,* 297–333.

Wilkinson, E., & Willoughby, L. A. (Eds. and trans.). *On the aesthetic education of Man by F. von Schiller.* Oxford: Oxford University Press, 1967.

Wilson, J. P. Nursing experience and the social smile. Unpublished doctoral dissertation, University of Chicago, 1963.

Witkin, H. A., Dyk, R. B., Faterson, H. F., Goodenough, D. R., & Karp, S. A. *Psychological differentiation.* New York: Wiley, 1962.

Wolf, T. M. Effects of live modeled sex-inappropriate play behavior in a naturalistic setting. *Developmental Psychology,* 1973, *9,* 120–123.

Wolff, P. H. Observations on the early development of smiling. In B. M. Foss (Ed.), *Determinants of infant behavior II.* New York: Wiley, 1963.

Wolfgang, C. An exploration of the relationship between the cognitive area of reading and selected developmental aspects of children's play. *Psychology in the Schools,* 1974, *11,* 338–343.

Yarrow, M. L., Scott, P., & Waxler, C. Z. Learning concern for others. *Developmental Psychology,* 1973, *8,* 240–260.

Zern, D., & Taylor, A. L. Rhythmic behavior in the hierarchy of responses of preschool children. *Merrill–Palmer Quarterly,* 1973, *19,* 137–145.

Zigler, E. Levine, J., & Gould, L. Cognitive processes in the development of children's appreciation of humor. *Child Development,* 1966, *37,* 507–518.

Zigler, E., Levine, J., & Gould, L. Cognitive challenge as a factor in children's humor appreciation. *Journal of Personality and Social Psychology,* 1967, *6,* 332–336.

Subject Index

A

Art, psychological dimensions expressed in, 122
Assimilation, reproductive and recognitory, 83

B

Behavior modification, 78, 116
Bubbling effervescence, 54
 in the creative process, 116

C

Career choices, 135–138
 field data, 136–138
 influence of developmental dynamics, 135–136
 playing with options in, 133–134
 role of the school in, 134–135
Childrearing, sexual stereotyping in, 79
Childrearing practices, 124–127
 cross-cultural aspects of, 120
 father's role in, 127
Combinatorial play as cognitive spontaneity, 84
 in different occupations, 139–140
 as ingredient of creative thought, 2
Competence, 70
Competition
 in games, 79
 and the ludic element, 118
Cooperation
 in classroom learning, 80
 in games, 79

D

Creativity, 3, 149
 and achievement motivation, 120
 influence of familiar elements on, 88
 in leisure activities, 147–148
 sex differences as a function of affect, 117
Culture, as an influence on play, 102–103

D

Daydreams, affect in, 125
Divergent thinking, see also Creativity
 in games, 113
 relationship to playfulness in kindergartners, 29
Divergent Thinking Tasks, 25

E

Education, 13
 play element in, 12

F

Familiarity, 109–111
 and function pleasure, 109, 114
 and role of collective unconscious, 111
Fantasy
 affect in, 78
 complex, 80
 measure of, 66
Fantasy assimilation
 in cognitive approach to humor, 66
 in creative process, 115
 in educational setting, 132
 and sense of humor, 110

A 7
B 8
C 9
D 0
E 1
F 2
G 3
H 4
I 5
J 6